D1329948

I T

IT

A History of Human Beauty

Arthur Marwick

Hambledon and London

London and New York

Hambledon and London

102 Gloucester Avenue
London, NW1 8HX

175 Fifth Avenue
New York, NY 10010
USA

First Published 2004

ISBN 1 85285 448 0

A description of this book is available from the
British Library and from the Library of Congress.

Typeset by Carnegie Publishing, Lancaster,
and printed in Great Britain by Cambridge University Press.

Contents

Illustrations

Preface

We know that people who are born into the upper class, or who are born rich, or who are born with a particular mental set which predisposes them towards aiming single-mindedly at amassing power, or at making pots of money, tend to do well in the world (become prime ministers, or generals, or company directors). But what of those men and women who are born beautiful – are their life chances affected thereby? That is the question I have set out to resolve. It quickly became clear that if my computations were to be valid ones I would need to adopt a rigorous definition of beauty, not rolling it up with all the other desirable qualities a person can have – such as kindness, intelligence, humour – as is often done in ordinary conversation. To Plato and then to the Christian Church a beautiful soul was more important than a lovely face and shapely figure, 'beauty of mind' more important than 'beauty of body'. What people like doing, of course, is muddling things up together: 'he's a beautiful man' can actually mean 'he's wonderfully kind and likeable and terrific to be with, though not actually physically very attractive'. Such sophistries are forbidden to me – in this book beauty is an attribute purely of the face and figure.

To begin with I accepted the conventional, though actually little examined, view that standards of beauty change from age to age. In human affairs much does change – ideologies and institutions, economic and social systems, class structures, the role and status of women; my own study of the evidence compelled me to the conclusion that, relative to these, beauty (in the western world that I am qualified to write about) has changed little. That is why I call it a 'relative constant', a 'relative universal'. To be honest I am not greatly impressed by the oft-repeated accounts of African tribes prizing fatness, South American ones lip plates, Burmese ones necks stretched and ringed like a snake – in these examples the admiration is for symbols of wealth and status, not beauty.

Indeed the whole subject is bedevilled by an elementary failure to distinguish between fashion and beauty.

This book makes a fundamental distinction between what I refer to as the 'traditional' and the 'modern' evaluation of beauty. Beautiful human beings (men as well as women) have always been objects of fascination to the less well-favoured majority but, up to the nineteenth century and even beyond, views about beauty were deeply confused. Status and wealth were still the major criteria upon which people were judged; beauty was recognised, but was seen as dangerous and disruptive, fomenting lust, tempting young people into socially disastrous marriages. Beautiful women could rise in society, but only by first falling on their backs as concubines, mistresses, courtesans, or as, in the nineteenth century, members of the select group known in France as *Grandes Horizontales*. Beautiful women became consorts to Kings, but seldom ever became their Queens; for that, regal status and exploitable dynastic connections were required. There were jobs (as footmen, for instance) for which beautiful men were particularly well qualified. Occasionally a beautiful man could do well out of sexual services rendered – where the King was gay, or where the head of the Empire was Catherine the Great. Only in recent times has the 'modern' view of beauty emerged. This sees beauty as a purely physical quality, embodying sex appeal, but no longer having to be parlayed into actual sexual congress; an independent characteristic whose value rivals that of status and wealth. Everywhere today, on film, on television, in public relations, in the whole celebrity circus, we are surrounded by evidence that good looks can readily be converted into hard cash. How far was that true in the past? How did we get to where we are today? In the 1980s I published a massive and extensively illustrated tome, *Beauty in History: Society, Politics and Personal Appearance, c. 1500 to the Present.* Fundamentalist feminism was then at its height: accordingly the book was blasted into oblivion by reviewers (not all female) who decided in advance that mine was the sort of book which imposes standards of beauty on women in order to oppress them, without pausing to read that what I was actually saying was that women are fully entitled to judge men by their looks in exactly the way that men have always judged women. *It: A History of Human Beauty* is a shorter, better and different book, drawing, however, upon research and reflection spread over a quarter of a century. As such, it owes much to the help I have received from curators, archivists and librarians, and the advice given by colleagues and friends.

First, I must single out Tony Coulson who, till his tragically early death, was Media Librarian at the Open University. Tony went far beyond the call of professional duty in tracing reproductions back to their original sources, in acquiring slides for me, and in guiding me through the morasses of attribution and misattribution. At the Hoover Institution Archives, California, Director Elena Danielson, together with her assistants, provided perfect service to a researcher on a most abstruse topic. In the Special Collections and University Archives of the Stanford University Libraries I also received immaculate service from Carol Rudisell, Sara Timby, Margaret J. Kimball and all the staff working there. Coming nearer home I must record with thanks the special assistance of Jack and Ann Flavell at the Bodleian Library, Geoffrey Marsh at the Museum of London, and John Jacob of Kenwood House. Among many academic colleagues I would particularly like to thank Professors Anne Lawrence of the Open University, Marc Ferro and Pierre Sorlin of Paris, and Dan Leab of New York; and also Agnes Petersen of the Hoover Institution.

Copyright holders have been generous in allowing me to make use of copyright material. I am grateful to Lord and Lady Monson for a letter from the sixth Baron to his son in the Monson Papers in the Lincoln County Record Office; to Mrs J. E. Nurse of Tunbridge Wells for an extract from the 'Memorial of James Howard of Manchester (1738 to 1822) by his daughter Rachel Barrow (1789 to 1870)'; to Patricia Anderson Liedke for the Melville Anderson and Charlena Van Vleeck material in the Anderson Papers in the Department of Special Collections and University Archives, the Stanford University Libraries; to Evelyn F. Gardiner and Janet Nicoleau for the Mary Hallock Foote Papers in the same department. I should like to thank the Hoover Institution, Stanford, for making it possible for me to use a number of important collections (listed in my sources) and the National Library of Scotland for the James Gall journal and the Robert Graham diaries. I have made strenuous efforts to trace all copyright holders. If in any instance I have failed to make due acknowledgement I shall be glad to put the matter right as quickly as possible.

1

Fascination

As every doctor knows, people habitually overstate how often they're having sex while understating how much alcohol they drink. But of all human attributes, the one over which there is most dishonesty, most persistent refusal to face the facts, most doublethink, is physical appearance. Much of this, of course, is in the cause of common civility and decency: far kinder to pour out the balm of gentle flattery than to fling the corrosive acid of honest judgement on, say, a pudgy nose, piggy eyes, and a receding chin, or a face and figure (I am speaking of males as well as females) which are nondescript, plain and utterly devoid of allure. Civilisation has always depended upon the observance of certain polite fictions, and nowhere is there a richer growth of such fictions than in regard to questions of human beauty. Partly this is because of the special resonances, and special ambiguities, of the very concept of 'beauty'; partly, it is because personal appearance is intimately bound up with the sense of self-worth, and, more critically, with sexuality, sexual attractiveness and sexual success. Look up the thousands of tomes and treatises on 'beauty' and you'll find that most of them deal with moral or aesthetic beauty, often representing the two as being inextricably intertwined, very few descending to the mundane topic of the physical appearance of human beings. This is because the eternal quest has been for a universal concept of beauty, one which will cover poems, paintings, symphonies, statues, sunsets and seascapes (natural and imagined), beautiful bodies and beautiful minds.

'Beauty' is itself such a 'beautiful' concept that the conviction is that it must connote something transcendental, something beyond human affairs, such as truth, purity, godliness, spirituality, 'the good' to the utmost degree. Outstanding physical beauty (in both males and females), the less privileged of us cannot help noting, offers its possessors sexual opportunity aplenty, and thus hints at promiscuity, lust and carnal gluttony – indulgences incompatible with any rarified notions of the meaning of beauty. For someone to be 'truly beautiful', the implication is, they must possess some moral or spiritual qualities beyond being 'merely beautiful'. They must be irradiated by, as it is often put, an 'inner light' – for 'beauty', as the oft-repeated, but seldom-examined cliché has it, 'is more than skin deep'. One might actually say of someone, 'He's a beautiful person, even though he's not very good-looking'.

Yet while much lip service is paid to the notion of the transcendental quality of beauty, the overwhelming evidence is that in our everyday lives we are actually obsessed by surface appearance, those enjoying great natural beauty always attracting special attention, sometimes adoration, sometimes hatred, there being frequent laments about the unfair advantages enjoyed by the comely and the cruel penalties imposed on the ugly. One much-quoted version of the transcendental concept of beauty was coined by the poet Keats, and represented as being expressed by the Grecian urn itself (the very quintessence of pure aesthetic beauty), in the last stanza of 'Ode on a Grecian Urn':

> Beauty is truth, truth beauty, that is all
> Ye know on earth, and all ye need to know.

In fact Keats was obsessed with the entirely carnal beauty of his fiancée, Fanny Brawne, somewhat to her annoyance. In a famous response to her protestations, he makes a forceful case for the importance of beauty as a merely physical quality (no high-blown stuff about 'truth' here!):

> Why may I not speak of your Beauty, since without that I could never have
> love'd you? I cannot conceive any beginning of such love as I have for you
> but Beauty. There may be the sort of love for which, without the least
> sneer at it, I have the highest respect and can admire it in others: but it
> has not the richness, the bloom, the full form, the enchantment of love
> after my own heart.[1]

The dishonesty and doublethink arise from our perfectly understandable desires to believe several different things simultaneously, together with the way in which the topic of beauty is encrusted both in age-old myths and our own strongly held personal feelings. Thinking straight on beauty is one of the most difficult tasks encountered by human beings. The most common circle of self-deception starts from the honest perception, 'I am not beautiful in the way that the television presenters, the models, the film stars I see all the time are beautiful', proceeds to the self-reassurance, 'But I do have qualities of intelligence and understanding, or charm and sympathy, or humour and sparkle, or ...' (fill it in accordance with your own personal conviction about what makes you attractive and desirable to others) ... and concludes, 'So actually I am beautiful' – and, because what everyone really wants (despite the transcendentalism) is to be accounted physically beautiful, the moral qualities of intelligence and understanding, charm and sparkle, or whatever, are, in the manner of the medieval alchemist (and with as much genuine success) transmuted into physical beauty. Then there are those who, while self-aware about their own appearance, are convinced they are capable of divining the 'inner light' in others which alone confers 'true beauty' and which, of course, excludes everyone they detest, annoying personal acquaintances or bumptious celebrities. Some commentators claim to be able to detect in a person's appearance the indications of 'character' which, they maintain, alone give substance to true beauty, as distinct from a merely decorative vacuity. Myth, prejudice, hyperintellectual fastidiousness and, above all, the failure to recognise that (perfectly legitimately) the word 'beautiful' is used in a number of distinctively different ways, account for our muddled thoughts on the topic of human beauty: we constantly slither from one meaning to another, so that moral beauty is passed off as physical beauty, or a physically beautiful person you don't happen to like or are jealous of, is denied the attribute of 'beauty'. In magazines and guides we find the word 'beauty' being used in yet another different way, to signify the preoccupation with making the most of our appearance through the use of powder and paint, hairstyling, 'beauty' aids, fashionable attire and, increasingly, cosmetic surgery; to mean, in fact, 'self-presentation', or 'grooming'. Heavy investment in self-presentation, in the simulation of beauty, comes to be passed off as beauty itself.

What I am doing is conducting a unique investigation: what part, historically, has personal appearance played in people's lives, in their successes and in their failures, in their own destinies, and, where I am dealing with monarchs and politicians, in the destinies of others, or, where I am dealing with humbler people, in opportunities for wealth and social advancement, whether through career, or marriage, or both? If my conclusions are to be of any value, I must be punctilious in

singling out physical appearance, beauty of face and figure, from all the
other qualities with which these are customarily run together. I must
take great pains to pin down what people actually did look like and not
be content with the usual conventional, but often wildly inaccurate,
formulae, which, the more one reads the biographies of those traditionally held to be comely, one finds simply to be handed down from one
author to another. Over the years, historians have expatiated on the
power conferred upon individuals through being born to high status or
great wealth; they have analysed the kinds of psyche which make for a
Washington, a Napoleon, or a Churchill; recently some have suggested
that the vital ingredient for exercising power in 'the professional society' is education.[2] Talents and gifts are unequally distributed. Strength
of will, physical courage, a mighty intellect, personal charisma, the gift
of the gab: these are personal qualities which may give certain individuals advantages over others. Despite all the confusion and doublethink,
it has, in reality, never gone unnoticed that a rather small number of
individuals enjoy great natural beauty, while the vast majority do not; it
also being observed that a fair number can be accounted personable,
with many others being positively plain or ugly. From comments frequently made, it would seem that these differences do matter. But in
exactly what way, or ways, has never been systematically established –
apart from earlier work of my own.[3] My present task is to pin down the
nature and extent of the power exercised, in the past, and on into
the present, by personal physical beauty; and also to assess the significance of being personable as against being plain or ugly – in all cases
examining both the public and private spheres. If I am to do that, I have
to isolate personal, physical, surface beauty from all other possible types
of beauty. And I will have to use all the sources available, visual and
written, to establish what the people I am discussing really did look like.
It will be no good saying of a certain duchess that she exercised great
power because of her beauty if in fact her power was really due to the
status and wealth she already possessed, and the description 'beautiful'
was simply flattery induced by that same status and wealth.

The first two things we have to do are these: first, distinguish between
'beauty' and 'fashion'; and, secondly, disabuse ourselves of any idea that
there is one single type of beauty – the most common candidate is the
so-called 'Greek ideal of beauty', when, actually, if we forget myth and

ideology, we can see that very many of those who have been accounted beautiful have nothing 'Greek' about them. Fashion is an integral part of human life. Those who wish to find greatest acceptance in society, to pass with least adverse comment, take care to dress, to style their hair, their beards, their wigs, their make-up, in accordance with current fashion; those who are out of fashion will always seem slightly odd, uneasily out of place. Fashion has been attacked, through the ages, by men for allegedly permitting plain women to pass themselves off as beautiful, and, more recently, by feminists for allegedly confirming women's role as sex objects. In the first decade of the sixteenth century Sir Thomas More was a lusty and hard-living critic of the conventions and pieties of his day: in the ideal society he envisaged in his *Utopia* 'natural bewtie and comliness' were so highly prized in both men and women, as compared with fashionable costume and cosmetics ('payntings') which concealed 'the endowments of the bodye', that before marrying each would-be spouse had to be exposed to the other completely naked:

> in cheusing wyfes and husbandes they observe earnestly and strayetely a custome whiche seemed to us very fonde and folysh. For a sad and honest matrone sheweth the woman, be she maide or widdowe, naked to the wowere. And likewise a sage and discrete man exhibyteth the wowere naked to the woman.[4]

It is absolutely clear from the context, incidentally, that More was not concerned with some kind of medical inspection (as distinct from an erotic one). The nineteenth-century American music critic and Darwinian philosopher, Henry Theophilus Finck, declared fashion 'the hand-maid of ugliness', arguing that it was a device of the ugly majority for compelling the beautiful minority to conceal their charms.[5] The most elaborate expression of this profoundly misogynous sentiment came from the French scholar Marcel Braunschvig, in his *Women and Beauty*, published in 1919. Fashion, he said, substitutes a false conception of beauty for the real thing:

> In the eyes of many beauty is confused with elegance, which is simply conformity to the latest demands of fashion. From this many aberrations in taste follow: luxurious grooming leads an ugly woman to be judged beautiful, while the beauty of a woman wearing an unfashionable costume passes unnoticed. Dress has constituted a beauty by conventions which

often supersede true beauty. The majority of women believe that this is to their advantage; for, lacking true beauty, so rare, a woman always has the money to procure the beauty that can be bought.[6]

Almost the whole of chapter two of volume two of Simone de Beauvoir's *The Second Sex*, the bible of post-war feminism, is taken up with fashion and cosmetics, representing them as integral to the oppression of women. Yet there is one sentence which suggests what the true significance of making up and dressing up may be to a woman: 'to care for her beauty, to dress up, is a kind of work that enables her to take possession of her person, as she takes possession of her home through housework, her persona then seems chosen and created by herself '.[7] For myself, I am in no way critical of fashion or of the use of cosmetics, both of which I see as a normal part of human life as it has evolved from the earliest times. My sole points are that, in an investigation such as this, fashion must be distinguished from natural beauty, and 'beauty' of the women's magazines, that is self-presentation, must be distinguished from natural endowment. Elegance and good taste are undoubtedly admirable qualities, but they are simply not the same thing as physical beauty, and truly sharp eyes will not mistake them for such.

From portrayals of Queen Elizabeth I, both in film and television productions and in portraits painted at the time, from paintings by Piero della Francesca and his contemporaries, we are familiar with the fact that in the fifteenth and sixteenth centuries it was fashionable for women to shave their foreheads. But this did not mean that a shaven forehead was in itself an indicator of beauty: a beautiful woman with a shaven forehead was beautiful; an ugly woman with a shaven forehead was not. Since the 1960s, extremely slim female figures have been in fashion. But the contention that fashion model Twiggy was beautiful only because fashion decreed skinniness to be beautiful is utterly absurd. In the sixties, as ever, there were very many skinny women who were not in the least beautiful. Twiggy was beautiful because her figure was perfectly proportioned and because she had an astoundingly lovely face. For much of the nineteenth century, it was not fashionable to be red-haired, since red hair was associated with freckles, taken to be a blemish on perfect beauty. However, a normal lusty young man, in this case nineteen-year-old Englishman, James Salter of Tolleshunt D'Arcy, attending the Lewes ball in December 1859, while affected by the fashionable prejudice was not blinded by it: 'singularly enough, I did not see one girl pretty enough to attract or detain the eye beyond the first glance, and another prodigy was that, of the most passable, three red-headed girls stood first, both as regards dancing and looks'.[8] Fashion, while never approving of the fat, did, in the nineteenth century, favour the buxom. Yet our connoisseur of female beauty, Henry Theophilus Finck, fell in love with, and married, an extraordinarily beautiful woman (we have her photograph) with, as he commented, 'no figure worth talking about'. In her late teens, the renowned actress, Sarah Bernhardt, still in the era when plump faces and ample bosoms were allegedly the ideal of feminine beauty, was also slim and girlish: that stopped no man from lusting after her astonishing beauty – and, as we shall see, giving her a golden start in her career. Too many writers on human beauty simply make facile readings from what painters painted or what fashion writers decreed: to see what was really beautiful, as distinct from what was in fashion, we have to examine the sentiments and reactions of flesh-and-blood beholders towards flesh-and-blood individuals.

A recent feminist writer on female beauty found it 'curious' that the winner of the second Miss America beauty competition, held in 1922, 'differed considerably in face and figure' from the first winner of the competition, launched in Atlantic City in 1921.[9] She had assumed, along with all those who theorise about the 'cultural construction of reality', that in any particular era only one style of beauty (allegedly 'constructed' by the dominant class in that society) is recognised. In fact, there are always many different styles of beauty, so that there is nothing 'curious' at all about the woman selected as the most beautiful in 1922 looking different 'in face and figure' from the one chosen in 1921. The point about a beauty competition is that *everyone* who enters for it has, if they are not to cause profound embarrassment, to be beautiful (indeed for an unambiguous fix on the beauty being discussed in this book, a good question to ask about any individual being considered is, 'Could they, without embarrassment, enter a beauty competition?'). Who actually wins a beauty competition is not, for our investigation, of any great significance, and an eventual winner is certainly not to be thought of seriously as being more beautiful than the other competitors: the boundary between beauty and absence of it is not between the winner and the others, but between those qualified to enter in the first place and those not so qualified. Those qualified, it quickly becomes apparent, 'differ considerably in face and figure'. There are many different types of human appearance. Among the main 'types' to be found in everday discourse (and associated loosely with geographic or ethnic origins) are 'Nordic', 'Mediterranean', 'West European', 'Slavonic', 'African', 'Arabic', 'Indian', 'Oriental' – these labels are not scientific, but their broad import will be readily apparent. In each of these groups (and several others one could no doubt think of) there are (a minority of) beautiful people, a proportion of personable ones, and a majority who are nondescript, or worse. Beautiful people are the most perfect representatives in face and figure of their own particular type; some of the most beautiful individuals are the products of inter-breeding between different ethnic or geographical groups: one thinks, for instance, of mixed Chinese or Japanese and European ancestry in California, or of mixed African and European ancestry in the former slave-holding states. Many of us have fixations on particular physical types and may find persons belonging to these types, even the ones less favoured in face and figure, beautiful to the exclusion of persons of other physical types. Apprehension of beauty is subject to much per-sonal idiosyncracy; but the definitions of beauty deployed in this study have to be those accepted by overwhelming majorities, not the out-comes of specific psychological imprinting or personal prejudice. Thin, aesthetic-looking men are not more beautiful than broad-shouldered rugged men (though they may be to certain women with particular out-looks and tastes); beautiful rugged men are more beautiful than ugly thin men, and vice-versa. Blondes are not more beautiful than brunettes; beautiful brunettes are more beautiful than ugly blondes, and vice versa. Joanna Pitman has recently produced a fascinating study, *On Blondes*[10] with much on the poetry and symbolism of 'abundant tresses' and 'women's crowning glory', particularly when these are blond, whether natural or dyed; my study is perhaps at once earthier and more ruthless, and I must stress that one single feature, even blond hair, will not render a person beautiful; beauty depends upon a holistic totality of alluring features (sometimes including just one, irresistibly, ever so faintly out of alignment). Chekhov presented the brutal truth when he had Sonya cry out that 'when a woman is plain, she is always told "You have beautiful eyes, you have beautiful hair" ...'[11] To resume. Buxom women are not intrinsically more beautiful than slim women. Properly proportioned buxom women with beautiful faces are more beautiful than scrawny slim women with plain faces; properly proportioned slim women with beautiful faces are more beautiful than ill-proportioned buxom women with plain faces. It's perfectly reasonable to say in ordinary speech: 'I like Italian men; they're so beautiful'. That might well mean, 'Among the Italian men I've encountered, a notably high proportion have been very good-looking'. One would not actually have to live very long in Italy to appreciate that, marvellous people as the Italians are, they have their own proportion of the plain and the ugly.

The beauty which I am concerned with is *not* 'more than skin deep', but is purely a surface quality, one which is registered on sight, and before one has any chance to appreciate the other qualities the person may possess. And it is *not* 'in the eye of the beholder'. Beauty goes far beyond personal predeliction or fancy; it appeals to *majorities*; it is 'in the eye of all beholders', or (given that the disgruntled and the idiosyncratic are always with us), '*almost* all beholders'. There would be no point in studying the influence beauty has on people's lives if it were simply a matter of personal taste or choice. Those who are beautiful for the purposes of the enquiry conducted in this book are those who are considered to be beautiful by an overwhelming majority of those beholding them. Many attempts have been made to say what precise mappings and measurements constitute beauty in human beings. None of them work in practice (many famous beauties, it has been gleefully reported, violate the basic measurements – that of proportion of lip to chin, to nose, to brow, being a favourite one) and none take into account my fundamental point about beauty coming in many different types. Outstanding beauty registers itself immediately and announces itself by the effects it has on beholders; we, most of us, recognise it when we see it. Even novelists are not strikingly successful in giving meticulous descriptions of individual beauty. We believe in the beauty of Gwendolen in *Daniel Deronda*, or Trollope's Lizzie Greystock, or Lyon Burke, the irresistible hunk in Jacqueline Susann's *Valley of the Dolls*, less through any painstaking descriptions provided by the authors than through the accounts given of their effects on other people. Beauty is that entirely physical phenomenon which has a disturbing, enticing, arousing effect on beholders.

Beauty is appreciated by (almost) all beholders, but the crude fact is that there is never enough of it to go around. What there is will be grabbed by the rich and the powerful. Thus if we wish to track down a cross section of the most beautiful women from any era in the past we should look to those chosen by the royal, the noble and the wealthy as concubines and mistresses – that is, for pleasure, rather than for matrimony, companionship and the breeding of children. Evolutionary theories which confuse physical beauty with breeding potential (and thus absurdly equate wide hips and big bottoms with beauty) fail to understand the lure, for those human beings in a position to achieve their goals, of the sexual possession of a beautiful body. Beauty is an independent quality, inextricably associated with sexual pleasure: it is differential genetic inheritance which leads to a few people being beautiful and most not, but, beyond the undisputed attraction of the aesthetically alluring and the even stronger one of sexual gratification, there is no need at all for evolutionary theories to account for the appeal of beauty. To dispose of arguments which too readily became eugenicist and racist let me state bluntly that the most beautiful is not axiomatically 'the fittest'; one strives to bed a beautiful partner not (despite even the wisdom of Shakespeare [12]) to improve the gene pool, but because the outcome is in itself wondrous. If evolution really tended to the consistent selection of the beautiful and the steady elimination of the plain and the ugly, why is it that, alas, there are still plenty of the latter in every population? The philosopher, Ellen Scarry, in a fascinating book, manages: to associate 'beauty' in the hallowed way with 'truth' (they are not, she says, 'identical', but 'allied', for beauty 'incites the desire for truth');[13] to find one universal beauty in 'a boy or a flower or a bird or in a poem or a painting or a palm tree or a person'; and to insist that beauty makes us want, equally, to beget children (if contemplating a beautiful person) or 'the begetting of poems and laws, the works of Homer ...' (if contemplating a beautiful object).[14] This equation of copulation with artistic creation or the promulgation of legal systems is the sort of drivel, gift-wrapped in olde worldly terms like 'begetting', with which philosophers habitually confuse such issues as human beauty.

Edward, Prince of Wales, who succeeded to the throne as Edward VII, was gross and unprepossessing, fully meriting his nickname of 'Tum-Tum'; his mistresses, who were presented to him on a plate, were all very beautiful (it was for that quality, of course, that they were selected). The same truism applies to the women bedded by Louis XIV, Charles II (he did have saturnine good looks, though whether he really needed them in addition to his king-size sex drive is an open question), Pablo Picasso, Benito Mussolini, Charlie Chaplin, and hundreds of other powerful, or celebrated, men in many walks of life. Until very recently, there are few analogous females: women usually had to find a husband or 'protector' to support them and were in no position to privilege the aesthetics of sexual pleasure. One of the few exceptions proving the rule that where they have an unfettered choice, human beings (male or female) choose their sexual partners from among the beautiful, is Catherine the Great: as all-powerful empress of Russia, she did not consort with fat old generals but with slim young guardsmen.

To sort out properly the relationship between beauty, desirability and sexual pleasure, we must distinguish between the initiation and the continuation of a sexual relationship, and between arousal and satisfaction. Beauty certainly creates arousal, which, of course, is essential to satisfaction, and is the most direct non-verbal indication of the likelihood of pleasure; in the well-known words – which we need not *fully* agree with – of Stendhal (himself an ugly little man), 'La beauté n'est que la promesse du bonheur'.[15] When it comes to realisation of pleasure (satisfaction), and to continuation of a relationship, then beauty, or its absence, can become critical (does one wish to contemplate one's partner, or does one bury one's head in the pillow?). All this is very well known, which is why, as I have just been stressing, the rich and the powerful, who can make choices, almost invariably have beautiful sexual partners.

Beauty in human beings is always perceived as sexually desirable, though everything that is sexually arousing is not necessarily beautiful. There exist such potentially erotic qualities as (in men) height or strength, and (in both sexes) voice, demeanour, self-presentation, and also such physical features as chest, breasts, legs or posterior (again both sexes). The genitals are not usually considered beautiful, though the sight of them tends to be sexually arousing – actually it might be more accurate to say that the genitals set within the entire context of a beautiful body and a beautiful face can be seen as a particularly exciting part of the total beauty; one breast taken in isolation, or a chin and neck, or a nose cut off from the rest of the face, or a loose pair of testicles, would be unlikely to seem beautiful. Our notion of human beauty is our notion of what a human being, in an increasingly recognised variety of types, ought to look like. Given freedom from all constraints, what we would like to unite with sexually are the most nearly perfect specimens of our species. What we find most desirable is most beautiful; what is beautiful we wish to possess. I believe that any analogies from the animal kingdom applied to human beings are deeply suspect, our evolution and acculturation having proceeded over thousands of years in highly distinctive circumstances. Despite Voltaire's famous 'Ask a toad what is beauty he will answer that it is his female with two huge round eyes coming out of her tiny head, large flat mouth, yellow belly and brown back',[16] and such obvious phenomena as the peacock's tail, it is unlikely that animals have any sense of beauty. Some animals *we* may find particularly fetching, for example domestic cats; thus seeing elements of feline grace in a woman may be a compliment to her appearance. But on the whole we prefer humans to look supremely human and not remind us of animal creation, and not, above all, of our near ancestors the apes.[17] Since Darwin's time it has been pointed out that a proper chin and a distinctive, free-standing nose, both attributes not possessed by animals, are absolutely essential to the notion of human beauty.[18] To these negative points (identifying indicators of ugliness rather than beauty) can be added any characteristics suggesting impotence, infertility or, above all, mortality. In our culture, bodily and facial hair are usually acceptable in males but not in females, probably because of these animal and mortality taboos.

Being about beauty, this book is also about its absence. Broadly what I have in mind is a fourfold taxonomy, but with a multitude of individuals and types who manifestly cross the boundaries (the man with the beautiful face, but the distressingly puny body; the *joli(e) laid(e)* – male as well as female; the lovely girl with the terrible legs). First, we have the *beautiful*, a tiny minority: perhaps, today, around five per cent of the male and female population between the ages of, say, sixteen and forty in any major country (from America to China, India to Australia). Then there are the *personable*, perhaps up to about a third of the same population – those who definitely have some of the qualities of beauty and who have a strong chance of doing well in the realm of self-presentation. After that come what I shall call the *ill-favoured*, rather more than half of the remaining population; these include those suffering from the ravages of ageing, and range from individuals who are widely recognised among those who know them to possess considerable sexual attractiveness (though, to repeat an absolutely key point, this will not be apparent *on sight* to beholders), to individuals who will be thought of as homely, to those who are termed plain, to those who are ugly (this term, it should be clear by now, is no more being used in a moral sense than is the term 'beautiful').

Finally there are those who suffer from some significant physical disability. To some readers this sort of taxonomy will reek of what is sometimes called 'body fascism'. Certainly the consciousness of imperfections and blemishes of face and figure causes much misery, and to dwell on them is to be cruel and oppressive. However, as already noted, an investigation of this sort must depend, in an area traditionally beset by polite evasions, on facing the truth. In some contexts the crucial distinction, with respect to life-chances and outcomes, is between being personable and being definitely ill-favoured. But then, manifestly, other qualities rather than sheer beauty will have come into the equation – intellect, talent, grace, say – and then it will be essential to guard against the elemental error of allowing a personable appearance together with a particular talent or talents to be counted as beauty. There will be many cases where success will be attributable wholly or partly to qualities other than beauty; the crucial task is to label these correctly and not somehow allow them to pass as a form of beauty.

Most studies of human beauty depend very heavily on the representations of artists and argue, say, that because Cranach painted Eve this way, Raphael his Madonnas that way, and Titian his female figures from Greek mythology in yet another way, this shows the manner in which standards of beauty change from age to age and are indeed socially constructed. Much of the evidence, in fact, contradicts the assumption that just because artists in any one era concentrated on one particular style of beauty that was the only style that princes, courtiers, merchants and all real living people in a position to make choices recognised. There is a further problem: it is too readily assumed that every painting of a woman by every artist must be intended to be beautiful, and (this is perhaps the more critical point) was widely accepted as such by a majority of contemporary viewers. It is not unreasonable to assume that in representing a powerful sitter an artist will introduce a dose of flattery (and so may be reliable on contemporary concepts of beauty, though not on the looks of his sitters); against that is the consideration that sitters do generally desire the portraits to present credible likenesses. At the very least, before reading off from a painting conclusions about concepts of beauty, we have to have information both on the artist's intentions and on contemporary reactions. I have already mentioned the difficulties novelists face in describing a beautiful individual: given that at the heart of human beauty lies the element of sexual appeal, it is not necessarily easy for painting, essentially a static art form, still less for sculpture, with its coldness, hardness and lack of colour variations, to render that beauty.

Artists in past centuries were often concerned to render such qualities as holiness or spirituality, nobility and dignity. It is profoundly significant that Botticelli was in his own day, and has been since, one of the most controversial of all painters of women. His women have a stunning beauty which exudes sexiness and speaks directly to us today. Some of Botticelli's paintings were burned by the pietistic monk Savonarola, undoubtedly because of the deeply disturbing allure of the women represented; learned scholars in the nineteenth century, made uncomfortable by these same representations of women, argued that the models were in fact tubercular – a complaint also raised against the women represented in Pre-Raphaelite paintings, who projected a similar sexuality.[19] The eighteenth-century English portrait painter Sir Joshua Reynolds aimed at a consciously dignified style with even his most beautiful female subjects. They tend, therefore, to lack sensuality; however, we can get a very clear sense of one uninhibited notion of beauty of the time from Reynolds's renderings of such abstractions as 'Theory' and 'Justice' – again they speak directly to us, as the universal quality of sexual beauty always must, and demonstrate that there was *not* a particular eighteenth-century canon of beauty monopolising the academic art of the time. Universal but not uniform: that is what I am saying about beauty. The range of types recognised today is great; it was more restricted in earlier more convention-bound eras. In some periods some types of beauty were less fashionable than others. At no time can perceptions of beauty be totally extricated from taboos and shibboleths, from fashion and convention; but the social and cultural inflections are minor compared with the fundamentals of beauty. It has become unexamined dogma that such qualities as beauty (and everything else!) are entirely relative, are 'culturally constructed', this dogma being derived from Marxism and being fortified by post-modernism and certain brands of feminism. But if we abandon dogma (and Marxism and post-modernism are simply belief systems bolstered by faith alone which we have absolutely no obligation to accept)[20] and focus instead on the kind of evidence I am examining here, we may well accept that, granting minor variations in emphasis, concepts of beauty throughout the history of western societies are basically unchanging. We have the paintings of Botticelli, of Reynolds, of the Pre-Raphaelites, of Greuze, of numberless other artists. For Greek ideas of beauty we are very largely dependent, as it happens, on Roman copies of Greek statues, with a few well-known Greek originals, all backed up by a certain amount of written material. For Roman concepts of female beauty we do have plenty of paintings (there is a fine collection in the Vatican), demonstrating that the Romans admired many of the types of beauty that we admire today. I am a historian, and so am very conscious that over time, and in different cultures, there are great changes and great differences in political and legal systems, social and economic organisation, belief structures, and in, for instance, the status and power of women; compared with these, any changes and differences in standards of beauty are rather insignificant.

Because a painting is acknowledged to be a great painting, and because it contains one or more representations of women, that does not mean that these women must have been, and that their portraits were necessarily intended to represent them as, beautiful. On the other hand, paintings of no great artistic merit can contain indisputably beautiful women: the paintings of Greuze provide cogent support for the contention that a woman desired for her beauty in the late eighteenth century would be so desired today – *The Broken Jug* is no masterpiece, but what a lovely young woman it portrays. So to the crucial case of the canvases of Peter Paul Rubens, with their masses of ponderous female flesh. Some art critics would argue that the women portrayed in

Rubens's paintings are beautiful and that it is only because we look at them wrongly that we get the sense of their being grossly overweight.[21] I think it has to be admitted that both in our own eyes, and judged by the types of women being painted just before, and just after Rubens, and indeed by other artists at the time of Rubens, his women are too fat to be beautiful. What I am going to suggest is that in Europe as a whole (Rubens was an international painter renowned throughout Europe), while the representations of women produced by Rubens were undoubtedly possessed of a strong erotic charge (for some beholders at least), they were not widely regarded as ideals of beauty, and that to see them as intended as such is to misconceive Rubens's own objectives.

Let us start with his treatise *The Theory of the Human Figure*. This work is based on Greek theories of art and on the careful study of surviving Greek statues. It is overwhelmingly devoted to the male figure, which is said to be based on the cube and the triangle. 'The male form', Rubens insists, 'is the true perfection of the human figure.'[22] In chapter 3 there is a section on antique statues, with some brief references to statues of woman, who 'differs from man in that she is more apprehensive and more feeble, because her centre of gravity, which passes through the middle of the throat, does not correspond exactly and perpendicularly with the centre of equilibrium which ought to be found in the middle of the back of the leg, as it is in a man ...'[23] Only chapter 7, the last one, is devoted entirely to 'the proportions of the woman'. Rubens writes:

> The elements of the human figure are different in man and in woman, in that in man all the elements tend towards perfection, as in the cube and equilateral triangle: in woman, on the contrary, everything is more feeble and smaller. From which happens that, in woman, the perfection is less, but the elegance of forms is greater: in place of the cube which is enfeebled in the figure of woman, there is a parallelogram ... From that one can infer that, with regard to the perfection of forms, woman takes second place after man ... the idea of the beauty of man having been created perfect, as it probably existed in Adam and in Christ.

Rubens then moves on to 'the perfection of the various parts of the body of a woman'. He says that the body must not be 'too thin or too skinny, nor too large or too fat, but with a moderate *embonpoint*, following the model of the antique statues'.[24]

Rubens, therefore, was concerned to paint women (and men) as in antique statues, and in accordance with his belief that women did not exemplify human beauty as perfectly as men. Before dealing with more of Rubens's aims as a painter, it is important to examine his personal circumstances. He was himself a beautiful man, and a great success in the world both as a diplomat and as a painter. In 1609, at the age of thirty-two, he married Isabella Brandt, who was eighteen. The double portrait which Rubens did of himself and his young bride is a charming one; Rubens is the handsome dashing figure, his wife youthfully enticing enough, but plumpish and with a round, personable face, rather than a strikingly beautiful one. From the available Flemish womankind Rubens had, as everyone does, made *his* choice, not expecting a woman to compete with him in beauty, and being personally drawn towards plumpness (a quality he did not confuse with beauty). The marriage was without doubt a happy and loving one; the couple had one girl and two boys. Then in 1626 Isabella died. Rubens's reflections on her death are preserved in a famous letter:

> Truly I have lost an excellent companion, whom one could love – indeed had to love, with good reason – as having none of the faults of her sex. She had no capricious moods, and no feminine weakness, but was all goodness and honesty. And because of her virtues she was loved during her lifetime, and mourned by all at her death. Such a loss seems to me worthy of deep feeling, and since the true remedy for all ills is Forgetfulness, daughter of Time, I must without doubt look to her for help. But I find it very hard to separate grief for this loss from the memory of a person whom I must love and cherish as long as I live.[25]

That there is no mention at all of Isabella's appearance, not even any conventional invocation of her 'beauty', may simply be in keeping with the elegiac tone of the letter; or it may add to our understanding of how Rubens perceived his wife.

Just over eight years later, Rubens did decide to marry again, this time choosing Hélène Fourment, a girl of sixteen with a remarkable resemblance to Isabella, whose niece indeed she was; Rubens was now fifty-three. The several portraits of Hélène show her as having even more of a pudding face than Isabella, and reveal also that she very quickly became obese. All this we can take as confirmation that Rubens had a proclivity for fattish women; clearly he became fixated on a particular facial type, and seemingly did not look for, nor expect to find, particular distinction of feature in a woman's face. That, *as a painter*, he could register more distinguished and appealing features is brought out in his famous painting (in the National Gallery, London) of Hélène's sister, Suzanne, known as *Le Chapeau de Paille (The Straw Hat)*. In his great mythological paintings filled with women who, both in their heavy limbs and rather boring faces, tend to be reminiscent of Isabella and Hélène, Rubens was, in part, following his own fancy. It may also be worth recalling that one of his most famous commissions was the cycle (in the Louvre) on the life of Marie de' Médicis, who was herself a heavy and plain woman. Rubens did his best with her, but maybe it was tactful to surround her with other female figures built on a similar scale. Then there were the theories we have noted on the proper way of representing human forms, female and male. Actually Rubens painted on a more voluminous scale than was to be found in the classical statues he studied, and this, to come to the absolutely fundamental point, was because he himself was busy pioneering the new baroque style for which massive proportions were required. Rubens was concerned with the overall artistic problems of composition and scale; and he was intensely preoccupied with the texture of flesh, and the play of light upon it. For artistic purposes, he needed immense expanses of ponderous flesh. A variety of evidence, then, indicates that Rubens's representations of women were not primarily intended by him to be models of female beauty – he had other purposes in mind. Without doubt there were contemporary patrons who rejoiced in the voluptuous displays of nudity (but, as already noted, while beauty is always sexually appealing, that which is sexually arousing is not always beautiful); there were others, however, who dismissed Rubens's models as overweight Flemish peasant women[26] To clinch the argument that they were certainly not *the only* model of female beauty at the time – which is really the minimum I have to establish for my purpose – I wish to take you into the Palazzo Bianco in Genoa: in one room, on opposite walls, painted within ten years of each other, are a gross female by Rubens, and a slim elegant one by Van Dyke. Rubens's women may well have been representative of a living, breathing, type which predominated in the Flanders of the day, but they were not taken throughout France, Italy and England to be generally representative of the highest female beauty.

Finally here are the views of an art historian who confesses to finding much of Rubens's work 'arousing' and describes *The Rape of the Daughters of Leucippus, The Three Graces* and *Hélène Fourment in a Fur Wrap* as masterpieces of erotic art (they may be, but, to repeat, that does not automatically make them exemplars of female beauty).[27] In trying to deal with the present-day view that Rubens's women are too fat, this critic, Keith Roberts, offers 'a word ... in Rubens's favour'. This 'word', in fact, supports my own contentions:

> Even now, very few women have figures as trim as Brigitte Bardot's. Undress any crowd of Saturday morning shoppers in one of the main shopping streets of Europe and the effect would probably be depressing and more 'Rubensian' than one might have imagined. A more important point is that in saying 'I hate Rubens's fat women' one is mentally taking them out of the picture and seeing them as real figures in the real world; but the degree of illusion Rubens creates through his brilliant painting of skin is, first and last, an *artistic* illusion.
>
> What is really significant about Phoebe and Hilaria in *The Rape of the Daughters of Leucippus* is not their bodies, judged as female bodies in this or any other situation, but their *poses* in this particular composition ... How the figures might have looked in other situations, or in life, was totally irrelevant.[28]

My case rests: Rubens as the painter of an everyday 'depressing' crowd of Saturday morning shoppers, or Rubens as the creator of great pictorial compositions, is fine: this is not the artist painting, as so often alleged, the early seventeenth-century ideal of female pulchritude.

My contention is that ideas of what, in the Western World, have constituted human beauty are more universal, and less subject to variation (though they have been subject to expansion and increasing flexibility), than is assumed, practically without reflection or examination, by trendy theory. What has changed though, and that is a central theme of this book, is the way in which beauty is *valued*. Today, the evidence lies all around us that our civilisation as it exists now has an intense preoccupation with personal appearance, and gives a very high rating to human beauty. Whether on the billboards which line our streets and stations, in the glossy magazines which jostle for position on bookstalls and in the newsagents, or during the regular assaults of the television commercials on our own living rooms, we see that the received method of marketing products of every type is to associate them with a beautiful human being, whether male or female. It is a commonplace that, as technology advanced in tandem with conflicts in Kosovo, Afghanistan, and Iraq, television also brought the heat of battle into our homes; at the same time one could not avoid noting that the new generation of war reporters were, to an astonishing degree, beautiful young women, with a scattering of beautiful young men, one of whom, Rageh Omar, a black BBC reporter, was apparently so attractive to American females he acquired the nickname 'The Scud Stud'. Today, in a wide range of jobs, particularly those in any form of communications, the possession of personal beauty is an enormous asset. Nearly twenty years ago I made the case that human beauty in the late twentieth century was coming to assume an independent value of its own, rivalling such qualities as status, wealth and education, and being possessed, indeed, of considerable commercial value. Since then a number of hard-headed economic studies have conclusively demonstrated that in many areas the beautiful get the better jobs, pull in the higher earnings.[29] Here, in prime Wall Street jargon, is the conclusion from the first of these studies:

> Holding constant demographic and labor-market characteristics, plain people earn less than people of average looks, who earn less than the good-looking. The penalty for plainness is 5 to 10 per cent, slightly larger than the premium for beauty. The effects are slightly larger for men than women; but unattractive women are less likely than others to participate in the labor force and are more likely to be married to men with unexpectedly low human capital. Better-looking people sort into occupations where beauty is likely to be more productive; but the impact of individuals' looks on their earnings is mostly independent of occupation.[30]

Ironically, this utterly practical research, demonstrating that, with respect to fundamental earning power, beauty was certainly no myth, had in part been stimulated by the runaway best-seller, *The Beauty Myth* by Naomi Wolf (1990), which argued that ideals of female beauty were deliberately constructed by men in order to perpetuate their rule over women; by writing off large numbers of women as 'not beautiful' they could, Wolf claimed, keep these women in a permanent state of oppression. Like all spinners of absurd relativist theory, Wolf was obsessed by the notion that men are driven by the search for power, when most, in fact, are driven by the search for pleasure. Hence her ludicrous and (at that time) intellectually trendy contention that: 'The beauty myth is not about women at all. It is all about men and power'.[31] If men actually could 'construct' female beauty, it would be in their interest not to restrict the amount of beauty but to create as much as possible, so that there would be plenty of lovely sex-mates to go round. In any case, as the survey I have just quoted brings out, the bonus of beauty was now being enjoyed by men as well as women. Wolf was herself a very beautiful young woman, and looked terrific in her many television interviews. It is, of course, one of the benefits of that distinctly non-mythical attribute, beauty, that it can enable its possessors to get away with talking complete tripe.

No doubt it *is* unfair that some individuals are beautiful and most are not; but then it is also unfair that a relative minority have musical talent, mathematical talent, artistic talent, literary talent, acting talent, business talent, sporting talent, the uniquely flexible cartilages and joints which make possible the exquisite contortions of the ballet dancer. It's true that exploitation of the main range of human talents calls for dedication, training and hard work in a way that exploitation of beauty generally does not, though, as we shall see in the course of this book, the exploitation of beauty usually does call for elements of thought, patience, strategy and, often, the exercise of another talent or talents. But whether we are talking of the most formidable intellect, the most sublime artistic genius, or merely great natural beauty, each is, ultimately, a gift from the genes. In the past the beautiful cashed in on their looks almost exclusively by granting sexual favours to the powerful. But in modern mass democratic society, though beauty, of course, continues to carry its elemental sexual charge, its commercial value, based on its appeal to masses of people, as consumers, viewers, audiences, no longer depends on sexual transactions (though jobs putting sexuality up for sale continue to blossom – from male prostitution to female lap-dancing). The advantages conferred by beauty can be irritating, even infuriating. But try this simple test: would you really prefer there to be fewer (perhaps even no) beautiful people in the world, or more of them? Most of us recognise that, in fact, we get immense pleasure from the company of beautiful people (of both sexes), from beholding them, and (generally) experience a sense of lift when a beautiful person comes into the room; and that, short of getting what we really want (a stunningly beautiful sex-mate for our ourselves) we would rather have more of the beautiful around than fewer of them. Thus, while I am not going to equate the possession of perfect form and features to the talent of a Luciano Pavarotti, or a Bill Gates, I do maintain that that particular and very specific gift does enrich the lives of others. What causes the agony is the mad pursuit of beauty when it is better to recognise that, like the vast majority, we do not possess it, and the failure to recognise that there are so many other worthwhile personal qualities, such as friendliness, generosity and understanding.

That beauty is fascinating, disturbing, intensely real (in other words no myth) is apparent from the (highly rational) attention it is receiving from the post-feminist generation. Ellen Zetzel Lambert in *The Face of Love: Feminism and the Beauty Question* (1995) poses the questions:

> What is the nature of the elusive but surely real relationship between a person's outward appearance and his or her inner nature? Why should some people seem so beautiful to us on a first meeting, then not so beautiful as we come to know them better, while the beauty of others reveals itself to us only over time?[32]

Wendy Steiner, in *The Problem with Beauty* (2001) has advised that instead of giving themselves eating disorders in the pursuit of perfect beauty, which, unlike many earlier feminists of a post-modernist persuasion, she clearly accepts does actually exist, women should 'see themselves as beautiful in a more human sense – valuable, worthy of love.'[33] This echoes the advice advanced fifteen years earlier by Nancy C. Baker in her *The Beauty Trap: How Every Woman Can Free Herself From It* – and, indeed, that of wise post-feminist women everywhere:

> Isn't it time that we redefined beauty for ourselves so that it includes far more than perfect features, artfully enhanced make-up, hairstyling and clothing. My own new definition, for instance, is that a truly beautiful woman makes the best of her physical assets but, more important, she also *radiates a personal quality which is attractive.* Unlike the woman with a gorgeous face and body who is obsessed with herself, my ideally beautiful woman exudes concern for others, as well as intelligence, enthusiasm, humour, and self-confidence. These are all qualities we can cultivate in ourselves, and they're qualities that will last us a lifetime.[34]

Sensible as these arguments are for the everyday living of life, they simply take us back to the subterfuges discussed at the beginning of this chapter, blurring the distinction (essential to the purposes of this book) between being physically beautiful (having 'a gorgeous face and body' – don't we need to preserve the obvious word for that rare and disturbing condition?) and being 'nice', 'human', 'considerate'. The curious point about these feminist and post-feminist works is that, while I have always been concerned with the implications of beauty in men as well as of beauty in women (though my feminist critics refused to give me any credit for this), they are exclusively concerned with looks in women. This book deals equally with 'the man with the gorgeous face and body'. I regret Baker's slander that the beautiful woman is necessarily 'obsessed with herself': many beautiful women are 'considerate' and 'human' – feminists ruin their own arguments when they suggest otherwise. Actually, I will be showing that, historically, gorgeous men (unlike most gorgeous women) have tended to be rather stupidly 'obsessed with themselves'.

My fundamental point is that beauty is no figment, no myth: beauty exists. It stands out, it arouses desire, it is disturbing; it may bring success, or it may bring tragedy. As two women psychologists, Elaine Hatfield and Susan Sprecher, have put it their brilliant synthesis based on masses of empirical work, *Mirror, Mirror: The Importance of Looks in Everyday Life*:

> Undoubtedly, it is good to be good-looking when it comes to developing and maintaining personal relationships. Those possessed with good looks seem to have many advantages in their social lives … people do desire the company of attractive men and women. In most people's fantasies, the 'romantic other' is someone who looks like he/she just stepped out of the pages of *Glamour* magazine. When men and women do not have to worry about the possibility of being rejected, they tend to prefer the most attractive partner possible … attractiveness can stimulate passion – the best aphrodisiac seems to be an attractive partner.

Hatfield and Sprecher point out some of the disadvantages beauty can have (Paul Newman, whom they do not mention, was not alone among beautiful males in complaining that constant reference to his blue eyes distracted attention from his achievements as a highly intelligent actor and director – personally I doubt whether such compliments to a man or a woman, or the ones to woman that feminists used to call 'demeaning': 'lovely face', 'nice legs', 'good body', 'stunning looks', etc, really are much of a burden.) Hatfield and Sprecher quote this from a 'beautiful' (their word) woman:

> I am small and blonde. Many men assume even before they've met me, that I am interested in romance. When men I don't even know start up with me, I get non-responsive and irritable. I know what it will lead to. It's embarrassing. It's exhausting. No one will take no for an answer. I'm tired of saying no, again, and again, ever so politely.[35]

To demonstrate that beautiful men suffer in the same way, Hatfield and Sprecher cite the case of a beautiful male journalist, Pat Jordan, who, in June 1982, published an article in *Mademoiselle*, entitled 'Confessions of a Handsome Devil':

> Everyone has fleeting sexual fantasies about one another. For some, however, these fantasies are not enough. When Jordan is not interested, some women feel betrayed and strike out. Friendship is not enough for them. Many beautiful women, attracted to him because of his looks, turned on him when he failed to respond.[36]

No doubt Jordan was the source for this account, but Hatfield and Sprecher authenticate it by presenting it in their own words.

Beauty as aphrodisiac and provoker of sexual fantasy, as well as beauty as enhancement of earning power: these are the blunt, unambiguous ways in which beauty is evaluated today. But throughout the centuries, up until very recently, beauty, while always perceived as exceptional, and therefore as exciting and disturbing, was thoroughly enveloped in ambivalence and confusion. These have their origins in the nature of early – basically agricultural and land-owning – society, its customs and superstitions, and in the more self-conscious programmes and codes worked out by the Ancient Greeks, then developed within the early Christian Church. It is to pre-industrial society, its beliefs and prejudices about beauty, and the practical implications of these, that I now turn.

2

Plato, Augustine and Mrs Astell

From classical times till at least the late nineteenth century the over-whelming majority of the inhabitants of the West scratched a living from the land. They were mobile neither geographically nor socially: the peasant lived, worked, married and died within his own community. Those who were mobile were still less fortunate, for their mobility was that of the vagrant and the tramp. For neither man nor woman was there much choice in the way of sexual partners: the notion of choosing someone because of their superior personal appearance was an almost meaningless one. Standards of nutrition and health were low and, there-fore, so also were sex drives: marriage was overwhelmingly a matter of stern practicality rather than sexual gratification. Again, therefore, per-sonal appearance was scarcely a matter of great concern. Even had private inclination existed, without the chance to travel or the chance to move up in society, the opportunity for comparison, and therefore for selection, scarcely existed. With illness, mortality and early decrepitude everywhere in evidence, an overwhelming priority was the rearing of (comparatively) healthy children for continuance of the family and, more to the point, support when earning powers failed. The impera-tives, then, were far other than those of sexual aesthetics. The outlook of the relatively well-fed peasants of medieval Franche-Comté in eastern France is encapsulated in a local proverb which, it should be noted, makes it perfectly clear the peasants fully understood the concept, and the (dangerous) joys of having a beautiful wife: 'When one has a beau-tiful wife, one has no fine pigs – Why? – Because the pigs, instead of eating, spend all their time staring at her'.[1]

Even for the highest born, life was brutish and potentially short: every sinew had to be stretched towards maintaining and, if possible, improv-ing the family fortunes (this was usually just as true for monarchies and

empires as for farming and professional families). For the most powerful (and, therefore, male) there certainly were opportunities for
exercising the eternal predilection for a beautiful sexual partner, but in
marriage, and all formal social and political relationships, considerations of wealth and status always reigned supreme over those of mere
physical beauty.

Pagan superstition blended with classical thought and Christian piety.
Common knowledge held it that a person's character was closely related
to their physical appearance. The ugly and the deformed were – one of
the cruellest aspects of traditional attitudes – automatically judged to be
guilty of the utmost villainy; a princess who said her prayers was decreed
to be beautiful, even if actually plain as a prune, and spurned by all
suitors who had any choice in the matter. Sexuality (this is where traditional attitudes contrast diametrically with modern ones) was a matter
for shock, horror and guilt. Practical parents, guardians of the family
fortunes, and of community values, joined with Platonic philosophers –
from whom came the governing concept of love without sex, 'platonic
love' – and the fathers of the early Christian church – who went one better in inventing procreation without sex, 'virgin birth' – in denouncing
the dangers and temptations of human beauty. The servants of a church
morbidly preoccupied with what it saw as the evils of sexuality railed
against such beauty – extolling instead the beauty of God – while prudent parents could see that lust for a beautiful face or body could be
totally disruptive of careful schemes for enhancing the family position.

Usually the lust was that of a man, in Ancient Greece the lust of a
man for a beautiful boy, and, in the middle ages and through to recent
times, the lust of a man for a beautiful woman. Even today most books
about human beauty focus exclusively on women. Though there are
exceptions, it is an important part of the traditional evaluation of beauty
that it is seen as a quality essentially pertaining to women. This book
will give examples from the past of beauty in man being of historical significance, and will trace the processes by which, in the contemporary
evaluation of beauty, that of males is considered to share in importance
with that of females. In this chapter such examples, as the chapter title
indicates, necessarily take second place to a discussion of the formation
of the traditional beliefs and prejudices about beauty. The first clear
injunctions are found scattered in the works of the ancient Greek

philosopher Plato (427–347 BC), who set out deliberately to influence behaviour. In this he was followed by the early Christians, most notably St Augustine (354–430), whose writings incorporate extensive commentaries on the scriptures. Certain figures in the Italian Renaissance, notably Agnolo Firenzuola (active in the early sixteenth century), brought some modern notions into their discussions and debates on beauty and self-presentation, while Shakespeare (at the end of the same century) simply commented with unique perceptiveness on the passions and foibles of the society around him. There followed many moralists and purveyors of advice, obsessed, of course, by sex and lust: Mrs Mary Astell (writing at the beginning of the eighteenth century) is the prime example of an English one.

Ancient Athens was in many respects a vicious society, founded, it could almost be said, on the twin institutions of slavery and capital punishment (and death by the swallowing of hemlock was, contrary to the suppositions of romantics like Keats, a horrible one).[2] The enduring appeal of ancient Athens is that the bright young men of its elite addressed themselves to the questions of human existence, in all its ramifications, which have remained on our agenda ever since. Plato was primarily a political animal, preoccupied with the questions of how the good life should be achieved and how the individual within the community should be governed. In Athens those dramatic instincts, which lie deep in human nature and gain other outlets through the flamboyance of fashion, were expressed in theatre and in political debate. Plato's chosen form, in which he explored the great questions, was the dialogue. In many of the dialogues the leading figure is Socrates (469–399 BC), Plato's revered teacher. Many of the other characters had a genuine historical existence; a few seem to have been invented. The words, and probably much of the thought, are almost certainly those of Plato and are usually thus attributed, as they will be here. The major discussions of beauty are contained in the *Georgias*, the *Greater Hippias*, the *Phaedras* and the *Symposium* (or 'Banquet'). The intention in the *Greater Hippias* seems to be to set up Hippias, so that the superficiality of his comments is exposed as Socrates goes on to reveal deeper and more subtle truths. Actually Hippias' response to Socrates' question, 'What is beauty?' both demonstrates that even the ancient Greeks were susceptible to the eternal lure of female beauty, and has an impressively modern ring to it: 'A beautiful young lady is a beauty'.[3] However, Socrates trumps that with what for more than two millennia has been taken for the very summit of wisdom: 'Is not the most beautiful of mortal women plain when compared with the perfect and unfading beauty of the immortal Gods?' It should be noted, however, that Socrates is recognising that among mortal women there are some accepted by all as being outstandingly beautiful. Their problem, if we read his words carefully, is not just that their beauty is not 'perfect' but that it is not 'unfading'; this became a favourite theme of moralists of all types, who delight in telling us that not only does mortal beauty 'fade', it rots away. Socrates (somewhat erratically and inconsistently, it seems to me), then moves to a much-quoted definition of beauty, suggesting that 'the useful and the effective directed to the achievement of a good end, are the beautiful'.[4]

It is in the *Phaedras* that one finds the core of the Platonic view of beauty which, in all its poignant ambivalence, formed the basis of the conception of beauty held throughout most of the history of the West. True beauty, Socrates says, is, together with the wise and the good, a part of divinity. But there is also 'mere bodily beauty' and, Socrates laments, it is ordained:

> that all men, even the wisest, shall be the slaves of corporeal beauty ...
> Base souls, almost all wholly embruted in sense, love, almost as brutes do,
> rushing in to enjoy and beget ...[5]

The idea that beyond mere bodily beauty there exists true, divine beauty and that the beautiful, the true, and the good are only different manifestations of one eternal divine perfection is repeated in the *Symposium*. Here there is, as it were, a dialogue within a dialogue, when Socrates reports on the interchange he has had with the wise woman Diotima of Mantinea. Why this character, almost certainly fictional, should have been introduced is not clear; both Plato and Socrates were generally contemptuous of the intellectual powers of women, but it may be that Plato wanted independent propaganda on behalf of homosexual love.[6] Anyway, it is in the reported words of Diotima that we have the famous passage about the ladder, or series, of ascending stages which leads from earthly beauty to absolute beauty.

> For he who would proceed aright in this matter should begin in youth to
> seek the company of corporeal beauty; and, first, if he be guided by his

instructor aright, to love one beautiful body only – out of that he should create fair thoughts; and soon he will himself perceive that the beauty of one body is akin to the beauty of another; and then if beauty of form in general is his pursuit, how foolish would he be not to recognise that the beauty in everybody is one and the same! And when he perceives this he will abate his violent love of the one, which he will despise and deem a small thing, and will become a steadfast lover of all beautiful bodies. In the next stage he will consider that the beauty of the soul is more precious than the beauty of the outward form; so that if a virtuous soul have but a little comeliness, he will be content to love and tend him, and will search out and bring to birth thoughts which may improve the young, until he is compelled next to contemplate and see the beauty in institutions and laws, and to understand that the beauty of them all is of one family, and that personal beauty is a trifle; and after institutions his guide will lead him on to the sciences, in order that, beholding the wide region already occupied by beauty, he may cease to be like a servant in love with one beauty only, that of a particular youth or man or institution, himself a slave mean and narrow-minded; but drawing towards and contemplating the vast sea of beauty, he will create many fair and noble thoughts and discourses in boundless love of wisdom, until on that shore he grows and waxes strong, and at last the vision is revealed to him of a single science, which is the science of beauty everywhere.[7]

This ascent from earthly to absolute beauty, Diotima concludes, should govern men's lives. What should be loved is beauty in general, beauty in the abstract, divine beauty, 'the science of beauty everywhere'; what is being warned against is obsession with one particularly (physically) beautiful body – it should be recognised (as moralists, and some feminists, like to tell us today) that all human bodies share in the quality of beauty. This is advice on how to lead the good life: what is openly admitted is the immense power of sheer corporeal beauty which, whether in young women or young men, makes 'slaves' of men, bringing them rushing in 'almost as brutes do' to 'enjoy', though obviously not always 'to beget' (indeed I suspect that 'beget' is used as a kind of poetic metaphor to signify 'copulate' or 'ejaculate'). It should also be noted that Diotima recognises that someone with 'a virtuous soul' may actually not be very good looking. It is perhaps a pity that future generations, including people in our own day, chose to heed the confused spiritual message wittingly propagated by the Greeks (perhaps to mollify their gods), and ignored their repeated insistence on the very real existence of a rare, but devastating, 'bodily beauty'. It is this 'bodily beauty', actually recognised, if a little surreptitiously, by all the greatest minds of the past, that my book is concerned with.

If we judge by Greek sculpture, then divine beauty was actually remarkably similar to human beauty, the theory being that to achieve it the sculptor had to take the best features from many different human beings (actually, as we all know, one of the points about a supremely beautiful human being is the impression he or she gives of having features which cannot be improved upon). Divine Greek beauty does not – though there is a certain cold lack of sensuality about marble sculptures – look a million miles different from the beauty which arouses brutish instincts to enjoy and 'beget'. In fact, as the probably deliberately 'spun' words attributed to Diotima revealed, where the powerful male Athenian sought beauty was not in the likes of the Venus de Milo but in young men. The true Athenian pin-up was perhaps Ganymede, the mythical figure described in Homer's *Iliad* as 'the most beautiful of mortal men', whose beauty excited the desire of Zeus himself – naturalistically represented on many a Greek vase. In the *Charmides*, whose central political topic is the desirability of moderation, we get a sharp illumination of what powerful, middle-aged Athenians really thought constituted beauty.

Socrates is the narrator; he tells of how he was in the palaestra of Taures after a considerable absence from Athens. He asks 'about the present state of philosophy, and about the youth ... whether any of them were remarkable for wisdom, or beauty, or both'. Critias speaks of 'the great beauty of the day' – Charmides. Charmides enters and

> At that moment, when I saw him, I confess that I was quite astonished at his beauty and stature; all the company seemed to be enamoured of him; amazement and confusion reigned when he entered; and a second troupe of lovers followed behind him. That grown-up men like ourselves should have been affected in this way was not surprising, but I observed the boys and saw that all of them, down to the very smallest, turned and looked at him, as if he had been a statue ... Chaerephon called me and said: What do you think of the young man, Socrates?
> Has he not a beautiful face?

Most beautiful, I said.

But you would think nothing of his face, he replied, if you could see his naked form: he is absolutely perfect.

And to this they all agreed,

Ye Gods, I said, what a paragon if only he has one other slight addition.

What is that? said Critias.

If he has a noble soul ...

He is as fair and good within as he is without, replied Critias.

Then before we see his body, should we not ask him to strip and show us his soul? ...

When Charmides comes and sits besides Socrates the latter's powers of conversation flee:

> I caught sight of the inwards of his garment and took the flame. Then I could no longer contain myself. I thought how well Cydias understood the nature of love, when, in speaking of a fair youth, he warns someone 'not to bring the faun in the sight of the lion to be devoured by him', for fear that I had been overcome by a sort of wild-beast appetite.[8]

Clearly Plato (or Socrates) did believe deeply in the distinction between the noble beauty of the soul and the wickedly tempting beauty of the body, though there does seem to be more than a touch of wanting to have your crumpet and moralise about it too. Writers such as George Eliot, Anthony Trollope and Jacqueline Suzanne evoke human beauty, not so much by direct description as by describing the impact the beautiful person has on others. Here Plato has just given us a classic instance of this. With respect to Charmides, we learn nothing of the shape of his nose, the height of his brow, or the thrust of his chin, but we are left in no doubt as to his devastating physical beauty – 'amazement and confusion reigned when he entered'; he engendered in Socrates 'a sort of wild-beast appetite'. Once more we have an unambiguous recognition of beauty in the modern (the guilt over sexual desire apart) sexual (in this case homosexual) sense. Once more we have that insistence upon the distinction between the beauty of the body and the beauty of the soul, within a further insistence on there being an absolute beauty, embracing everything, including institutions, science and noble thoughts and discourses, which generated the appalling muddle which has bedevilled the study of human beauty ever since. Among the Greeks, the ambivalent and potentially hypocritical notion of beauty went hand in hand with the relegation of women to a thoroughly subordinate status, and a contempt for real wives, mothers and daughters (as distinct from goddesses). The emergence of the modern conception of beauty was to depend, not on the continuing subordination of women, but upon their increasing liberation. To their Roman and medieval successors, the Greeks transmitted their confusion and guilt about human beauty, though not, on the whole, their homosexuality. While Athenian males relegated their womenfolk entirely to the private sphere of home and kitchen, only applauding beauty contests among young males, and leaving beauty contests among girls entirely for female audiences,[9] the Romans did allow their women some part in social life and applauded young female acrobats and other performers clad in the scantiest 'bikinis'.[10]

St Augustine was born on 13 November 354 at Tagaste, a small town in the Roman province of Numidia on what is now the eastern border of Algeria, the son of a minor, and, therefore, moderately paid Roman village official. His father was a pagan, but Augustine, though not baptised, learned the rites and beliefs of Christianity from his mother, a devout Christian. First he studied grammar and literature, then in 370 he went to Carthage to study rhetoric. Shortly he revealed his own interest in that subject of perennial fascination by writing a book about it: *On the Beautiful and the Fitting (De Pulchro et Apto*, 380); meantime he had settled down with a woman whose looks greatly appealed to him, though he was inclined to agree with his mother that, being of lowly social status, she was not really a suitable partner, eventually dropping her after a ten-year relationship. As he tell us in the *Confessions* (400?), written after he had become a Christian, a bishop, and the leading theologian of his day, he frequently succumbed to the temptations presented by attractive young women. After teaching, first at Tagaste, then at Carthage, he moved in 383 to the centre of the empire, Rome, going on the following year to the municipal chair of rhetoric at Milan. In 386 he decided to become a Christian, leading a group in philosophical dialogues which he published as *Against the Academics: On the Happy Life and on Order*. After demonstrating the breadth of his interests with his *On Music*, he then concentrated on what was now his central concern, publishing *On the Morals of the Catholic Church and of the Manicheans.* At this point, he returned to North Africa, where he sold up all his property, devoting the proceeds to the poor, and taking up the monastic life. On a visit to Hippo in 391 he was ordained into the priesthood. Achieving fame for his sermons and debating abilities, in 395 or 396 he was elevated to the bishopric of Hippo. In 397 there appeared the first of his three books *On Christian Doctrine.* Many other works followed until the first instalment of *The City of God* appeared in 413, the remainder coming out serially over the next thirteen years.

Writing in the *Confessions* of his salad years, Augustine tells us:

> I went to Carthage, where I found myself in the midst of a hissing cauldron of lust ... I muddied the stream of friendship.[11]

He explains:

> I was in love with a beauty of a lower order and it was dragging me down. I used to ask my friends 'Do we love anything unless it is beautiful? What, then, is beauty and in what does it consist? What is it that attracts us and wins us over to the things we love? Unless there were beauty and grace in them, they would be powerless to win our hearts.'[12]

He became fascinated by what he took to be the part played in beauty (manifestly he is referring to women) by what he called 'the due balance' between the whole and its parts, as in 'the balance between the whole of the body and any of its limbs', physical beauty being dependent, he declared, 'on a harmony between the parts of the body, combined with an attractive complexion'.[13] This was the fundamental subject of his book on Beauty (this book was lost during his lifetime as he no doubt came to regard the subject as too redolent of his early carnal interests and inappropriate to his later godly ones).

Augustine made clear his immense debt to Plato, and in his own writing all the abhorrence of lust, all the guilty fastidiousness we find in Plato, appears in spades. This is how he addressed Plato:

> You have persuaded me that the truth is seen not with the bodily eyes, but with the pure mind ... Nothing hinders the perception of the truth more than a life devoted to lusts, and the false images of sensual things, derived from the sensual world and impressed upon us by the agency of the body.[14]

We noted Plato's argument that divine beauty eclipses human beauty because it is 'unfading'. As a few glances around any old church and churchyard will demonstrate, the medieval church was steeped in morbidity and a fascination with death and decay. Augustine was an energetic agent in the creation and spread of this culture of the shroud and skeleton, particularly in his discussions of human beauty. The flesh, he declared, was 'but a covering of rags, always decaying towards final death'; bodily beauty would always putrify and disappear.[15] This was true, of course, and obviously a vital consideration in the evaluation of human beauty to those who shared Christian (and Platonic) preoccupations with the contrast between eternity and the evanescence of human life. If, of course, you accept, as we tend to do in our secular age, that you are only going to be around for a short time anyway, you also accept that the enjoyment of beauty is necessarily going to be short-lived; beauty is not associated with eternity, but with youthfulness.

Augustine also goes on for page after page, and with great gusto, about the evils of sexual desire and sexual activity. Here are a few sentences extracted from over sixty close packed pages in *The City of God*:

> the word lust usually suggests to the mind the lustful excitement of the organ of generation. And this lust not only takes possession of the whole body and outward members, but also makes itself felt within and moves the whole mass with a passion in which mental emotion is mingled with a bodily appetite, so that the pleasure which results is the greatest of all bodily pleasures. So possessing indeed is this pleasure that, the moment of time in which it is consummated, all mental activity is suspended.[16]

This is immediately followed up by the, let's face it, rather laughable suggestion that the wise and holy man would prefer it if he could actually have children without going through the disgusting business of sex, along the way invoking a misogynous verse from I Thessalonians, 4.4:

> What friend of wisdom and holy joys, who, being married, but knowing as the apostle says, 'how to possess his vessel in santification and honour, not in the disease of desire, as the Gentiles who know not God', would not prefer, if this were possible, to beget children without this lust, so that in this function of begetting offspring the members created for this purpose should not be stimulated by the heat of lust, but should be actuated by his volition, in the same way as his other members serve him for their respective ends?[17]

Here we have the origins of that twisted puritanism, Catholic and Protestant, which had such a devastating impact on ideas about sex, and, of course, about sexual attraction. At the same time, of course, Augustine is recognising sex as 'the greatest of all bodily pleasures', and for all of his strictures against it, he does linger sensuously over the beautiful woman that he imagines Philosophia, or Wisdom, to be: anyone seeing Philosophia's face 'would fly, an impassioned and holy lover, amazed and glowing with excitement to the beauty of Philosophia'.[18] And at one point he recognises female beauty as 'certainly a good, a good of God', but then adds (rather clear-sightedly, actually, considering one of the enduring conventions about beauty and goodness) that God 'bestows it on the evil as well as the good'.[19] The cumulative message of Augustine's strictures, and a most important one when it comes to assessing the real outcomes of being endowed with true physical beauty, is that there is a desperate competition between the love of female beauty and the love of God.

Through all medieval discussions of beauty, the insistent theme is that corporeal beauty, where openly recognised to exist, is something for males to admire in females. In medieval Europe the convention became established of beautiful women as the inspiration for male action and heroics. Beauty certainly was considered a valuable asset in medieval monarchs, and the medieval romances do not entirely neglect male personal appearance, but the emphasis is on stature and strength, broad breasts and shoulders, thick strong thighs, and on such characteristics as valour and endurance, rather than on distinction of facial features.[20] Discussing male beauty in the manner in which female beauty had always been discussed is, of course, in large measure unique to the modern, post-1960s evaluation of beauty. In introducing his hero Thomas Randolph, the Scottish poet John Barbour (c. 1320–1395) requires a full twenty-two lines to catalogue his virtues of prowess, loyalty and honour, while his personal appearance can be dealt with in three:

> He weas of mesurabill stature,
> And portrait weill at all mesur'
> With braid visage, pleasant and fair.[21]

Although much more detail is given on the attributes which make up the personal appearance of heroines, it is highly stereotyped: her figure is small, well rounded, slender and graceful, with a small willowy waist as a prime standard of excellence; the feet are small, the flesh white, save for her rose-red cheeks, the hair blonde, the eyes blue and sparkling.[22]

Among the many departures from tact that the strict pursuit of the aims of this book forces me into is the comment that slimness is always prized in women, and that while the canonisation of that quality may have gone to health-threatening extremes in our own day, it is a complete myth that, in the West, fatness was ever prized. 'I wouldn't chuck her out of bed,' was once a frequent but, one now hopes extinct, expression of crude male chauvinism. Philippe I of France (1180–1233) did indeed, we are told by the medieval chronicler William Malmesbury, chuck his first wife out of bed, because he found her '*trop grasse*' (too fat).[23]

In the later middle ages, and on into the sixteenth and seventeenth centuries, there were standard summaries of what was held to constitute beauty in a woman: first there are seven essential qualities, then nine, then eighteen, and then the elaborate and very popular thirty, grouped in threes: three to be long – hands, legs and hair; three to be white; three to be pink; three to be round; three to be narrow; and so on. Clearly the magic was as much arithmetical as sensuous.[24] We are very short of biographical information for the middle ages, but it would certainly be unwise to conclude that even those men who were in a position to make choices exclusively favoured blondes, or went around ticking off the long items, the pink ones, the round ones, etc. On the point that beauty was felt to be a characteristic of women rather than men, however, the evidence is sound. This is borne out further by the fact that there are very few descriptions of ugly women in medieval literature and that, where they exist, wicked witches apart, their purpose is usually to bring out the beauty of the heroine.[25] Overall what we have is a very strong emphasis on the conventional and even the artificial, an emphasis which precludes a proper appreciation of natural beauty in its many types, a key element in the way beauty is appraised today. Absolutely central is the association between looks and character: in the romances, the villains, from the devil upward, are all extremely ugly.[26] From classical times there had been treatises on physiognomy translated, retranslated, and hawked around medieval Europe, treatises which reinforced the contempt and cruelty habitually shown towards the physically ill-favoured and deformed. *Certeyne Rewles of Phisnomy* (a fourteenth- or fifteenth-century translation from the Arabic) tells us that: 'ye face that es playne with outen rounde hilles, signyfies a strydiefull man, truandous wrong-wyse and unclene ... Grete lippes are token of a folische man'.[27]

The theory, then, was that bodily beauty went with goodness and godliness: along with their conventionalised physical attributes, heroines always have a string of oft-recurring and rather bland epithets applied to them: worthy, godly, virtuous, gentle, meek.[28] But of course, even in the most ritualised society, reality keeps breaking in. With its strong (official) hatred of sexual pleasure, the Christian Church was overly aware of the sinful temptations besetting a beautiful woman since, even if she was inherently virtuous, she would be the object of persistent attentions from desirable males to a degree not encountered by her less well-favoured sisters. Through to at least the early seventeenth century writers from within the Christian fold constantly repeat the same confl-icting and hypocritical utterances: within a few pages a writer can define beauty as goodness, attack it for arousing lust, and then proceed to dwell lubriciously on the unseen intimate beauties of a woman's body. The stylistic trick used by medieval painters to give an almost tactile sense of physical intimacy was to paint palpably round stomachs (the 'bellies' so lovingly described in the literature). The proper place to look for a rep-resentation of what really was regarded as physical beauty is in a painting where the women genuinely are meant to be tempting. A per-fect example is provided by that ultimate Christian painting, *The Temptation of St Antony*, painted in the mid-sixteenth century by the Dutchman Henrick Met de Bles (known as '*Il Civetta*' – the Owl).[29] Antony is being tempted by two dolly-birds with sweet young faces, perky breasts and round tummies; the contrast between them and the overdressed old hag who is showing them off could not be more strik-ing, nor more striking testimony to the absurdity of the theory that men invent the distinction between beauty and ugliness simply in order to put women down.

Everybody knew there was a distinction, not least the wealthier women of the sixteenth century. Thus, already, 'beauty guides' were beginning to appear, designed to help women present themselves in the most comely way. The most famous pioneer of this genre was the Venet-ian physician, Giovanni Marinelli, author also of *Medicines for the*

Treatment of Infirmities in Women (1563). His *The Embellishments of Women* (in Italian *Gli ornamenti delle donne*) came out in Venice the previous year. Naturally there is no suggestion that there is anything wicked about aspiring after a beautiful appearance: on the contrary this is 'a useful work ... essential for every gentle person'; and, to enhance marketability, the claim is made that it is 'translated from the writings of a Greek Queen'.[30] Advice will be given on how the beauties of the body can be improved 'by art' and by 'human industry', care being taken, however, to stress the importance of 'graceful manners' and a 'virtuous spirit'.[31] The quality of the advice offered is not actually very impressive, with much on the desired proportions of the various parts of the body, less on how this is to be achieved. One gets a sad insight into the prevalence of 'infirmities of the body'; much of the solid advice concerns potions, paints and 'scented waters', with about a quarter of the whole devoted to the treatment of the hair (perhaps this became 'woman's crowning glory' because it was one feature that was actually amenable to 'art' and 'human industry'). An abundance of literary references lend the book a certain dignity, though scarcely increased utility for the purposes in hand.

In these early years of the printing press, plagiarism and piracy were rampant. In 1582 there appeared in Paris, *Three Books on the Embellishment and Ornament of the Human Body*, which, though claiming to be 'translated from the Latin by M. Jean Liebaut, Doctor of Medicine in Paris', bore a strong resemblance to the book by Marinelli, with, however, additions and omissions and the material ordered in a different way. We start with 'waters and powders' and move immediately to 'the hair' and then 'all the parts and dependencies of the head'. The French book gives much longer and more searching treatment to 'The Chest and the Breasts' than does the Italian version:

> The chest is considered beautiful when it is large, full of flesh, without any bone appearing, while in colour tinted with vermilion; accompanied by two fine round apples, small and firm, which are not too solid but which come and go like little waves.
>   This beauty of the breasts is ruined when they are flat, puny and flaccid: or when they are huge, like a beggar's bag: or too hard: or inflamed, chancrous, or hairy.

Various potions are recommended for external application. Then there is further discussion of the breasts which, it is said, this time directly repeating Marinelli's comments, should 'not be too big, pendulous, or too droopy'.[32] The treatment recommended was probably quite sensible, though may not have been very reassuring: 'a good, hot, moist and nourishing diet, including good wines, good soups, jellies, pressed meats, and similar foods'.[33] Once again it is unambiguously clear that fatness is not an esteemed attribute in women, a point driven home in the references to 'buttocks' and 'thighs' which should not be at all big and fat ('*seulement médiocrement grosses et amples*').[34] That male deportment, if not exactly beauty of feature, was of significance, is brought out by occasional mentions of matters affecting men as well as women – notably bad breath.[35]

There we have the directness of a book designed (however optimistically) for use. With Gabriel de Minut's *Of Beauty* (1587), we are back in the morass of Platonic-Christian morality. Dedicated to Catherine de' Medici, it specifies its purpose as 'to signify that what is naturally beautiful is also naturally good' (quite a job, since, as I have already mentioned, Catherine de' Medici was far from 'naturally beautiful' – traditional philosophy, however, was well suited to coping with such problems). In one of the essays there is a description of one of the great reputed beauties of sixteenth-century France (on whom, however, we have little detail), La Belle Paule. Although we are told that she was completely free of the vice which renders ugly the most beautiful person, Minut does insist on how corporeal beauty can, in the context of someone with a 'black soul', give rise to 'the pollution and contamination of vice and ordure'.[36] The same idea is expressed with equal intensity in a slightly later book which, judging by the title, ought to have had the same useful aims as the books by Marinelli and Liebaut, *L'art d'embellir* (Paris, 1608), by David de Flurance Rivault: before offering any advice on self-embellishment, the author denounces 'the beauty which rules over our affections, dominates our will and enslaves our liberty, causing unbelievable desires, excesses of passion and fires of sensuality' (the beauty, of course, is in women; the 'fires' in men).[37] Minut praises La Belle Paule precisely because she has to fight over and over again – 'a hundred plus a hundred times', he says – to defend her honour; she therefore merits the crown of glory far more than a woman who is not thus tempted.[38] Quite palpably, though, he utterly relishes contemplating those beautiful women who, being tempted, succumb, weeping crocodile tears over 'the poor hymen totally broken and torn'.[39] Then comes his description of the physical attributes of La Belle Paule.[40] In the usual way we have the conventional allusions to her forehead, eyes, eyebrows and nose – hers, we learn, is perfect, and the further improving information is thrown in that, according to Aristotle, different shapes of nose indicate different types of personality. There are standard phrases on the ears, chin, throat and so on, while the mouth, intriguingly, is compared to that of a handsome young man. Then we come to the breasts (de Minut uses the respectable, but sensual *tétin*), which de Minut describes as 'fine', while noting (a point not made in the beauty guides) that we don't get to see or touch them. There is much on the thighs and buttocks, but, in the same vein, we are told that we can only guess at these since again they are concealed from us. Now the belly is caressingly described 'with the entry that babies come through'. But this entry, again we are warned, is accessible to only one person, the many others who lusted after it having been bravely fought off, so that, says de Minut, 'we may decorate and embellish this zone of the very centre of which we are now speaking … the Temple dedicated to Venus'.[41] But, after this excursion into eroticism, we are, by the last page of the book, back to the insistence that beauty and morality are interrelated, with the closing words: 'beautiful is good, and good is beautiful'.[42]

It is important not to exaggerate the social and cultural changes (confined anyway to the elites) taking place during the Italian Renaissance (centring on the sixteenth century), but undoubtedly there was an airing of new and modern-sounding ideas about human beauty. Art and philosophy, culture and behaviour continued to be pervaded and dominated by religious categories and religious modes of thought and expression. The single, central, indisputable feature of what Italians themselves at the time recognised as the *la rinascita*, the 'rebirth' or 'Renaissance', was the revival of classical learning. Inevitably there was a re-emphasis on Platonic ideals. Yet in the early part of the sixteenth century a debate was initiated in which, whatever the surface formalities, a challenge was mounted to both the Athenian and medieval evaluations of human beauty. This challenge was related both to the general ideas of Renaissance humanism (as expressed, for example, in

More's *Utopia*) and to the special features of urban culture in such city states as Florence, Venice, Mantua and Urbino.

The city states offered a unique urban environment in which comparisons and choices could be made between attractive members of the opposite sex, and a unique form of courtly life wherein questions of beauty and sexual attractiveness were openly discussed: the whole process was greatly enhanced by the mobility which existed between these north Italian cities. Secondly, humanist thought, which was at full strength at the beginning of the sixteenth century, while not to be identified with secularism, certainly encouraged hedonism and the belief that 'pleasure is the proper purpose of every human act'. As early as 1430 Lorenzo Valla had written that 'pleasure is the true good'. Bringing our central topic back into focus, he had then continued, 'what is sweeter, what more delectable, what more adorable, than a fair face?', recommending that in summer beautiful women should go lightly clad or not at all.[43] Thirdly, in the Italian city states were gathered the finest artists, and the finest collections of paintings; how beauty should be painted was an important matter for discussion; aesthetic standards were high and could actually be applied in the pursuit of sexual pleasure. Finally, among the privileged of Florence and Urbino, Mantua and Venice, Ferrara, Siena and Lucca, women were less trammelled by conventions and stereotypes than they had been in medieval courts and castles; questions of male beauty came into the reckoning, as well as the more traditional ones of male valour. Indubitably, the position of women, even in circles where 'modern' ideas about beauty were being canvassed, remained very much one of dependency. Yet, if the reputation of Urbino had been built by Duke Federigo di Montefeltro, the dominant figure at the end of the fifteenth century was Elisabetta di Gonzago from Mantua, wife of Federigo's son, Guidobaldo, who was himself incapacitated by gout. In running the brilliant court society of Urbino, Elisabetta was assisted by her lady, Emilia Pia.[44] During the discussions of beauty he conducted at Prato with the women of nearby Florence, Agnolo Firenzuola went out of his way to insist that he believed women to be the equals of men, though the very insistence suggests that this view was not very widely held.

The confrontation between the Platonic and the modern view of beauty can be seen at its sharpest in a too-much-neglected section of the

fourth book of *Il libro de cortegiano* (*The Book of the Courtier*) by Count
Baldesar Castiglione, which was based on real conversations held on
four evenings during March 1507 in the palace of Urbino (under the
general sponsorship of Elisabetta and immediate chairwomanship of
Emilia Pia), though undoubtedly much edited and revised before eventual publication in Venice in 1528. Thereafter it became one of the most
influential of sixteenth-century books, there being, for instance, an English translation by Sir Thomas Hoby in 1561.[45] The discussion is opened
by the humanist cleric Pietro Bembo, Platonist scholar and, later, a Cardinal. He begins (I use the Hoby translation, with phrases from the
original Italian where there may be ambiguity; more modern translations seem to me not always to get things quite right) by distinguishing
between the beauty which applies to all things 'framed in good proportion' and the rather more interesting subject, now the immediate topic
for discussion, the beauty 'that we meane, which is onlie it, that
appeareth in bodies, and especially in the face of mann' (that is, 'in the
face of human beings', *nei volti humani* in the original), proceeding
immediately to a moving invocation of the power of beauty (in both
males and females) to arouse sexual love. Such beauty, he declares,
'moveth thys fervent covetinge which we call love'. But after much more
in this vein, comes the conventional moralising (hypocritical also, since
Bembo's own life fully demonstrated his own carnal interest in female
beauty):

> When the fool is taken with covetting to enjoy the beauty as a good thing
> he falleth into the most deep errors and judgeth the body i.e. in which
> Beawty is discerned, to be the the principall cause thereof: whereupon to
> enjoye it, he reckoneth it necessary to joigne as inwardly as he can with
> that bodye, whyche is false.

Our senses, Bembo concludes, are the cause of wretchedness, while
beauty is always good. Others follow along similar lines, till Federigo
Fregoso (courtier, diplomat and scholar) brings them to a halt with a
blunt and modern statement of beauty (in men as well as women) as
independent of all moralising. Beautiful women, he says, have caused
wars; then he continues:

> There be also manye wicked men that have the comliness of a beautiful
> countenance, and it seemeth that nature hath so shaped them, because

they may be the redier to deceive, and that this amiable looke were like a baite that coverth the hooke.

But after this sane, and very modern, appraisal, Bembo has the last word, returning us totally to the old superstition: 'Beawtie is a face pleasant, merrie, comelye and to be desired for goodnesse: and Foulness is a face darke, uglesome, unpleasant and to be shonned by yll'.[46]

But there were other persuasive opponents of tradition (including, as we have already noted, from northern Europe, Sir Thomas More). Pride of place, however, must go to Agnolo Firenzuola's *Dialogue on the Beauty of Women*, first published in 1548. Of a number of similar works from the sixteenth century this most unambiguously presents the notion of beauty as an independent characteristic, esssentially sexual and unrelated to morality. Over a period of several years Firenzuola had been providing at Prato a series of lectures on and discussions of the nature of beauty. His book, like *The Book of the Courtier*, is a record, again no doubt suitably polished and embellished, of actual conversations with real participants, who, in this case however, are concealed behind fictitious names, Firenzuola taking the name of Celso Selvaggio.[47] There is an agreeable informality and naturalism about the discussions which indicate that one is indeed in touch with real people expressing genuine opinions. Firenzuola (under his pseudonym of Celso) constantly expresses amused irritation when, just as he is talking about the shape of female breasts, the women go out of their way to conceal their own. Some of the qualities of informality and naturalism are apparent in Niccolò Franco's *Dialogue on Beauty* (1542) and Lodovico Domenichi's *The Nobility of Women* (1549), both of which deal with real living contemporaries and not simply abstractions, and, to a lesser degree, *The Book of the Beautiful Women* (1554) by Federigo Luigini and *The Chief Beauties of Women* (1566) by Niccolò Campani.[48] Rather different are the books simply designed to instruct painters on how to achieve the effects of perfect beauty, such as the famous work of Giovan Giorgio Trissino.[49] Even Firenzuola's *Dialogue* provides some elements of this kind of instruction, which is not directly relevant to this study, but in fact he does agreeably distance himself from such abstract discourse when he says: 'There are many other measurements which, however, are of no importance and as Nature even rarely conforms to them, we will leave them to the painters, who with a stroke of the brush more or less, may lengthen or shorten them as seems good to them'.[50] This is the best riposte I know to all the assertions about beauty requiring that the height of the forehead should be as one-third to two-thirds for the rest of the face, etc., etc.

Although the exchanges from *The Book of the Courtier* already quoted referred to beauty in both men and women, a previous discussion in the same book had discussed the medieval precept which undoubtedly continued to hold sway in most circles throughout the Renaissance and for a long period thereafter: 'Methinke well beawty is more necessarie in her then in the Courtier, for (to saye the truth) there is a great lacke in the woman that wanteth beawtie'.[51] The very fact that all the books mentioned indicate in their titles that their prime concern is with the beauty of women shows how firmly their authors were constrained by the existing convention; but I do want to bring out the extent to which beauty is being treated as pertinent to men as well as to women. In Firenzuola's *Dialogue*, Celso, responding to a question from one of the women, declares that it is proper for women to contemplate the beauty of men and for men to contemplate the beauty of women, concluding 'when we are speaking of beauty in general, we mean your beauty, and our beauty', but then adds that a particular concern will be with what he calls the more delicate beauty of women.[52] In their discussions of the proper portions of the body, both Firenzuola and Niccolò Franco refer as much to men as to women. Firenzuola observes along the way that a shapely nose is as important for a man as it is for a woman,[53] while Franco has a brief description of the proper styling of the beard.[54] Furthermore the first part of Franco's work actually concludes with glorifications of the beauty of two men, Alfonso Davalo and the French invader, King Charles VIII (1470–98). However there is a continuance of the medieval tradition in that other qualities such as strength, diligence and intellect are integrated into the descriptions of physical features, and in the strong elements of sheer flattery.[55] Domenichi is entirely conventional in declaring that women are more beautiful than men, but he does recognise that certain physical characteristics in men will be attractive to women.[56]

What is most significant in Firenzuola is that beauty and sexual gratification are presented as good ends in themselves, without any need to link one to godliness and condemn the other. For beauty, he says, 'we see a man forget himself; and on beholding a face graced with this celestial gift, his limbs will quake, his hair stand on end, and he will sweat and shiver at the same time'.[57] Beauty, this natural attribute, the 'celestial gift', is very much *not* something merely in the eye of the beholder, a matter of subjective judgement:

> When we speak of a beautiful woman we mean one whom all alike admire, and not this one or that one only; thus Nova, so ill-favoured as she is, appears most pleasing in the sight of her Tomaso, albeit she is as uncomely as she possibly can be … a lady fair in all points, like yourself, must necessarily be pleasing to all, as you are; *albeit few are pleasing to you*, as I know full well.[58]

The phrase I have italicised, spoken with personal feeling as Celso addresses the gorgeous Madonna Selvaggia, brings out again Firenzuola's recognition that women too can be fussy about beauty in the opposite sex. More than a century later the French social commentator, La Bruyère, expressed women's liking for beauty in men with great cynicism:

> A vain, indiscreet, garrulous and vulgar man, who speaks confidently of his faith and of others with contempt, impetuous, haughty, conceited, lacking in morals and probity, with a crippled mind, bad judgement and free imagination, he needs nothing more in order to be thoroughly adored by women than to have a beautiful face and a fine figure.[59]

The attitudes towards beauty which, in all their ambiguity, dominated the early modern period are, as one might expect, most neatly encapsulated in one pregnant line by William Shakespeare. At the end of Act I of *As You Like It* (written in the closing years of the sixteenth century), Celia and Rosalind decide to flee from the court of the wicked uncle who has usurped the throne.

> | Rosalind | Why whither shall we go? |
> | Celia | To seek my uncle in the Forest of Arden. |
> | Rosalind | Alas! What danger will it be to us, |
> | | Maids as we are, to travel forthe so far? |
> | | Beauty provoketh thieves sooner than gold! |
> | Celia | I'll put myself in poor and mean attire, |
> | | And with a kind of umber smirch my face; |
> | | The like do you; so shall we pass along, |
> | | And never stir assailants.[60] |

Beautiful women attract assailants; plain ones on the whole do not. The line 'Beauty provoketh thieves sooner than gold' captures both the power of beauty and, through the association with thieves, its dangerous, even disreputable quality. In Shakespeare's time, of course, both Rosalind and Celia were played by young male actors. Only from the 1660s were female roles on stage consistently and continuously played by women. This in itself was an important, if relatively small, step in a more candid evaluation of beauty in both sexes. There then came to be a different kind of resonance about the disguises adopted by Rosalind and Celia. A gorgeous actress would be no less fetching for having a besmirched face nor, still less for, as in Rosalind's case, being dressed as a page boy. Popular Restoration and eighteenth-century plays frequently contained a part (for actresses who specialised in this role) which required the adoption at some point of masculine disguise: this provided the opportunity for the actress to show off, and the audience to appreciate, the shape of her legs.[61]

Naturally, the perception of beauty as a desirable commodity in its own right did not suddenly disappear with the collapse of the Italian city states: in secure, affluent environments (for example the courts of Louis XIV and Louis XV, or the great houses of some of the most eminent English aristocrats) beauty could be an independent characteristic of great value to its possessor. But the publication of dialogues openly praising sexual beauty ceased; mistrust and moralising took over.[62] For almost all sections of society in the seventeenth and eighteenth centuries life was too serious for beauty to play a significant role. For families at the top of the social scale, as also in the relatively comfortable middle, the most pressing requirement was the consolidation or improvement of social status, and the acquisition of a beautiful spouse did not automatically secure that.

Squire Allworthy in *Tom Jones*, by the eighteenth-century English novelist and magistrate Henry Fielding, was all in favour of marriage being founded on love: he regarded as equally deplorable parental compulsion, avarice for a great fortune, snobbery for a title and lust for a beautiful person.[63] The wisdom, and the fears and prejudices, of the day had been well summed up at the very beginning of the century by Mrs Mary Astell, a prolific commentator on proper and improper behaviour, in *Some Reflections on Marriage* of 1700. Choice in marriage, she says quite reasonably, should be 'guided by Reason', as against what, rather heatedly, she calls 'Humour or brutish Passion'. What, she asks, 'Do men propose to themselves in Marriage?', and quickly answers: 'What will she bring is the first enquiry. How many Acres? Or how much ready Coin?' Mrs Astell, a true daughter of her time, does not altogether disapprove, 'for Marriage without a Competency ... is no very comfortable condition'. A few pages later comes an immensely rich passage, whose heavy mistrust of beauty makes a fitting note on which to end this chapter, which has brought our study of traditional evaluations of beauty from Ancient Greece up to the eighteenth century:

> But suppose a man does not Marry for Money, though for one that does not, perhaps there are thousands that do; let him Marry for Love, and Heroick Action, which makes a mighty noise in the World, partly because of its rarity, and partly in regard of its extravagancy, and what does his Marrying for Love amount to? There's no great odds between his Marrying for the Love of Money, or for the Love of Beauty, the Man does not Act according to Reason in either Case; but is governed by irregular Appetites.[64]

3

Kings and Concubines

Prevailing ideas about how far, and in what senses, beauty should be valued obviously affected how far, if at all, beautiful individuals were able to cash in on their looks. One gigantic problem is that in the more remote periods (the sixteenth century and earlier, say) it is very difficult to be sure just exactly what any one particular person looked like. Sticking to my fundamental point that beauty, in individuals that we will ourselves never see, is very largely to be recognised by the reactions it provoked in other people at the time, I consider that the handful of women (and the odd man) reputed the great beauties of their age pretty certainly were great beauties (I do not, remember, accept the unexamined cliché that each age constructs its own ideal of beauty), though I always seek corroboration in the visual, as well as the detailed written evidence. Among 'reputed great beauties' were Veronica Franco, sixteenth-century Venetian courtesan; Gabrielle d'Estrées (mistress of Henry IV, Bourbon King of France, 1589–1610), known to many of us through the double portrait in the Louvre of her and her sister, bosoms boldly exposed; Madame de Montespan, who was readily tempted into the bed of Louis XIV, and Françoise Marguerite de Sévigny, who was not; Marion de Lorne, high-class courtesan, 'the marvel of her age' (the mid seventeenth century) with 'the body of Aphrodite';[1] Lucy Walter, mistress of the prince who was to become Charles II; Barbara Villiers and Hortense Mancini, among the many mistresses of the King who was Charles II; Madame Du Barry, mistress of Louis XV. Among men with analogous reputations were: Robert Devereux, second Earl of Essex, who touched the heartstrings of his Queen, Elizabeth I; George Villiers, Duke of Buckingham, who touched those of his King, James I; the Marquis de Cinq-Mars, protégé of Richelieu, madly loved by Marion de Lorne and dozens of other women; James, Duke of Monmouth, Pretender to the English throne; John Churchill, successful soldier who became Duke of

Marlborough. Those women rated stunning beauties in some circles inevitably incurred hostility and jealousy in others, and so had their detractors: I reserve for further scrutiny such women as: Louise de la Vallière, Ninon de Lenclos, Nell Gwyn, Madame de Pompadour.

None of the six wives of Henry VIII can assuredly be described as a reputed beauty, though, in at least three cases, the evidence in is conflict. Thanks to the brilliant work by Sir Roy Strong and others in the authentication, or the opposite, of portraits, we have a firmer base than ever before for making judgements, though sometimes we are left with only one authenticated portrait for each wife, and that frequently in a rather austere and colourless style, so that we may be left puzzling over whether a face is simply quietly well-proportioned, but otherwise rather plain, or whether it manifests the very fundamentals of beauty. Fortunately I have the conclusions of present-day historical experts to draw on, though sometimes those at the popular end of the market resort to the reassuring, bet-hedging cliché. On Anne Boleyn, Alison Weir writes that while 'not pretty', she had 'that indefinable quality, sex appeal'.[2] I must confess to having little patience with 'indefinable qualities'. Undoubtedly sex appeal can be found in people who are not beautiful, though whether it has the universal and immediate impact of physical beauty may be questioned. If we can recognise it, surely we can identify the possible ways in which it can be attained. From time to time, the posh English Sunday newspapers publish (inconclusive) articles about the alleged secret odours which (in a woman) make men (or in a man, women) their sex slaves. More basically, certain women are reputed to 'turn tricks', certain men to be 'sexual athletes' or possessed of exceptional endowment. These, presumably, are thoroughly definable elements of sex appeal. Many women have ways of indicating – through walk, use of eyes, lips, hips, voice, display of cleavage, of thighs – a profound interest in sex, perhaps a readiness to 'turn tricks'.

It is certainly an observable fact that a woman who knows herself to be less than beautiful may put extra effort into hinting at a possible readiness for sex. Sometimes what is meant by 'indefinable sex appeal' is a selection of the other qualities which endear a woman to a man: style, elegance, wit, intelligence, talent, understanding and compassion. This, however, seems to be to stretching the term 'sex appeal' into meaninglessness, rather as, traditionally, the word 'beauty' has been stretched into meaninglessness. In a man without beauty, sex appeal may consist in some or all of the following: great height, great strength, strongly masculine attitudes and behaviour, assiduous attention to a woman's needs and interests, a comedic personality, a highly romantic outlook. The possession of power by a man is said to be a sexual turn-on for some women – the possession of power by a woman, to date, not seeming to have the same effect on men; my own suspicion is that the attraction of power is often rather akin to that of wealth, it's the fringe benefits it brings that count, rather than any special sexual excitation inherent in power itself. Anyway, I'm keen to drive home once again my determination to isolate beauty as a quality in its own right, and then to be as precise as possible about any other qualities which may add to a person's attractiveness. One caution must constantly be kept in mind: men, deplorable creatures that they are, will often jump at the offer of bed and board without finding the woman concerned particularly attractive – the circumstances which get him into bed, or even a relationship, may not be 'indefinable sex appeal' but just lust or loneliness.

It cannot be claimed that looks played much part in the winning of thrones, though a good presence – as with Henry VIII, Louis XIV, Charles II, Louis XV – could be a positive asset. 'Queens', Lady Antonia Fraser has told us, 'were not expected to be great beauties.'[3] In the rare cases where they ruled in their own right, royal blood was what counted; as consorts they were selected for their value as diplomatic pawns. The young Prince Henry, later Henry VIII, had actually complained that it is 'the fate of princes to be in marriages of far worse sort than the condition of poor men. Princes take as is brought them by others, and poor men commonly at their own choice'.[4] Actually Henry did make his own choices. What he wanted was a comfortable marriage and a male heir; his lust for beauty he satisfied inconspicuously with a succession of short-term mistresses. At other courts, beautiful women could, with patience and skill, aspire to considerable worldly success as mistress of the king, but, at all courts, were very unwise even to think about becoming queen. Queen Elizabeth I was already in her late thirties when she began to sit for the portraits we are familiar with. However, the one early portrait of her, aged thirteen (actually a common marriage age for royal and aristocratic females) does, in contrast to an early one of her decidedly plain elder half-sister, the future Queen Mary, suggest the irony that, as a young queen she was definitely beautiful.[5] Ironical because, though her beauty entitled her to a happy marriage to the handsome object of her love, Robert Dudley, reasons of state prevented this; and because she is usually remembered as the rather sad painted and bewigged old maid of the later years of her reign.

If that sounds like a poisonous compound of ageism and sexism, then I fear that in a study of beauty ageing is not a factor that can be ignored; we are constantly coming up against it, not least in the lives of Henry VIII's six wives. The first, Catherine of Aragon, was betrothed, sight unseen, to Henry's elder brother, Prince Arthur. The father of Arthur and Henry, Henry VII, was desperate for an alliance with Spain, yet when Catherine finally arrived in England he insisted on inspecting her personally (to check her potential as a breeder of heirs) before allowing the marriage to go ahead. She was nearly sixteen, pleasant-faced, plump-ish, and with the intense appeal of young girlhood. Arthur was just fifteen, and (despite myths) was actually handsome and healthy enough; yet, such were the risks of the time, he was ill and dead within the year. With Henry VII dead, and his second son now Henry VIII, the latter, by his own choice, married Catherine. At twenty-three the face was less pleasing, the plumpness more pronounced; however, at eighteen Henry was contented enough, and desperate for Spanish support in his war against France. But Catherine failed to produce the urgently needed male heir; furthermore, as Alison Weir puts it succinctly, her 'gradually fading looks were brought increasingly into contrast by the maturing beauty of her younger husband'.[6] Meantime Henry had become infatuated with Anne Boleyn, whose dark colouring did not conform to the courtly conventions already noted, and whose social status rendered her an inappropriate consort for a king. By my own rules I have to deny her the accolade of beauty – there are many contemporary criticisms of her appearance,[7] and the one portrait in the National Portrait Gallery is so austere as to be, at best, inconclusive; additionally, I have to record the melancholy fact that (while I personally suspect that she was, in youth, beautiful in a convention-defying way) her looks quickly faded.[8] She would have been wise to settle for being a specially favoured mistress instead of playing for the highest stakes. Henry succumbed. Having divorced Catherine, he married Anne, but she too failed to produce the crucial male heir. On trumped up charges of sexual misbehaviour, perversely at a time when quite palpably she was no longer sexually appealing, Henry had her executed. Her successor, Jane Seymour, it is universally agreed, presented Henry with a welcome contrast to Anne, being modest and demure and, while quite personable, lacking in any claim to outstanding physical allure. Jane gave the king what should have guaranteed her a long reign, the male heir he so desired (the future Edward VI), but herself died a few days later. Henry had been in love with Jane, and did not immediately seek a replacement. None the less, the search was soon on for a queen who would serve Henry well on the international stage, cementing his position as a champion of Protestantism. Thus the king's advisers lighted on Anne of Cleves; Henry was enthusiastic about the *idea*, but, unfortunately, on first sight of Anne, took an instant dislike to her. Thus the legend grew up that she was physically repulsive (she did have an unpleasant body odour),[9] that written accounts of her appearance were unreliable, and the portrait of her which Hans Holbein was specially dispatched to paint for Henry's benefit was overly flattering. Taking all the evidence together, and reminding ourselves that repulsiveness is in the eyes of all beholders just as much as beauty is, we have to conclude that Anne was quite personable – and that Henry's aversion was personal to him. Anne was divorced, and treated reasonably well thereafter.[10] Again Henry turned back to the English court and, now a fat, unsavoury fifty year old, married the teenage niece of the Duke of Norfolk, Catherine Howard. She was the wife Henry loved most (though the visual evidence does not show her appearance to be a great improvement on that of Anne of Cleves), but he was correspondingly offended by the discovery of her platonic affair with courtier, Thomas Culpepper, and so had her executed. Henry was now ready for a mature bride, twice married, just thirty something – Catherine Parr, herself in love with the beautiful Sir Thomas Seymour, brother of Jane. Despite her age, Catherine was, on the evidence of a recently authenticated portrait,[11] quite certainly the only one among the six wives to rival the young Anne Boleyn in having claims to beauty. She wanted to marry Seymour and did not want to marry smelly old Henry. Her beauty brought her tragedy in that she had to give up the love of her life; but she was a dignified queen with considerable influence over the continually developing Protestant settlement; and, thanks to a wise and patient strategy, she survived.[12]

The mother of Louis XIV, the formidable Marie de' Médicis, who had brought a vast dowry to the debt-ridden Henry IV, was, as the many portraits demonstrate, fat and plain. Louis, too, performed his dynastic duty, marrying the daughter of Philip IV, King of Spain, Maria Teresa, who was short, fat and ugly. Her royal status and the power of Spain had made her Queen of France, but she had no hope of holding the marital attentions of the King. The *maîtresse declarée* (or *maîtresse en titre*) for most of the 1660s was a shy, reticent girl of, by court standards, low social status (she was from the minor nobility and had suffered the double blow, not so much that first her father, then her father-in-law, had died, but that before doing so, each had amassed substantial debts), Louise de la Vallière, who had come to the court as maid-of-honour to the King's sister-in-law, Henrietta of England. By the second half of the decade, as contemporaries remarked, Louise was being strongly chal- lenged for the King's favour by a woman four years older than herself, Madame Françoise de Montespan.[13] By birth Madame de Montespan was a Mortemart, one of the oldest families of France. By the end of the decade Françoise had supplanted Louise. The two best-known portraits of Madame de Montespan are by mediocre artists (one literally unknown, the other, Henri Gascar, so nearly unknown as makes no diff- erence), which may explain the bland, sexless, sub-Venus de Milo appearance in both; however, the portrait by the highly competent Pierre Mignard shows a very striking and sensual woman. Two well- known renderings of Mlle de la Vallière, both enamels by Jean Petitot, suffer from the medium and also, again, from being in the Grecian mode. But for their conveyance of vivacity and freshness, they beat the two mediocre Montespan portraits hands down.[14] The truly lovely por- trait of Louise, the Jean Nocret at Versailles, renders her by about the same margin more beautiful than the Mignard Montespan.

The written testimony is far from conclusive, though, on balance, it favours Madame de Montespan. What is clear is that the latter was lively, witty and strong-willed in a way Mlle de la Vallière was not; also that she made a quite determined and calculated bid to oust Louise and become chief mistress. The Prince de Condé said of Mme de Montes- pan in November 1666 that 'no one could have more spirit or more beauty'; an Italian gentleman at court, Primi Visconti, lyricised over her 'blonde hair, large azure blue eyes, well-formed aquiline nose, vermilion

mouth, beautiful teeth', making, 'in a word, a perfect face'.[15] Was it perhaps the eminence of the Mortemarts that was being admired, or did
Mme de Montespan more closely fit the courtly convention of the time?
(This was a time, we know, when conventions in beauty were of considerable importance, though that doesn't mean everyone was taken in
by them.) There were many comments on the fresh beauty of Mlle de
la Vallière, but the famous one by the Abbé de Choisy hits off the
impression that Louise stood outside the pale of courtly convention: she
was not, he said, 'one of those perfect beauties that one often admires
without loving' (a delicate way, I surmise, of referring to someone who
fulfils the arithmetic and the colour scheme but still fails to be beautiful).[16] The boring magistrate Olivier Lefèvre d'Ormesson, keeper of a
massive journal, found Louise 'not at all beautiful', but 'skinny' (she was
certainly slim), with 'a long face' and 'nose too wide at the bottom' (this
actually agrees with the fetching Nocret portrait). But d'Ormesson, who
had been scorned by the King, was a supporter of the Queen. He later
refers to Mme de Montepan's power, but not at all to her looks.[17]
(Because he disliked her too? Or because they were not so remarkable?
– I don't know).

It may well be that Louis, with so much choice on easy offer, could
see beyond the conventions which bound sycophantic observers and
appreciate, as we would today, the more unusual beauty of Louise. What
he also appreciated (I stress this, since I want to bring out the balance
between beauty and other qualities in affecting a person's life chances)
was the fact that Louise was a magnificent horsewoman; she was, in fact,
something of a tomboy (a characteristic at odds with the seventeenth-
century courtly image of womanhood) and, from a childhood accident,
resulting from a dangerous jumping game practised with her brother,
had the very faintest suspicion of a limp – a matter, inevitably, seized
upon by her detractors.[18] In the end, the spirit, wit, determination and
confidence of Mme de Montespan won out over Louise, who twice
retired to a convent, being, the first time, deliberately brought back and
openly cherished by Louis, who created her duchess and recognised
their daughter, Marie-Anne. Finally retiring to a life of piety, Louise had
not done badly from her looks – certainly immeasurably better than
Anne Boleyn. Eventually, at fifty-two Louis fell for Marie Angélique de
Fontanges, an eighteen-year-old maid of honour to Henrietta. Every

piece of evidence demonstrates that she was outstandingly beautiful, though apparently rather stupid.[19] As soon as she became pregnant Louis made her a duchess, but the child was stillborn and she herself never recovered. Of course, there were always hazards attached to careers based on the granting of sexual favours.

Of all the women associated with Louis XIV, the one best known to history is Madame de Maintenon, who, as Madame Scarron, had, despite being poor, moved in intellectual circles in the 1650s and 1660s; even then, as a Mignard portrait indicates, she was no more than personable. But she attracted the attention and gratitude of the King by looking after the children he had had by Mme de Montespan, and was rewarded with the estate of Maintenon, and the title of marquise. As her niece observed, Mme de Maintenon was welcomed by the Queen: unlike the three women just discussed, she posed no threat.[20]

In later middle age, as the country was shaken by a series of poisoning scandals, the King turned towards a kind of evangelical religiosity, reinforced by the death of the Queen in July 1683. The prim and deeply religious Madame de Maintenon, three years older than Louis, matched his mood exactly. She had been establishing a stronger and stronger hold over him, and at some stage, possibly even as early as 1683, they were secretly married. As is well known, the whole tone of the later years of the reign of Louis was pervaded by the puritanism of Mme de Maintenon. Looks had played no part in her triumph.

If we look back across the Channel to the court of Charles II matters are more straightforward. In that environment beauty certainly brought rewards. Charles's first mistress after the Restoration was Barbara Villiers, Mrs Palmer. Charles created her husband Earl of Castlemaine so that Barbara could have the rank of Lady Castlemaine. Financially she did well out of Charles (or, more accurately, the public purse), and she was able to ensure a secure future for her children. She was undoubtedly a woman of strong personality and great spirit, not only greatly influencing Charles, but taking a number of other lovers even while she was his mistress. The foundation of her career was the astonishing Villiers good looks (an earlier, male, Villiers will be discussed shortly). Later portraits from the studio of Sir Peter Lely tend to approximate to the same stereotype, but the stunning one of 1663 was done when the artist was still giving careful individual attention to his most important clients. Of the many written tributes to her beauty,[21] I want to focus on those of the civil servant and celebrated diarist Samuel Pepys, a choice representative of *l'homme moyen sensuel*. In Whitehall, seeing Lady Castlemaine, he 'glutted' himself 'with looking at her', the 'only she', as he put it on another occasion, 'I can observe for true beauty'. Several years later he confessed to the best dream he ever had when with Barbara in his bed he 'was admitted to use all the dalliance I desired with her'. Most significant of all is the reflection, after seeing her at the theatre, that though he knows 'well enough she is a whore' – and it must be stressed that he did recognise this, beauty not being confused here with morality or truth – because of her beauty he is ready to think the best of her and even to pity her.[22] There was no possibility of Lady Castlemaine becoming Queen. In accordance with dynastic imperatives, in 1662 Charles married Catherine of Braganza, once more, as portraits do not conceal (one suspects the artists of not trying very hard), a dumpy and unattractive woman; but Barbara continued to influence ministerial appointments in a way that the Queen simply did not.[23]

Many other beautiful women served as mistresses to the King and were rewarded. While manifestly the crown itself provided the seductive magic, one element in Charles's successes with women was his own striking physical appearance, along with his general good humour and graciousness. While Louis XIV was short, Charles was six feet two inches tall, a very considerable height for that age. His swarthy, sexual looks are familiar from portraits. Madame de Motteville's description of him as a young man matches the portraits and indicates that sort of male appearance which, while definitely not beautiful, certainly has impact: 'well-made, with a swarthy complexion agreeing well with his fine black eyes, a large ugly mouth, graceful and dignified carriage, and a fine figure'.[24]

We all know about Nell Gwyn, but none of us know for sure what she looked like. Time was when art galleries happily displayed any number of 'Nell Gwyns'; now the poor historian risks being crushed to death in the stampede to deny that *any* portrait could possibly be of that notorious lady. A further problem arises from the procedures followed in the studio of Peter Lely. Already by 1661, when this Dutch-born artist was appointed Court Painter to Charles II, Lely had developed a technique of overemphasising the lower part of the eyelid which, when sensitively done, gave his sitters a slumberingly sensuous look. But soon 'Lely' portraits, often in several copies, were being manufactured at great speed by his many assistants. The well-known and much-reproduced portrait sold as a postcard and slide by the National Portrait Gallery, London, dates from the mid 1670s when the eyelid trick had become an ugly mannerism producing protuberant eyeballs. Nell may well not have been the sitter;[25] certainly it has to be doubted if this representation can be taken as a good likeness. Nell, the humble tart who consorted with royalty, has not been well treated by the British establishment. To the less than stunning image purveyed by the National Portrait Gallery must be added the insult offered by the *Dictionary of National Biography*: 'She appears to be low in stature and plump, to have had hair of reddish brown. Her foot was diminutive, and her eyes when she laughed became all but invisible.' The source for this is the highly dubious *Memoirs of the Life of Eleanour Gwinn* published in the middle of the eighteenth century.[26] The jibe about the smallness of her eyes is utterly inconsistent with the over-prominence given them in the National Portrait Gallery 'Lely', and the total impression is much at odds with Pepys's repeated emphasis on her 'prettiness', Madame D'Aulnoys's admiration for her figure, and the fact that on stage she could successfully impersonate a male gallant. Because there was so much emphasis on her wit, her vivacity and gaiety, it may be wise to conclude that she was highly personable rather than ravishingly beautiful, but near enough to beauty for her appearance indeed to have been a crucial asset.

By 1667 Nell Gwyn was an established comic actress and had become briefly the mistress of Lord Buckhurst. Charles already had on his team a pretty actress, Moll Davis; late in 1667 he signed on Nell, who from then on played an important part in the life of the King, though as a former actress from origins still more humble, she could not be *maîtresse en titre*. That role, as Charles tired of Lady Castlemaine (though she continued to enjoy public benefits, receiving a personal title as Duchess of Cleveland in 1670), went to Louise de Kéroualle, twenty-one-year-old daughter of an ancient Breton family and maid of honour (yet another one!) to Charles's sister, Henrietta. Louise had a baby face and haughty aristocratic manners. It took Charles a year to seduce her. Louise's son by Charles was legitimised as Charles Fitzroy, Duke of Richmond, and she herself in 1673 became Duchess of Portsmouth. Briefly her position was shaken by the arrival of a woman who, even more than Barbara Villiers, had used her personal beauty to lead a life as liberated as was possible for any woman in that age. Hortense Mancini was the niece of the powerful French statesman Cardinal Mazarin. Sensitive no doubt to the dangerous emotions her great beauty aroused, he married her to the Marquis de la Meilleraye, making over to him a substantial fortune and the title of Duc de Mazarin. Unfortunately the newly created duke was quite mad, a sad punishment,[27] though an appropriate one, some no doubt thought, for exceptional beauty. Hortense escaped and boldly travelled all over Europe, skilfully exploiting the devastating effect she had on men. Her first great love was the Duke of Savoy, with whom she spent three years. The second was Charles (she arrived in England in 1675). But this affair was in full flood for only three months, after which Hortense simply joined the team, with a generous pension till the end of her days, while the Duchess of Portsmouth was restored as principal mistress, her main rival thereafter being the popular Nell Gwyn. Mobbed in Oxford by a crowd who mistook her for the hated Catholic royal mistress, Nell put her head out of the coach window, crying: 'Pray, good people, be civil; I am the Protestant whore.' Charles's mistresses did well out of their looks; the more high-born were raised in status and were able to provide security for their offspring. Nell did well also, Charles supporting her in her great extravagances, and creating their first son Duke of St Albans. However, Charles's very first mistress, Lucy Walter, fulfilled that part of popular lore which charges that beauty can only bring tragedy (she certainly demonstrated one truism: better an ugly old king than a handsome young claimant). She had given birth to the son, James (later Duke of Monmouth), who was one of Charles's own favourites, but she herself lost all contact with him and died a miserable death in 1658 at the age of around twenty-eight.

This draws our attention to an important point. One cannot predict that a person born beautiful will automatically enjoy happiness and success. What one can predict is that their lives are likely to be different from those led by the less comely. For good or ill they will draw attention to themselves: they will have opportunities not open to others. What is made of these opportunities will depend on other personal qualities, and on circumstance. Beauty affects life *experiences* rather than necessarily life *chances*. This is brought out rather sharply by the careers of certain male beauties of the period. Let us go back to the reign of James I, and to 1614 when James, then forty-seven, met George Villiers, then twenty-two. Villiers was an extraordinarily handsome and highly sexed young man, quite happy to exploit James's rampant homosexuality. His physical presence gave him power over women and also heterosexual men; but now it was the King's favour that counted most, enabling Villiers to establish himself at the centre of a web of patronage which brought him good profits. In 1616 he was appointed Master of the Horse, dubbed a Knight of the Garter and created Viscount Villiers. The following year James conferred an earldom on him, giving this charming explanation to the Lords of the Counsel:

> I, James, am neither God nor an angel, but a man like any other. Therefore I act like a man, and confess to loving those dear to me more than other men. You may be sure that I love the Earl of Buckingham more than anyone else, and more than you who are here assembled. I wish to speak on my own behalf, and not to have it thought to be a defect, for Jesus Christ did the same and therefore I cannot be blamed. Jesus had his John, and I have my George.[28]

Buckingham shortly became a marquis and then, eventually, a duke, receiving the only dukedom granted outside the blood royal between 1485 and 1660. Meantime he captivated the utterly heterosexual heir to the throne, Charles (later Charles I). As well as charm, Buckingham had much skill and cunning, but in devising the scheme whereby he and Charles went to Spain in search of a Spanish consort for Charles he showed how far arrogant self-confidence could outrun political judgement. The scheme was a humiliating fiasco; none the less, even after the accession of Charles I in 1625, Buckingham remained the single greatest influence in the kingdom. But for arrogant beauty, Nemesis was at hand: to wide rejoicing, Buckingham was assassinated in 1628.

Something very close to an action replay took place a decade later in France, though on a rather more heroic scale. Under the regency of Marie de' Médicis and, more critically, in the early years of the reign of Louis XIII, the man who steadily concentrated power in his own hands was Bishop, and later Cardinal Richelieu, a highly active heterosexual, who, however, warmed to the delicately featured Henri d'Effiat, created Marquis de Cinq-Mars. As part of his scheme to dominate the sickly King, Richelieu pushed Cinq-Mars forward as a court favourite, Louis being completely captivated by this beautiful young man whose real talents, in fact, lay in seducing women: Marion de Lorne was madly in love with him, provoking the jealousy of the King, and the mother of Cinq-Mars to bringing accusations of rape against Marion.[29] Like Buckingham before him, Cinq-Mars came to feel himself all-conquering and invulnerable. In 1641 he joined the Spanish government in a conspiracy to assassinate his former patron, Richelieu, and take over power in Paris. Cinq-Mars and his cronies were no match for the Cardinal's espionage system. Nemesis once again overtook overweening male beauty: Cinq-Mars was executed.

Three dead swallows do not make a winter; still, let us look at the third in the gorgeous, tragic trio. The early pages of Madame d'Aulnoy's memoirs of the British court are dominated by Charles's son by Lucy Walter, James, Duke of Monmouth. As portraits show, he had inherited the beauty of his mother. Madame d'Aulnoy wrote admiringly that he had many mistresses, but that men also admired his beauty.[30] Monmouth lived the life of a brutal rowdy, interspersed with hectic periods of soldiering. Yet he had the gift of gaining the sympathy and support of his social inferiors, a gift greatly aided by personal beauty, but not created by it alone. He won a striking victory over rebellious Scottish Covenanters in 1679, and then good repute for the clemency he showed to the defeated. Charles II died unexpectedly in February 1685, to be succeeded by his openly Catholic brother, James II. Monmouth, an uncompromising Protestant, resigned himself to what seemed likely to be a long exile in Brussels. Yet within months (on 11 June to be precise) he had landed at Lyme Regis on the Dorset coast to head a rebellion against James. Though he rallied considerable support in the West Country, he was soon defeated and, on 11 July, beheaded on Tower Hill as a traitor. To get these events, and the place of Monmouth's looks in them, into perspective, we have to go back to 1680 when the Earl of Shaftesbury, seeing the possibility of making Monmouth the puppet of the Whig grandees who wished to exclude James from the throne, deliberately organised for him a kind of royal 'progress' through the West Country. Looks *were* important here: Monmouth could only gain in popularity through being shown off. The Whig conspirators continued to work on Monmouth, appealing both to his religious principles and to his vanity. He was impeccably qualified to raise a movement of the poor to middling interests in the West, but lacked the organisational skills and the decisiveness (he fumbled any chance of seizing Bristol) to lead them to victory.[31] Had he done so, he would be one of the heroes of British history. That he had that opportunity was due to a combination of birth and beauty. But consider: had Lucy Walter herself not been beautiful, and had her looks not been bequeathed to her son, would there have been a Monmouth's rebellion?

It is a relief to turn to a man who did manage to use his good looks to get him started on the road to the highest peaks of success. John Churchill's career began in service to James, Duke of York, later the James II Monmouth rebelled against. At twenty-one, Churchill, with his slim elegant figure, brilliant grey-green eyes, long eyelashes and long fair hair, noble nose and well-proportioned features, almost merits the adjective 'pretty', save that the word is too weak for the powerful impact he had on those around him. It was at this age that he was taken up by Barbara Villiers, now twenty-nine and Duchess of Cleveland. Although the King himself acknowledged her daughter Barbara, born in 1672, the father was almost certainly Churchill.[32] The proposition that Churchill owed the financial security upon which he built his subsequent glorious career to the loving generosity of Barbara Villiers is based on the testimony of the fourth Earl of Chesterfield, writing to his son in 1748, but seems plausible – the receipt for the annuity which Churchill purchased certainly exists, and there would not appear to be any other possible source for the purchasing price than Villiers, known to have been very generous towards those with whom she was enamoured. Marlborough the great general and national hero obviously called on many other qualities than those of personal appearance. The only point being suggested here is that Marlborough's beauty brought him the security and independence of a regular income upon which he was able to build his political and military career, and that that security might well not have come any other way. Indeed it seems possible to venture the generalisation, perhaps an obvious one, that beauty has its most critical effects in the early stages of a career, other qualities then becoming increasingly important; but between getting a start and not getting a start there can sometimes be the whole difference.

If we move to Madame de Pompadour and Madame Du Barry, we come to the heart of some of the main issues this book is intended to explore. Neither was of noble birth, but the former was extremely rich and had powerful connections and an exceptionally good education, while the latter was extremely poor, dependent on the charity of the church for her education, and, indeed, a classic instance of the woman whose sole asset is her looks. But what of the looks of Jeanne Antoinette Poisson, born in Paris in 1721 and later the Marquise de Pompadour? The problems are similar to those with Nell Gwyn, though in this case we do have a dozen or more thoroughly authenticated portraits. Many of us are familiar with those by François Boucher, very regal, very dignified, but showing a woman whose face is just too pinched, whose nose is just slightly too beaky and chin just slightly too weak to be beautiful. Now, almost all of these were painted when Madame de Pompadour was reaching the peak of her power, but passing the peak of her physical attractiveness. Earlier authenticated portraits, however, indicate the same personable, but scarcely beautiful, features. Paintings presenting an alluring young woman, once casually labelled 'Madame de Pompadour' have now been discredited. The stale argument that Pompadour as rendered by Boucher represented the ideal of beauty of the day is completely subverted by the large number of Bouchers featuring truly luscious young women, not differing one whit from *one* of the types which we find beautiful today. There are many written tributes to the beauty of Madame de Pompadour, while foreign observers expressed surprise at her lack of looks. There is a long, flattering, but, if we read it carefully, revealing description by Georges Leroy, Lieutenant of the Hunt at Versailles.[33] Leroy stresses noble deportment and facial expressiveness, speaking of the 'fire', 'spirit' and 'brilliance' of her eyes. Then comes the key sentence: 'She absolutely extinguished all the other women at the Court, although some were very beautiful.' Madame de Pompadour, I conclude, was not 'very beautiful', but had spirit and vivacity which rendered her very attractive. She also had a trove of appealing talents.

Without extreme good fortune in birth and upbringing, however, Mlle Poisson would neither have been able to develop these talents to the full, nor have been in a position to exploit either them, or her qualities of vivacity and personableness. When her wealthy father had to go into temporary exile following a financial scandal, four-year-old Jeanne Antoinette was taken into the guardianship of the powerful and wealthy

M. le Normant de Tournehem, who provided her with the best education obtainable, so that she developed into an immensely cultivated
young woman, a lively conversationalist and brilliant musical per-
former. He also provided her with a husband in the form of his nephew
Paul le Normant de Tournehem or le Normant d'Etioles, as he now
styled himself, whose reluctant agreement may suggest that he found her
less than irresistably beautiful. With the marriage (March 1741, when she
was nineteen) came a substantial income, an elegant Paris address, the
Chateau d'Etioles in the Forest of Sénart and the fine-sounding name of
Madame d'Etioles. At Etioles she built her own theatre, where she
became famous for her dramatic and musical presentations. In Paris
she was on show in the salons and at supper parties.

The events which followed are explicable only as part of a deliberate
campaign by Mme d'Etioles to establish herself as mistress to the King,
Louis XV, a campaign she waged with courage and resourcefulness.
Louis regularly went hunting in the Forest of Sénart, so, to attract his
attention, she took to following the hunt in a brightly coloured chaise.
She adopted the same tactics in Paris, where she would ensconce herself
at the theatre in full view of the King. The climax came in 1745 when a
series of masked balls were held in honour of the marriage of the
Dauphin. Under cover of the festivities, Mme d'Etioles succeeded in lur-
ing the rather timid Louis into her bed. Shortly afterwards she was
acknowledged as *maîtresse en titre* and given the title of Marquise de
Pompadour. For almost twenty years, till her death on 15 April 1764, she
was in all but name Queen of France, with a strong influence over affairs
of state – almost entirely for the worse. On the other hand, she played
the leading part in maintaining the high aesthetic standards of the court.

That the King had taken a bourgeoise as *maîtresse en titre* was quite
shocking, though so cultured were Pompadour's graces, and so regal her
style, that criticism was muted. The woman who eventually took her
place and reigned as *maîtresse en titre* until the King's death came from
an altogether lower social position, a fatherless child from the provinces.
Educated by the church, Jeanne Bécu was, at fifteen, given employment
as a companion to the widow of a tax-collector. The first description we
have of her is at age sixteen when we are told 'she was already built to
ravish; a figure both lithe and noble; an oval face as if drawn with a paint
brush; large eyes, clearly set apart, with that slumberous glance, which

made them a constant invitation to love; lovely mouth; small feet; hair so abundant that I could not have held it in my two hands'.[34] With such looks there were two obvious careers for Mlle Bécu: she could go into the theatre, where, however, the pay was tiny, or non-existent, or she could serve in an elegant shop, patronised by rich Parisians always on the lookout for beautiful potential mistresses. Bécu, at the age of seventeen in fact took employment as a *vendeuse* in the select fashion shop Labille, in rue Neuve-des-Petis-Champs. Jeanne attracted enormous attention, and her potential was appreciated by at least two commercial specialists in female beauty: Madame Gourdan, a well-established procuress, and Jean Du Barry, always known, accurately, as 'le Roué'. Jeanne, now calling herself Jeanne Beauvarnier, because it sounded grander, became the mistress of Du Barry, who was not so much interested in his own pleasure as in the hard cash value of such an outstanding beauty. The police were interested as well, and in their journal of 19 December 1764, two inspectors reported of Mlle Beauvarnier; 'She is a person nineteen years old, tall, well-made and of distinguished appearance, with a most lovely face'.[35]

She could not attract the attention of the King with quite the elegant panache shown by Mme d'Etioles, but she deliberately made visits to Versailles, positioning herself so as to be noticed by him. Here there is no question but that physical beauty was the sole, unalloyed element in the chemistry which followed. The King, now fifty-eight, did notice Jeanne and instructed his valet-de-chamber to find out more about her. Jean Du Barry acted as the middleman, making the profit he had always counted on; as the King found Mlle Beauvarnier in all respects to his pleasure, Du Barry, in fulfilment of the King's requirements in the matter (he didn't wish to be lumbered with illegitimate children), had Jeanne married to his own brother, Count Guillaume Du Barry, in July 1768. In April 1769, Mme Du Barry was formally presented at the Versailles Court, remaining *maîtresse-en-titre* till the King's death in 1774. Her lower-class origins and lack of aristocratic graces meant that she continued to be a subject of scandal to a degree that Pompadour never was, and it is significant that she was never elevated beyond the title which, for convenience, she had already acquired as the Comtesse Du Barry.

Du Barry, in almost every way, represents the idea of human beauty as itself, not something else: she pioneered the greatest simplicity of dress, making absolutely the most of her natural attributes, and, to the great vexation of older women, she put no powder on her hair. But it would be wrong to discount the personal qualities which she did possess. She was high-spirited and cheerful, learned to speak French correctly and was a brilliant storyteller. Obviously, she suited the King perfectly in his declining years. But she had no security for the future, and with the King's death was forced into an uncomfortable retirement, still occasionally visited and praised by former admirers. Her associations with the old regime were nevertheless too evident, and under the Terror she was dragged from her seclusion: understandably her spirit cracked and she died a sad, undignified death at the guillotine. The message does not need to be underlined that there was often little security for a woman whose social ascent was dependent upon granting sexual favours to powerful men. At the same time, had little orphan Jeanne been born plain she might well have perished of malnutrition at an early age.

Let us conclude this chapter by considering what happened when the boot was on the other foot, securely in the case of Catherine the Great, loosely in the case of Queen Christina of Sweden, though that could not have been predicted from their different situations at birth. As daughter of the great warrior King Gustavus Adolphus, Christina succeeded legitimately to the throne of Sweden, in the seventeenth century a major European power. As Princess Sophia of Anhalt-Zerbst, the future Catherine the Great was born a penniless minor German princess who had to deploy courage, skill and ruthlessness to become Empress of Russia. Christina converted to Catholicism, abdicated and, based in Rome, lived a life of great notoriety, chortled and gasped over throughout Europe.[36] Sophia was no more than personable, though as Catherine the Great she was, in middle age, statuesque, with a commanding presence. Christina verged on the plain, and, having been dropped as a baby, had a deformed shoulder. One cannot but admire her energy, stamina, boldness, support for the arts, determination to be her own woman and defiance of convention. If only she had had the beauty to go with these qualities she would, quite probably, have been a very happy woman. In Rome she fell passionately in love with the distinctly odd-looking Cardinal Decco Azzolino.[37] He, while flattered to be associated with a former queen, quickly lost whatever sexual appetite he may have had for her and could raise no more than (in the words of her authoritative biographer Georgina Masson) 'a sympathy and kindliness for this strange and really pathetic woman whom he knew depended on him for all her happiness in life, as well as wise counsel and support'.[38]

For over fifty years, with only the slightest interruption, the Russian Empire was ruled by two strong-willed, but not specially good-looking women, Elizabeth I and Catherine II (Catherine the Great).[39] At the Russian court, did beautiful men have the advantages of a Villiers or a Du Barry, or were other qualities demanded by the imperial rulers? Elizabeth, daughter of Peter the Great, achieved the throne through a well-conceived bloodless coup against her female cousin, the Regent Ann. She had a number of not particularly handsome lovers when the equivalent of a *maîtresse en titre* appeared in the form of Alexis Razumovsky. Razumovsky was of even lower social status than Du Barry – he was a Ukrainian peasant. Clearly he was a man of sense, patience and skill, but above all he was beautiful in the most virile way. Elizabeth created him prince and field marshal. As he grew older, the Empress kept him on the strength, but added three very good-looking younger men, Shuvalov, Kachinersky and Beketov. As her heir, Elizabeth, for romantic reasons of her own, chose a grandson of Peter the Great, who was a German prince, naming him Grand Duke Peter Fedorovich; she also decided that the appropriate wife for the Grand Duke was the Princess Sophia, who, along with her mother, was summoned to Russia. As she recorded in her *Memoirs*, Sophia was not specially impressed by the sixteen-year-old Grand Duke Peter, a feeble creature, whose looks were shortly totally destroyed by a smallpox attack.[40] The young Sophia, who had converted to the Russian Orthodox Church and taken the name of Catherine, had exactly the same excuse as Henry VIII, Charles II, Louis XIV or Louis XV for seeking a good-looking lover (or half-a-dozen).

The first was Serge Saltikov, of whom Catherine later wrote: 'unfortunately I could not help listening to him; he was handsome as the dawn'.[41] Her next lover, the Polish Count Stanislaus Poniatowsky, was generally reputed to be one of the best-looking men of his time, though Catherine herself commented on his extreme short-sightedness[42] (which may account for his rather flattering description of her).[43] In 1759 Catherine turned to Gregory Gregorievitch of the powerful Orlov family. The classic perfection of his features was commented upon by both women and men, as also the virile strength of his body. Orlov was a Barbara Villiers, with rather more power: he had his pick of all the most beautiful young women at court, while he treated Catherine in a very casual way (he was twenty-five and Catherine thirty). At this stage, of course, she was not yet Empress, though she was very carefully preparing herself – she was far better informed, as well as being inherently far more intelligent than anyone else at court. On the afternoon of Christmas Day 1761, the Empress Elizabeth died. The Grand Duke Peter became Tsar Peter III. By now estranged from his clever and highly sexed wife, he hoped to be able to get rid of her and establish as Empress his homely mistress, Elizabeth Worontsov, with whom he felt at ease. As it turned out, he assisted Catherine's cause by making blunder after blunder. The first quality Catherine showed was cool, calculating courage; secondly, she showed sensitivity and skill in choosing her moment. Undoubtedly her physical presence counted for much, but it is unclear that her sexual favours to Orlov made much difference. She had the support of the Guards regiments and personally led them against Peter, who abdicated without bloodshed. Reminding us of the world we are in, Peter was murdered on 5 July 1762.

Now Empress in her own right, Catherine could fully indulge her tastes in men. Orlov remained her principal lover till 1772. If one runs through the list, the qualifications clearly were beauty and youth. It is true that her long-term lover after Orlov, Gregory Potemkin, was all of thirty-five years old, but then she was forty-five. Potemkin was large and dramatic rather than beautiful, being very dark, with an aquiline nose, and by the time his relationship got going he had lost an eye (probably due to a neglected abscess) and had developed a facial tic. She wrote to him as 'My beauty, my marble beauty',[44] but obviously, like Pompadour, he had other qualities than the purely physical, and she kept up her correspondence with him long after she was devoting herself amost exclusively to handsome young soldiers. In the late 1760s there had been the gorgeous twenty-seven-year-old Plato Zubov, whom she showed off publicly as a man would show off a beautiful girlfriend. For two years in the early 1770s there was the handsome guardsman Alexander Vasilikov. In 1775 there began the most famous period when she had a series of beautiful young soldiers, each one appointed to a post as Adjutant General, and each one around twenty-three at the time of his appointment.

Very, very few women indeed find themselves in a position anything like that of Catherine the Great. She had achieved that position in part by the decisions of another woman, the Empress Elizabeth, but ultimately through her own intelligence, courage and hard work (not least in learning the Russian language and Russian ways): personal beauty did not enter into it, and she could never have made a career as a Du Barry or even as a Barbara Villiers (that is dependent on pleasing a powerful male). She is of interest for our purposes in showing what could happen when a woman did have freedom and power.

4

Something Handsome and Cheap

All of the women, and some of the men, cashing in on their looks were in fact doing so by granting sexual favours to one of more persons in positions of power. For Jeanne Bécu an important stage along that road was serving in a shop; for Nell Gwyn it was displaying herself as an actress. There were, indeed, a number of occupations whose doors were more readily opened to beautiful women than to plain ones, though until the twentieth century the greatest material rewards continued to be secured through some branch of the sex trade: prostitution, concubinage and, in certain circumstances, marriage. Eventually, as actresses mutated into film stars, a beautiful woman could earn millions because of her appeal to millions and not because of a sexual relationship with a single powerful man. Actually, before going on stage, Nell had occupied the coveted post of orange-seller in the newly opened King's Theatre, her looks giving her the edge over the stiff competition;[1] while, as we saw, Jeanne's first occupation had been in service, as a lady's companion. Thus the 'occupations' I have just referred to can be summarised as 'the four esses': service, selling, show business, and, of course, sex. There is a fifth, but very different, 's', that of *salonière*. This was an avocation rather than an occupation, one in which beauty was not an essential qualification, but where the good-looking were often of particular renown. Here we touch on the general point that in some environments, or some situations, highly praised looks are a comparative, or relative, matter: *salonières*, ladies who organised and acted as hostesses in 'salons' to which they invited the leading intellectuals and artists of the day, were not, as a group, outstandingly beautiful, but some achieved special eminence because, *compared* with other women of similar intelligence, talent and culture, they were at least highly personable and sometimes genuinely beautiful. Women who were both eminent and beautiful were much painted, the artist never the less *being paid* for what were, presumably, congenial commissions. In a later chapter we'll encounter another occupation which often offered open arms to specially good-looking women, that of artist's model, for which the artist (whatever else he might do) *did pay*. And during the course of this chapter I'll indicate how service, selling and show business could sometimes also offer special opportunities to beautiful men.

In sixteenth-century Italy, and most notably in Venice, there was a special class of sex-worker, the *cortigiana onesta* (the 'honoured' courtesan, 'honest' in the sense of being 'valued' in a way in which the common prostitute, the *meretrice*, was not), who, recognised by the state, basically earned her keep from sexual services rendered, but who was also expected to offer cultured and intellectually stimulating companionship. Most famous of all was Veronica Franco, undoubtedly a poet and intellectual in her own right. Margaret F. Rosenthal has written a brilliant analysis of contemporary writings by, and about, Franco, *The Honest Courtesan: Veronica Franco, Citizen and Writer in Sixteenth-Century Venice*, declaring that 'Playing music, singing, composing poetry, and presenting a sophisticated figure were the courtesan's necessary, marketable skills'.[2] Being a feminist, Rosenthal leaves out the number one 'marketable' quality, beauty. That Franco was beautiful we know from contemporary accounts and can see for ourselves from three surviving portraits, particularly the famous one attributed to Tintoretto, now in the Worcester Art Gallery, Massachusetts; that her beauty was critically important to her and to the maintenance of her eminence in Venetian society we know from the way in which a jealous rival (male) poet made a special point of attacking her as 'ugly', writing that her looks 'could not fool a blind man nor a horse's arse'.[3]

In seventeenth-century France, Marion de Lorne was simply a high-class sex-worker, a courtesan. The less beautiful, but infinitely more talented Ninon de Lenclos (sometimes spelt Lanclos) was both courtesan and *salonière*, intimate with such intellectual giants as Molière, Bayle, Saint-Evremont and probably Pascal.[4] A leading light in the libertarian, anti-authoritarian movement in seventeenth-century Paris, and an author, she has a reputation akin to that of Queen Christina. Simone de Beauvoir, describing her as a 'seventeenth-century woman of wit and beauty', has called her 'the French woman whose independence seems the most like that of a man', adding:

Paradoxically, those women who exploit their femininity to the limit
create for themselves a situation almost equivalent to that of a man ...
Free in behaviour and conversation, they can attain – like Ninon de
Lenclos – to the rarest intellectual liberty. The most distinguished are often
surrounded by writers and artists who are bored by 'good' women.[5]

Clearly de Beauvoir did not share my ruthlessness in the assessment of
beauty. However, surviving portraits (in Versailles and Brussels) confirm the many contemporary written comments on Ninon, such as that
of Tallement de Réaux, 'as for beauty she never had a great deal, but
she always had plenty of spirit'.[6] She lived into her eighties, amazingly
well preserved, and had lovers almost to the end. Undoubtedly, as a
personable woman, she was much happier than the ill-favoured
Queen Christina. As she herself is reputed to have commented, 'Beauty
is a letter of recommendation which has no fixed limit'. Asked how
she managed to preserve her looks, she replied that that was because she
didn't indulge in 'cards, wine or women'.

The great age of the salons was the eighteenth century, and the golden
era is that of the thirty years after 1750, the years of brilliant and sus-
tained criticism of the authoritarianism and irrationality of the *ancien
régime*. Particularly interesting and instructive are the cases of Madame
Geoffrin, who had a husband but no title or noble *particule* ('de'), and
Mlle Julie de Lespinasse, who had the *particule*, was still relatively young
(having been born in 1732), but had no husband. François Geoffrin was
the ultimate bourgeois, a wealthy glass manufacturer, who, at the age of
forty-eight, took a wife, Marie-Thérèse Rodet, whose father had been a
valet at the royal court; her appeal was more her youth (she was fourteen) than any great distinction of looks. Geoffrin could readily provide
the wherewithal for lavish entertaining, but he himself had no interest
in the world of wit and intellect. Worse, he lived to the age of eighty-
four. Only with his death in 1749 was Mme Geoffrin able to realise to
the full her ambition of providing dinners for the intellectual giants of
the day, such as Montesquieu, Helvétius, d'Holbach, and Diderot and
D'Alembert, editors of the *Encyclopédie*, together with many of their
famous contributors. At fifty she was a plain woman, plainly dressed in
prim, almost spinster-like fashion.[7] The very reticence and sexlessness
was a strength: her dinner parties, held in the afternoon, were deeply
serious and highly moral, without any distraction of flirtation or

amorous exchange. If any woman made a signal contribution to the twenty-five-year production of the thirty-five volumes of the *Encyclo-pédie* (1751–76), the Enlightenment dictionary of universal knowledge, it was the prim, even prissy, Mme Geoffrin.

She also made a protégée of the young Julie de Lespinasse, who thus became the only other woman to be present at the afternoon salons held at the Geoffrin house on rue St Honoré. Julie was illegitimate, and, though cherished by her mother, had in adolescence no prospects other than entering a convent. Extremely intelligent, she had the lively charm that often goes with that, but she was not particularly pretty. She attracted the attention of members of the Parisian elite, one of whom (Jean-François Hénault, President of the Court of Appeal) informed her: 'Though not actually beautiful, you are distinguished-looking, and attract attention'.[8] Supported by the admiration of such *lumières* as D'Alembert, Julie graduated to holding her own salons from 5 to 8 p.m. in her house on rue de Belle Chasse. In the autumn of 1765 she caught the fearsome disease by which around one Frenchwoman in four at that time was disfigured, smallpox. D'Alembert despaired that she might die; she recovered, but with her eyesight seriously weakened, her health impaired and, the dread of so many women, such agreeable cast of countenance as she had possessed, totally destroyed. The faithful D'Alembert wrote to their common friend the Scottish philosopher David Hume: 'She is a good deal marked by the smallpox, but not the least in the world disfigured'. This judgement was praised by de Lespinasse's Edwardian biographer Camilla Jebb as 'touchingly charac-teristic of a sex most unjustly charged with inconstancy and an excessive regard to external appearances'.[9] The critical point is that the disfigure-ment in no way interrupted de Lespinasse's brilliant career at the soul of Enlightenment Paris.

D'Alembert was himself no beauty: the blunt truth – plain women preferring beautiful men just as plain men prefer beautiful women – is that, despite his devotion to her, Julie did not fancy him. She preferred the Spanish Marquis de Mora, then fell totally for the glamorous Comte de Guibert, whom she met at a garden fete on 21 June 1772. She was thirty-eight; he, eleven years younger, was enjoying the successful recep-tion of his preliminary 'Discourse' to his *General Essay on Tactics*, a powerful plea for social and political reform. With Guibert off on his travels, Julie overwhelmed him with passionate letters, while at the same time keeping up a more measured loving correspondance with Mora. Mora died of tuberculosis. Guibert married the sixteen-year-old Alexandrine de Courcelles, a very lovely girl, as we can see from the portrait by Greuze. Still at the height of her reputation as a great conversationalist and hostess, Julie de Lespinasse died on 22 May 1776, not yet forty-four. Could she have heard Guibert's funeral oration, would it have consoled her?: 'her plainness had nothing repulsive about it, at the first glance; at the second one had accustomed oneself to it, and as soon as she started speaking one forgot it'.[10]

The relationship between wealth and beauty in social mobility; the way in which wealth can render beauty inessential; the power of personal qualities other than beauty: all these are illustrated in the histories of two *salonières* of the later eighteenth century, Madame Necker, and her daughter, Mme de Staël. Susan Curchod was the daughter of a Swiss Calvinist clergyman, well educated and undoubtedly beautiful, but poor. She attracted the young Edward Gibbon, until his father forbade any idea of marriage. She then cashed in her looks to their fullest value, marrying the Swiss banker Jacques Necker, one of the richest men in Europe, who became Louis XVI's Finance Minister. Alas, in looks, their daughter Anne-Louise-Germaine favoured the father rather than the mother.[11] Mme de Charière, whose novel *Caliste* Germaine had read twenty times by the age of twenty, thought her plain and this was the, strictly accurate, verdict of most women who knew her. The same Edward Gibbon who had admired her mother described her as 'wild, vain, but good-natured and with a much larger provision of wit than beauty.' However, as her subsequent life was amply to demonstrate, she had her attractions for many men. The Comte de Guibert, seducer of the disfigured, middle-aged Mlle de Lespinasse, declared: 'Her great dark eyes are alight with genius. Her hair, black as ebony, falls around her shoulders in wavy locks. Her features are marked rather than delicate ... She has that which is more than beauty. What variety and expressions in her face! What delicate modulations in her voice! What perfect harmony between thought and its utterance!'[12] But beware the phrase 'more than beauty'; invariably it means 'less than beauty'.

There now enters one of those men whose primary, if not only, qualification was his good looks. Eric-Magnus, Baron de Staël, was an attaché to the Swedish ambassador in Paris, Count Creuze. Because of his looks he was something of a favourite with the Swedish King Gustavus II, and through his popularity with the Parisian ladies he managed to make ends meet, though personally very poor. Creuze informed Gustavus: 'Monsieur de Staël leads a very busy life. He is very well received at court, and all the young women of France would tear my eyes out if I did not show great concern for him. Madame de la Marck and Madame de Luxembourg would exterminate me.'[13] De Staël even had private access to Louis XVI's Queen, Marie Antoinette, something which Creuze himself was not able to obtain. Gustavus was prevailed upon, with Necker putting up the hard cash, to give de Staël a life tenure on the ambassadorship in Paris. On that basis a marriage contract with Germaine was agreed. Necker had not so much lost a daughter, he had gained a beautiful son-in-law, with a title and a post of high social status.

Mme de Staël was a woman of considerable talent and great creative energy. She had great self-confidence, a powerful personality, a liberated psyche and strong sexual appetites. No doubt she was proud of her handsome husband. When she first saw the tall, awkward Benjamin Constant, his appearance, she admitted, 'filled me with an insurmountable physical revulsion'.[14] But she had a daughter by him, as she had two sons by the Comte de Narbonne, in addition to the three children she bore her husband. With her father's immense riches behind her, with her own literary talent, with her strong personality and brilliant wit, she established unchallenged eminence as literary hostess and *salonière* in the period which followed that of Madame Geoffroi and Julie de Lespinasse, the period which embraced the last years of the *ancien régime*, the Revolution, the Napoleonic era and the Bourbon restoration.

There was, indeed, only one real challenger, the exquisitely beautiful Mme Récamier to whom Mme de Staël wrote the vibrant words: 'I would give half of the wit with which I am credited for half of the beauty you possess.'[15] Juliette Bernard was scarcely into her teens when her looks were being widely remarked upon. Having no money of her own, though her mother had been the mistress of a rich banker, Jacques-Rose Récamier, she was highly vulnerable. It seems likely that Récamier thought Juliette was, or at least might be, his own daughter. At any rate, in the interests of securing her position, she was married to him at the age of fifteen, he then being forty-two. It was common knowledge that the marriage was not consummated. If her husband's wealth provided the basis, Juliette's beauty was undoubtedly one of the prime attractions of her salon; but the testimony is unanimous that she was a gracious and sympathetic hostess, testimony all the more impressive since she held on tenaciously to her virginity. Juliette Récamier was not a rival to Germaine de Staël in wit and literary flair, but she monopolised attention as a beauty whom painters loved to paint and whose complete simplicity of dress exposed the empty pretentiousness of *les merveilleuses,* the elaborately overdressed ladies of the 1790s.

Mme Récamier had her setbacks, particularly when her husband went bankrupt: that she managed to re-establish her place in Parisian society must be largely attributed to her beauty. Although at times men were attracted away from Mme de Staël in her direction, she led nothing of the former's sex life. At the age of thirty she was engaged to Prince August of Prussia, but the engagement came to nothing; it has been suggested that the Prince was impotent.[16] Passionate love did not come to her till the age of forty when her famous affair with Chateaubriand, who was nine years her senior, began. Apart from the astonishing beauty of her youth, which certainly helped to launch her on her particular career, Mme Récamier was remarkable in sharing with her infinitely randier predeccessor, Ninon, a facility for preserving her looks: a drawing of her by Gérard in 1829, when she was fifty-two, makes her look like a young woman in her twenties; and similar thoughts are even stirred by a medallion of 1846. Here we have a woman whose life experiences were basically determined by her beauty, but whose success and popularity were as great as they were because of her warm personal qualities; other factors, both personal and external (she lost the favour of Napoleon for a time), brought reverses of fortune and long periods of unhappiness.

The only English woman who can be directly compared with those French sponsors of philosophy, social criticism and good conversation is Georgiana, Duchess of Devonshire, whose cultured, talented gatherings at Devonshire House in the 1770s were the nearest thing we have to the salons of the *lumières* . Furthermore Georgiana led 'a beauty chorus of aristocratic ladies' in charming lower-class citizens into supporting the Whig leader Charles James Fox at the Westminster constituency (where the franchise was unusually wide) in the general election of 1784.[17] How beautiful was the Duchess? Her best-selling biographer,

Amanda Foreman, concurs with established tradition in telling us that she was 'not classically pretty', 'not a conventional beauty'; her previous biographer wrote that she 'was not especially beautiful in the classical sense'.[18] Ruffled once again by imprecise use of language, I am unsure what exactly 'classical' or 'conventional' mean in this context: does the latter mean 'in accordance with the conventions of the eighteenth century', and the former 'in conformity with the ideal represented in the Venus de Milo', or, as I suspect, are we in the realm of the familiar comforting phrase which circumvents rigorous definition? There is the usual difficulty of contemporary accounts being in conflict. Horace Walpole declared Georgiana 'a phenomenon' who 'effaces all without being a beauty', while the actor David Garrick, something of a connoisseur in respect of his own leading ladies (Mary Ann Yates, Mrs Abington, Sophia Baddeley, Sarah Siddons), found her 'a most enchanting, exquisite, beautiful young creature. Were I five and twenty I could go mad about her, but as I am past five and fifty I would only suffer martyrdom for her'.[19] The double portrait by Jean-Urbain Guérin of Georgiana and Lady Elizabeth Foster gives the Duchess an exquisite profile; other portraits, unfortunately, are less unambiguous. Her hair was unfashionably reddish, but there is no doubt that she was widely perceived as having immense physical attractiveness. Among ordinary people who had no personal contact with her vivacity and charm, she was reputed beautiful. It seems worth seeking a verdict in the many satirical prints relating to the Duchess. If she had had definite defects of face or figure, these would undoubtedly have been caricatured; in fact Georgiana is always rendered in such a way as to make her sexual allure her most distinctive feature, singling her out from the plainer members of her 'beauty chorus'. She was also the subject of such popular ballads as 'The Piccadilly Beauty'. Beauty, I have said, comes in many types – many of them, certainly, not being appreciated in earlier ages. I conclude that her physical appearance fitted in to one of these types, and that, had that not been so she would not have been the celebrity that she was, and would not have been able to make such a stir in the Westminster campaign.

Similar uncertainties exist about the looks of England's most notorious courtesan, hard at work in the early part of the nineteenth century, author of the greatest kiss-and-tell masterpiece of all time, to which the Duke of Wellington apparently did not actually respond, 'Publish and

Be Damned' – I am referring to Harriette Wilson (1786–1845) and her *Memoirs* (1825). One of the fifteen children of a London watchmaker, Harriette, everyone agrees, had a quite extraordinary career, trading sex for social advancement and a life of luxury among the grandest in the land. A female rival called her 'superlatively lovely', but she attracted hostile as well as adoring comments. Some men were critical, or affected to be, of her boyish figure. Historian Kate Hickman insists, 'Harriette was not beautiful, but she was clever and spirited enough to make men think she was'. To me this is simply another phrasing of the comforting fairy tale we have already encountered, that, through spirit and cunning, women can make themselves beautiful in the eyes of the befuddled male beholder. I don't believe it; what I do believe, from the way men reacted to her, from the portrait engravings reproduced in Frances Wilson's *The Courtesan's Revenge: Harriette Wilson, the Woman who Blackmailed the King*, and from the intensity of feeling apparent in the written descriptions by both men and women, is that Harriette had a beauty which we would instantly recognise today, as most men and women, a few hidebound snobs and fops apart, recognised it then.[20]

From courtesans and *salonières* at the top of society, let us move to servants near the bottom. Servants formed a sizeable social group, from 8 to 13 per cent of the population in French towns at the end of the seventeenth century; most households that could afford domestic service at all had one servant, usually female. Male servants were more often found in the grander houses. In the earlier part of the period the main concern was over their honesty, for servants were generally regarded as belonging to the 'dangerous classes' and feared by those striving to establish a respectable living and life style.[21] But as we move into the eighteenth century it is clear that for the ambitious, elegant and presentable male servants were important status symbols. The connection between the employment of male servants and ostentatious ornamentation was recognised in Lord North's tax of 1777 of a guinea per male servant per year. And it was at this time that the word 'flunky' came into use.[22] For beautiful young men there were openings as footmen and valets; there was little likelihood of meteoric elevation through sex appeal, though Dr Cissie Fairchilds has shown that, with their good looks, fine clothes and sophisticated manner, male servants often did marry up – with daughters of artisans and shopkeepers, or even surgeons

and schoolmasters and, sometimes, merchants.[23] At least they ran no
risk of being cast into the streets seven months pregnant. Using the formal statements which the *ancien régime* required of all unmarried
mothers, Dr Fairchilds has also shown how, apart altogether from
unscrupulous employers, female servants were often seduced by their
male counterparts: 'menservants were usually handsome, because they
were hired to look well in livery, and their fine clothes and sophisticated
manner might well turn a woman's head'.[24] There were some special
opportunities for 'a few well-educated, well-groomed, and presentable
women' as well as men,[25] but, on the whole, domestic service was one
of the professions which bears out the novelist Henry Fielding's obser-
vation – running counter to the main tenor of my book – that 'beauty
was the greatest fortune for a man and the greatest misfortune for a
woman'.[26]

One celebrated escapee from domestic service was Emma Lyon, who
became successively mistress of Sir Harry Fetherstonehaugh (at the age
of sixteen), mistress of the Honourable Charles Grenville, and mistress,
then wife, of Grenville's uncle, Sir William Hamilton, British Plenipo-
tentiary in Naples. Her celebrated affair with Admiral Nelson is less
germane to this study than her remarkable social progress. She was born
in Cheshire, daughter of a blacksmith. Unfortunately we do not know
the vital stages by which she moved into gentry circles. She had a job
locally as an under-nursemaid, then her mother, who had herself moved
to the great metropolis, got her a post as a nursemaid in London (a crucial geographical move). She may then have moved to Mrs Kelly's very
high-class brothel, which was possibly the central stepping stone, but
we don't know for sure. What we do know, from the many Romney
portraits, is that she possesed, as Sir William (long before he had any
notion of marrying her), and almost everyone else, perceived, 'exquisite
beauty'.[27]

Once again, whatever the job that got a woman started on the career
ladder, rapid social promotion depended on the granting of sexual
favours to a small number of influential or powerful men. For a good-
looking man making a career out of his looks, sexual activity was usually
(though not always) incidental to social success. As old families grew
wealthier through collaboration with industrial enterprise, and new
families pushed their way in amongst the old, the premium placed upon

what was considered the cultured display of elegant, appropriately dressed male servants greatly increased. At grander English country houses in the mid nineteenth century, 'the first requirement of a foot-man, groom or coachman was that they should have the physique to show their liveries off to advantage'.[28] In her meticulous study, *The Rise and Fall of the Victorian Servant*, Pamela Horn has pointed out that 'Personal appearance was very important for any boy aspiring to the position of footman or page in a large household, for only the tall and well-built were considered'. She continued, 'wages often related to height, with the tallest men or boys receiving the highest pay'.[29] Similar considerations affected the American upper class as it developed in self-consciousness in the late nineteenth century. 'Among the "smart set" of the post-1870s', writes the historian of *Americans and their Servants* in the period 1800–1920, 'an imposing looking butler was a must. A "good" five-foot, three-hundred-pound, balding butler was impossible.'[30]

Even in the later eighteenth century, female servants were not intended for display. By the later nineteenth century, however, it was becoming a matter of prestige to have personable female servants: 'no one wanted a squat, thickset chambermaid; tall comely ones were required in wealthy homes'.[31] There was at least a chance now of a good-looking girl getting a position, principally for the attractiveness of her appearance and for display to envious guests, rather than for satisfying the desires which that appearance aroused. Of course the beautiful servant still ran special risks: either of being seduced by one of her masters (if not a fellow servant), or being sacked as a potential temptation to a growing son. But the main point stands: in the humblest jobs (where competition was often severe) beauty could be an asset, and did not always lead to the granting (or, more likely, exaction) of sexual favours; as always, these might lead to better positions where sex was a central consideration. Being a servant, obviously, was no wonderful achieve-ment with respect to conditions of work, earnings or status. It was seen by working-class and lower-middle-class men, by shopkeepers, trades-men, peasants and farmers as an excellent preparation for the duties of a wife.[32] Given that marriage remained the basic 'career' for most women, a comely girl who got a good post was twice blest in the marriage stakes – she had the skills and the looks.

The jumping-off point for Madame Du Barry was one of the shops

developing in the seventeenth and eighteenth centuries to meet the
needs of fashionable ladies, and providing employment for pretty young
women and showcases in which they could display their endowments to
rich men. The career of Kitty Fisher demonstrates the potency of beauty,
but was also suffused with that sense of tragedy insisted upon in so
much of the folklore about beauty being no real blessing for a woman.
Born in Soho, London in 1738 Kitty was, in recognition of her looks,
apprenticed to a milliner. She came quickly to the attention of London's
leading gallants and had a succession of increasingly famous lovers.
Twice painted by the best-known artist of the age, Sir Joshua Reynolds,
she was for six years reputed the capital's outstanding beauty, at the
centre of the aristocratic social scene, but not, however, eligible for marriage into the aristocracy. Then, suddenly, she fell ill, due to overuse of
the poisonous cosmetics of the day. She retired from high society,
marrying the humble John Norris. Within five months, at the age of
twenty-nine, she was dead.

The overwhelming number of pretty young women who became
salesgirls of one sort or another did not become celebrities though, one
hopes, they usually lived longer than Kitty Fisher. Ned Ward, the pioneer investigative writer, who began his *London Spy: The Vanities and
Vices of the Town Exposed to View* in 1698, described the New Exchange
(the fabled shopping centre of its day) as 'this seraglio of fair ladies', and
noted that 'the chiefest customers ... were beaux' who 'were paying
double price for linen gloves or sword-knots, to the prettiest women,
that they might go thence and boast among their brother fops what sin-
gular famous and great encouragement they had received'.[33] Earlier,
Pepys had reflected on his paying the glove-seller Doll twenty shillings
for one pair, 'she is so pretty that, God forgive me, I would not think it
too much'.[34]

We know of no male Kitty Fishers, but perhaps not sufficient attention has been paid to the way in which shops catering mainly for women
often found it advantageous to employ good-looking young men. Since,
in general, it was less easy for a rich woman to take a lower-class lover
than it was for a rich man to take a lower-class mistress, the prospects
for sharp social promotion were not great for handsome young shop
assistants – still relatively comfortable, if still demeaning and penuri-
ous, employment in a city shop was a distinct improvement upon the

furious struggle for subsistence permanently waged in the great metrop-
olises, as in all towns and villages. The appearance and style of some
shop assistants were referred to by Mrs Mary Manley in her *Female
Tatler* (1709):

> This afternoon some ladies, having an opinion of my fancy in cloaths,
> desired me to accompany them to Ludgate-hill, which I take to be as
> agreeable an amusement as a lady can pass away three or four hours in.
> The shops are perfect gilded theatres, the variety of wrought silks to many
> changes of fine scenes and the Mercers are the performers in the Opera ...
> dished-out creatures; and, by their elegant address and soft speeches, you
> would guess them to be Italians.[35]

On a shopping expedition the fictional character Evelina (in Fanny Burney's acutely observed novel of that title) remarks that 'there seems to
be six or seven men belonging to each shop'. 'And such men!', she adds.
Real-life shop assistants at the London Bridge drapers Flint and Palmer's
had their hair curled, powdered and starched each morning before
appearing in front of their customers.

We saw that the expanding economies of the nineteenth century and
the expanding desires of the rich created expanding opportunities in
service. So too in selling. The first successful department store entrepreneur in the United States was Alexander Turney Stewart, whose
emporium in New York City was completed in 1846. Stewart very deliberately and positively catered to women: accordingly, 'he chose his
salesmen for their "gentlemanly" manners and pleasing appearance';
each female customer was greeted at the door by the general manager
who 'assigned her, if she desired, a special salesman who escorted her
through the store'.[36] In the journal of Louis Fissner, a Prussian Jew
employed as a clothing shop salesman in Newburyport, Connecticut, in
the 1850s, there is a marked preoccupation with personal appearance.
On 14 April 1854, he noted the arrival of a new salesman from Boston:
'he is good looking but in my opinion he will stay but a short time'.[37]
Henry Mayhew, the London journalist, tells us of dress shops in the
1860s with 'fifty gentlemen behind the counters',[38] the fine personal
appearance necessary being demonstrated visually in such engraved
advertisements as that for Farmer and Rogers Great Shawl Emporium,
Regent Street, where we see the female shoppers and the male sales
staff.[39] John Bird Thomas, writing of his experiences as a shop boy in

the 1870s, recorded the importance of a good appearance even in ordinary grocers' shops. He had been advised that 'a good appearance and plenty of cheek will get you anywhere'. But apparently careful attention to dress was not enough, genuine good looks being an important requirement: 'I think that dressing up better helped because when I applied in answer to advertisements I generally got an interview, but there were so many taller and better looking applicants that all that happened was that they took my name and address and "would let me know"'.[40] The best summary of the relatively secure but also relatively menial prospects in this occupation for the handsome lad is provided by a satirical cartoon of 1881: 'Yes, Madame?' enquires a shopwalker of a customer entering the shop; the Lady replies, 'I want something handsome and cheap'; 'Certainly, Madam,' replies the shopwalker, 'Mr Jones, step forward.'[41]

My category 'show business' is, of course, anachronistic, but I have used it to highlight a realm of employment which continues, grows and mutates right through to the age of film and television. For a woman, going on stage could simply be a planned first step towards attracting the attention of some rich 'protector'; for a successful theatrical career, dramatic talent, as well an attractive appearance, was required (it must be remarked that many leading male actors had little or no claim to personal beauty). We last encountered Nell Gwyn, that model of beauty-fuelled social ascent, as an orange seller (born in 1650 into a completely destitute family, she had previously been a hawker of fish and a servant in a brothel);[42] she consolidated her position by demonstrating in brilliant degree the wit and power of repartee expected in this job. Wit, but mainly looks, gained Nell's promotion to the stage itself. To hold her place there, she had to manifest great talent for comedy (for tragedy she had little bent). Pepys hit off her various talents with his usual acuity: 'Pretty witty Nell', he called her. Seeing her at her lodging house door in Drury Lane on May Day 1667, he remarked that 'she seemed a mighty pretty creature'. Seeing her dressing herself backstage, he described her as 'very pretty, prettier than I thought'. Appraising her performance in Dryden's *The Mayden Queen*, he declared:

> So great a performance of a comical part was never, I believe, in the world before as Nell doth this, both as a mad girle and then most and best of all,

ANNA BOLINA VXOR— HENRI· OCTA

1. Anne Boleyn (1507–1536), second of Henry VIII's six wives. Was she beautiful, was she plain? This portrait is so severe – in painting royalty, artists aimed at dignity rather than sexiness – it's hard to tell. Unknown sixteenth-century artist. (*National Portrait Gallery*)

2. Henry Wriothesley, 3rd Earl of Southampton (1573–1624). His Greek nose and long auburn hair touched the heartstrings of the ageing Elizabeth I. Conceited and arrogant, he took part in Essex's rebellion in 1601 and was lucky to escape execution. Unknown artist, *c.* 1600. (*National Portrait Gallery*)

3. George Villiers, 1st Duke of Buckingham (1592–1628), with his long slim legs and wearing the Order of the Garter. Adored by James I and many, many women, he was also detested for his arrogance. Attributed to William Larkin, *c.* 1616. (*National Portrait Gallery*)

4. Nell Gwyn (1651–1687). As the whore who captivated Charles II, Nell has had her looks much traduced by the British establishment. This portrait is probably a good likeness. Painting by Simon Verelst, *c.* 1680. (*National Portrait Gallery*)

5. George Gordon Byron, 6th Lord Byron (1788–1824). Thanks to cheap engravings, the poet was one of history's first pin-ups. He followed a deliberate slimming regime, curled his hair and loved dressing up. Replica, *c.* 1835, of an original of 1813 by Thomas Philips. (*National Portrait Gallery*)

6. Emma Hamilton (1765–1815). Emma Lyon followed the paradigmatic career of the village beauty (the blacksmith's daughter), from service as a nursemaid, to metropolitan courtesan, to wife of Sir William Hamilton, with the added celebrity of becoming Lord Nelson's mistress. Painting by George Romney, c. 1785. (*National Portrait Gallery*)

7. Marie Duplessis. Slim and pale (and not, a contemporary thought, to the taste of the Turks), Alphonsine Plessis was carried by sheer beauty from grinding poverty in Normandy to becoming a leading courtesan, celebrated as La Dame aux Camélias and in *La Traviata*. It was TB, not the poverty (from which she did escape) which destroyed her. Portrait by Edouard Viénot, 1845.

8. Lola Montez. Born Marie Gilbert to a respectable English family in Limerick, she became one of the most famous of all the *Grandes Horizontales*. She eventually became *maîtresse en titre* to King Ludwig I of Bavaria. Portrait by Joseph Carl Stieler, *c.* 1845, Schloss Nymphenburg, Munich.

when she comes in as a young gallant; and hath the motions and carriage of a spark the most ever I saw any man have.[43]

But talent would not have triumphed unsupported by the granting of sexual favours. From the start of her stage career Nell was the mistress of the leading actor, Charles Hart (a great-nephew of Shakespeare), who provided her dramatic training and arranged for her to be taught to dance by another actor, John Lacey.

In seventeenth-century France it was generally the players of minor, and usually unpaid, parts who aimed to move quickly to the role of courtesan or kept woman. Let us turn instead to La Champmesle, a great tragedienne and a supreme interpreter of Racine. She was born into a family of middling prosperity and no social status in Rouen in 1642. She had had one husband before settling permanently into a theatrical career and marrying a fellow actor, Champmesle.[44] Her advantages were sheer talent, a marvellous voice and the ability to play the most passionate parts with complete authenticity, allied to a figure and appearance which seen on stage were acceptable to audiences. Mme de Sévigné, a devotee of her acting, said that she was ugly when seen close up, with small round eyes and a poor complexion. 'It is', explained the celebrated writer of letters, 'the player not the play that one comes to see. I went to *Ariane* only to see her. That tragedy is feeble ... But when La Champmesle appeared, one could hear a murmur, everybody was ravished and moved to tears by her despair.'[45] For seven years Racine and La Champmesle were lovers, though often the relationship seemed more like a marriage of convenience than a love match. During the same period La Champmesle had four or five other lovers, in this case the rightful prerogatives of professional success and membership of elite society (one of the lovers was the serial womaniser, Charles de Sévigné) rather than means to further social advancement.

Moving into the eighteenth century, and back across the Channel, the most important theatrical figure was David Garrick (1717–1779), a pupil of Dr Johnson's at Lichfield, whose theatrical career began in 1740 and who from 1747 was joint manager of London's Drury Lane theatre. Garrick wrote, acted, managed, directed and brought a new naturalism and professionalism to the theatre. Accounts dating from the 1740s describe him as 'a very sprightly young man, neatly made and of an expressive countenance', and 'little Garrick, young and light and alive in every muscle and every feature'.[46] From the various portraits, we can see that he was comely, but not strikingly beautiful. However, many of the other dominant male figures in the theatre of the day were scarcely even personable, whatever the roles they played might seem to demand. The rival whom Garrick effectively eclipsed, Quin, was now old and paunchy, but even in youth had not been much to look at.

Garrick had difficulty in finding and retaining actresses of the quality he insisted on, sometimes because of his own stinginess, or even because of jealousy of their successes. His favourite in the earlier years was Mrs Mary Ann Yates, a notable beauty and highly talented actress. She, however, moved to Edinburgh. Her own appraisal of her qualities – in which she clearly saw beauty as paramount – and the price they should command, can be seen in her reply to Garrick's determined effort to get her back:

> On considering every circumstance in my situation here, and my novelty, to say nothing of my beauty I think I cannot in conscience take less than £700 a year for my salary. For my clothes (as I love to be well dressed, and characters I appear in require it), I expect £200.[47]

In the event, the two-year deal concluded was for £750 per annum plus a further £50.

Garrick's other female star at this time was Mrs Abington (formerly Fanny Barton). Fanny Barton's history is the proverbial one of beauty providing the springboard and talent the wings for a girl to soar from penury to a secure and respected celebrity. Fanny Barton was born sometime in the 1730s, her mother dying when she was young. As a child she earned pennies selling flowers (which earned her the nickname of 'Nosegay Fan'), singing or reciting in public houses, or simply running errands. Sometimes she wangled a way into the private rooms of better establishments, doing recitations from a tabletop, 'her efforts and beauty winning the reward of a few pence from her auditors'.[48] While still very young, she became a servant in the house of a milliner in Cockspur Street, where, displaying the aptitude for learning which was one of her characteristics, she acquired the beginnings of a knowledge of dress and fashion, and also of French. It was almost inevitable that she should also have worked as a prostitute, her good looks presumably securing her better than average earnings. The gloss on this

part of her life in the Victorian biography from which I have just quoted
was:

> Fanny underwent many painful and ignoble experiences, that her early
> days were miserable, squalid and vicious, but that she strove after a better
> life. She may not be judged with severity, at least the circumstances of her
> condition must be remembered in passing sentence upon her, and some-
> thing of the evil of her career must be charged to the heartlessness of the
> world in which she lived.[49]

The striving after a better life cannot be doubted since at some stage she
added to her French an ability to converse in Italian, and, in the early
1750s, sought to put her natural and acquired talents to use by turning
to the theatre. After immediate successes at the Haymarket, she came to
the attention of Garrick, who presented her first appearance at Drury
Lane on 29 October 1756. Meantime she was taking music lessons from
a trumpeter in the Royal Service, James Abington; by September 1856
she had become Mrs Abington.

Garrick offered little in opportunities or wages, so she moved to
Dublin, where a critic described her as 'more womanly than Farren,
fuller, yet not heavy'.[50] A contemporary engraving after Gosway certainly
shows her to have had a fine bosom and a plump, wide face, with a
shapely nose in proportion, big eyes and a smallish, but very sensual
mouth; indeed, whether by design of the artist or not, an appealing
physicality is projected. If we are fully to understand the rise of Fanny
Barton, this is a far more relevant portrait than the well-known, but
much later, 'dignified' one by Reynolds. Her husband grew jealous of
both her success and her many admirers; finally she made him regular
payments in exchange for a full separation. She now took, as a lover the
elderly but rich Member of Parliament for Newry. Again there is a choice
piece of Victoriana:

> This connection, brought about through an approving choice of the mind
> on both sides, rather than the gratification of any other wish, the pleasure
> arising from this intercourse became gradually so intense, that he
> delighted in no company so much as her's, each was a great and irresistible
> attraction to the other ...[51]

He died, leaving a settlement on her which, as surely as the Villiers gift
had provided for John Churchill, provided her with the financial

platform upon which she could display her talents, and which, as surely, was earned through the lure of beauty. Beauty gave her security, but it was talent that gave her fame: Garrick now offered her £5 a week to return to Drury Lane (far short, though, of what he had paid to get Mrs Yates back).

Throughout the 1760s and 1770s Mrs Abington was firmly established as a brilliant player of comic parts, a leader of fashion and welcome visitor in high social circles.[52] In 1782, still at the height of her popularity, though now around fifty, she fell out again with Garrick and moved to Covent Garden, where her successes continued; at Drury Lane her place was taken by Elizabeth Farren. Three major contemporary sources attest to the turbulence stirred up by the advent of Eliza Farren. First, The Memoirs of the Present Countess of Derby (Late Miss Farren) by 'Petronius Arbiter', which, published in 1797, went through five editions in that year at the price of 1s 6d; secondly, a response to this critical account published in the same year and entitled The Testimony of Truth to Exalted Merit: or A Biographical Sketch of the Right Honourable the Countess of Derby in Refutation of a False and Scandalous Libel; and a satirical and critical poem, Thalia to Eliza, published in 1789. The second has as its frontispiece an engraving of her, showing an alluring face, with large, lustrous eyes, long, exquisitely formed nose, sensuous lips and rounded chin – in short, a beauty (a beauty, neither 'classical', nor 'conventional', but simply a beauty, in one of beauty's entrancing variety of types).

Elizabeth Farren was born in 1759 into a family of strolling players then operating in the north east of England. Her father died when she was very young. Eliza, with her elder sister Kitty, was put on the stage. Evidently talented as well as good-looking, Eliza was snapped up by Joseph Younger, the patentee of the Liverpool Theatre, and launched on an acting career. Through Younger's recommendation to Colman, manager of the Haymarket Theatre in London, Farren moved to the capital in 1777, where she was usually cast in tragic roles. She had no difficulty, however, in taking over Mrs Abington's position as leading comic actress. Critics, while finding her face 'handsome', commented unfavourably on her lack of 'embonpoint';[53] she may have been accounted unfashionably slim, but, demonstrating a point which occurs over and over again, Eliza was adored by audiences and lusted after by the mighty. Tall, with a neat figure, she was perfect for 'breeches parts', where, dressed up as a man, she could show off her elegant legs and shapely bottom. She attracted the attentions of the Whig leader, Charles James Fox (nobody accused him of lacking *embonpoint*), though not even the hostile *Memoirs* accused her of becoming his mistress. Her virtuous reputation stood her in good stead when Fox was succeeded as her principal admirer by the elderly Earl of Derby. With the Countess still alive, Eliza was given an understanding that she could consider herself the *expectant* Countess of Derby. True enough, on 8 April 1797 Eliza Farren made her last stage appearance preparatory to her marriage to the Earl of Derby on 8 May.

The greatest English actress of the eighteenth century, Sarah Siddons, is remembered as such rather than as a society beauty; but without her strong, distinctive and utterly seductive features it is unlikely that she would ever have stepped from her provincial touring company into the pages of history. She was performing with her company at Cheltenham when a number of aristocrats in the audience, who had come expecting some hilarity at the expense of incompetent mummers, were so taken with her that they wrote to Garrick. Garrick immediately sent out his talent spotters. Catching up with the company at Worcester, one of them, the Reverend Henry Bate, reported of Mrs Siddons that her face is 'the most strikingly beautiful for stage effect that I have ever beheld'.[54] In fact Siddons was so nervous in her first performance in London that she was not a great success. She therefore moved to Bath, where she steadily built up an immense reputation, laying the basis for her eventual triumph in London, where she soon became the sole dominating figure, holding that position till her retirement, at the age of sixty-seven, in 1812. With so many portraits of Sarah Siddons, few of us today would deny her claim to beauty, though her strong nose was not universally approved among the hidebound arbiters of eighteenth-century taste.

The career of Sarah Siddons points in the direction of the modern evaluation of beauty: her beauty allied to her great talent brought her huge success without her having to grant sexual favours. There was, of course, an entire profession founded solely on the selling of sex for instant cash. Telling the readers of his *Tableau de Paris* (1781) that there were thirty thousand prostitutes in Paris, Sebastien Mercier remarked upon the enormous social distance between them and courtesans, though, he declared primly, they 'have exactly the same goal'.[55] The 'enormous distance' is an undisputable fact, though women who supported themselves as manure-gatherers, salt-spreaders and the like 'might well envy the financial rewards of prostitution'.[56] On the other hand, good looks might be a contributory cause of a woman's downfall in the first place, leaving with her no choice but to go into prostitution. Harris's *List of Covent Garden Ladies* of 1793 tells us of a beautiful servant, employed in a 'gentlemean's family', who, on walks, attracted the attention of a 'gentleman of the law', who invited her to his chambers: 'The sequel it were needless to relate: she was debauched and after deserted by her betrayer. The consequence of which was, having lost her place, and being destitute of a character, she was obliged to have recourse to her beauty for subsistence.'[57] This publication, as does *Ranger's Impartial List of the Ladies of Pleasure in Edinburgh* of 1775, gives insights into the importance of personal beauty to a prostitute and its relationship to other desired qualities. In discussing another Covent Garden lady, Harris declared that 'Beauty ... is generally looked upon as the first and chief requisite; and, next to it, an agreeable conversation'. What this lady has, however, is 'good nature'; but then 'her favours may be had on very moderate terms'.[58] The seduced servant, on the other hand, being 'one of the finest women upon the town ... accordingly made one of the best figures from the emoluments of her employments'.[59] There was an Edinburgh girl of sixteen whose 'youth and beauty procure her a great many admirers'; another young lady was not pretty, but 'makes a tolerable livelihood'.[60] Descriptions of appearance are usually quite meticulous: the ill-favoured could expect half a guinea, while a 'beautiful lady' newly arrived from Wales charged five guineas.[61] In the Edinburgh guide musical talents and the ability to be a congenial drinking companion were also prized attributes, and in the London guide the epithets 'well bred' or 'well educated' indicated high prices. Both guides, as is the custom in such publications, and often in identical language, stressed the skills in the arts of love-making of their subjects: however, since this skill is allowed to every single one, it does not amount to a characteristic upon which discrimination between different prostitutes could be based. Self-evidently, very many prostitutes cannot have been at all beautiful, and obviously basic professional skills were important, at least among the brothel- or home-based ones featured in these guides.

That beauty was a most important asset for the woman who hoped to do particularly well is clear from the open attention paid to it, and from some of the downright offensive (in our eyes) comments. Of one Edinburgh lady it was reported: 'If it was not for this Lady's inordinate desire for the sport of Venus, she would certainly never have followed the game, as she does not possess one outward accomplishment to recommend her'.[62] On the customer's side, as Antonia Fraser has neatly put it, 'it was a case of striking a balance between what his purse could afford and what his sensibilities could stand'.[63] But if a woman was to derive real advantage and significant social promotion from her looks then she had to get out of common prostitution as quickly as possible before it destroyed her. (Emma Lyon – later Lady Hamilton – if she ever was a prostitute, had escaped by the time she was sixteen.) The seduced servant of the Covent Garden list did do well for a time as a kept woman, but when her protector died 'she was compelled to have recourse to a more general commerce, in which she has not been so successful as before'. Although the guide concluded that 'she may, nevertheless, still be pronounced a very good piece, and a desirable woman', the reasons for her diminished success and, evidently, hope of escape were clear: 'Chagrin added to the usual irregularities accidental to her profession, has diminished those charms which were before so attracting; her face is now rather bloated, and she is grown somewhat masculine in her person.'[64] For all prostitutes the risks were high, especially from venereal diseases and pregnancy. The prostitute could not insist that her customer wear 'armour': if he did, it was to protect himself against disease. The standard contraceptive method, a sponge soaked in alcohol, was not very effective.

We come to a fundamental proposition in this analysis of beauty, sex and social success. If a woman was to sell sexual favours and retain some kind of security, or attain further social advancement, she had to reach a level of society where she could have pregnancies without sabotaging her entire career. One route was across 'the enormous distance' into the world of kept women and courtesans: on the whole the better looking were more likely to achieve this, but the overwhelming majority, including the truly beautiful, failed, never really having had a chance in the first place. The other route was to become a brothel-keeper, like the celebrated Mrs Hayes in mid eighteenth-century London, who, reputedly, retired worth £20,000[65] Essential requirements were high initial earning power (good looks), immense good luck and managerial ability.

Male prostitution, much of it child prostitution, for male customers was not a glamorous business. Male prostitution for female customers, however, was a much more select affair and here men with the right attributes, which might include beauty of face and form, could add to their economic, and even improve their social, prospects. It seems unlikely that anyone would waste money placing this advertisement in the *Nottingham Weekly Courant* of 26 November 1717 if it were not genuine – why shouldn't it be?

> Any able young Man, strong in the Back, and endow'd with a good Carnal Weapon, with all the Appurtenances thereto belonging in good Repair, may have Half A Crown per Night, a Pair of clean Sheets, and other Necessaries, to perform Nocturnal Services on one Sarah Y-tes, whose Husband having for these 9 months past lost the Use of his Peace-Maker, the unhappy Woman is thereby driven to the last Extremity.[66]

To what profession should we allocate Casanova? As with Veronica Franco, recent work stresses his intellectual powers and high level of culture. One could describe him as a sort of male 'honest courtesan', save that he wasn't very honest and was constantly in trouble with the authorities. He was, therefore, something of a cross between a gigolo and a con man. He was tall (over six feet), dark and personable (we have a couple of portraits): he lived off his quick wits, his intriguing range of knowledge and talents, his plausibility and flair, his imposing person and his agreeable looks. One of the many spies employed to keep an eye on him reported (with absolutely no reason to varnish the truth):

> He is a man of forty years at most, of high stature, of good and vigorous aspect, very brown of skin, with a vivacious eye. He wears a short and chestnut coloured wig. From what I am told he is of a bold and disdainful character, but, especially, he is full of the gift of the gab, and, as such, witty and learned.[67]

Though his autobiography (our main source) is undoubtedly full of fantasy and exaggeration, Casanova was strikingly successful with women, over whom he was generally quite fastidious. He himself was not a stunning beauty, but good company, and physically fairly attractive. What did it mean to be ugly or deformed? Some made a sort of profession out of misfortune by becoming beggars. But without doubt the whole cast of pre-industrial society was to be inconsiderate to the extent of cruelty towards the ill formed. Women in the seventeenth century ran the risk of being identified as witches. Those who were successful with the pen, but not actually seen by the readers of their books (a condition which obtains less and less today) could generally afford to be ill-favoured. How far was this true of the spectacularly misshapen, and highly celebrated, Augustan poet, Alexander Pope? A victim of Pott's disease, Pope was a dwarf of four feet six inches, crippled by arthritis. In his own poignant words he referred to 'this long Disease, my life'. It may be that some of the passion which drove him on to success as a poet derived from his deformity. But though contemporaries had to recognise his genius, it cannot be said that they behaved well towards him. Official recognition of his merit, and the religious tolerance of Catholicism granted to many others, were withheld from him. His private life was scarcely happy. His over-strained attitude to sex, mingling boyish smut with elaborate gallantry, it has been authoritatively claimed, 'must derive from feelings of being unattractive, if not grotesque, to the women he desired'.[68] It may be noted that most of the unhappiness and much of the wayward behaviour of another seventeenth-century poet, Oliver Goldsmith, was caused by his consciousness of his own ugliness. 'Look at that fly with a long pin stuck through it!', a passing bully once shouted.[69] Lisa Jardine's recent biography of the brilliant and intensely industrious polymath, Robert Hooke, suggests possible connections between his failure to fulfil his potential, his lack of concrete achievements, his personal loneliness and misery, and his unappealing, misshapen appearance.[70]

Looks mattered in the pre-industrial world. The penalties for being ill-favoured or worse were more severe than they are today. Beauty was noticed and sought after, but attitudes towards it contained much of the traditional ambivalence, and conventions about what constituted beauty and what did not, though ignored by the clear-sighted and the lusty, remained strong. It always had profound effects on the lives of those who possessed it, but did not guarantee happiness and success, and could bring tragedy. Social status and wealth were still more important than personal appearance.

5

Getting Married

Those individuals (male and female) who profited from their good looks appeared beautiful to almost all who saw them. To get married one only has to appeal to one other person of the opposite sex, hence the understandable but misleading aphorism about beauty being in the eye of the beholder. Undoubtedly the phenomenon known as 'love' exists, and has (despite the attempts of some historians to limit it to modern times) existed throughout the ages. It is not necessarily a life-long phenomenon, nor an exclusive one; it is possible to fall in love several (or many) times in a lifetime, and possibly to be in love with more than one person at any one time. Since there are not nearly enough beautiful people to go round, it is just as well for the survival of the human race that the phenomenon does exist. Evidently, many marriages were and are contracted without the existence of mutual, or even one-sided, love. Motives for marrying were usually mixed, with economic and social considerations often predominating; for women marriage was frequently the only alternative to poverty and the loss of whatever social status they might have. The range of choices for men might not be much greater than that for women; an important sub-theme of this book is the manner in which the transition from pre-industrial society to industrial society is accompanied by a leap from limited marital (and extra-marital!) choices to extended ones.

We've already seen something of traditional moralistic and perhaps slightly inconsistent and confused views on beauty, duty, marriage and temptation. A sixteenth-century Bishop of Exeter, Miles Coverdale, struck an agreeable balance. Arguing that a spouse should be chosen for true riches of mind, body, and, of course, earthly possessions, he did have the grace to add that 'if beside these, thou foundest other great riches (beauty and such like gifts) ... thou hast the more to thank God for'.[1] However, his near contemporary Philip Stubbes, a perennial critic of society and its morals, was more in tune with *public* (never exactly the same as *private* – another theme of this book) morality when he complained of feckless marriages, with a boy not caring whether he had sufficient funds as long as 'he have his pretty pussy to huggle with all'.[2] Throughout the seventeenth century, 'passion, alias infatuation, alias lust' was seen, with respect to marriage, as 'a noxious ingredient, rather than a pre-requisite yeast', with 'sex and mere looks' being regarded as 'special snares'.[3] On into the next century it was strongly urged that sexual desire was not a proper motive for marriage.[4] Mrs Astell's turn-of-the-century denunciation of beauty for arousing 'irregular appetites' we have already encountered. Choice in marriage, she said, sensibly enough, should be 'guided by Reason' ('Marriage without a Competency', she explains realistically, 'is no very comfortable condition'); not – here comes the puritan fire – by 'Humour or brutish Passion'.[5] For the period 1680 to 1760 Dr Peter Borsay (admitting to considerable simplification, and including, I feel I have to add, a certain exaggeration) has summed up marriage among the middle and upper classes as follows: 'the woman brought wealth and the man status; a woman was as beautiful as she was wealthy, a man as handsome as he was superior'. He also quotes 'An Epistle to a Friend' from the *Tunbridge and Bath Miscellany* for the year 1714:

> With scorn Clodalia's haughty face we view,
> The deadn'd aspect, and the sordid hew,
> Her wealth discover'd gives her features lies.
> And we find charms to reconcile our eyes ...[6]

Beauty, or in this case its absence, *is* recognised to exist; but, where marriage is contemplated, beauty, as compared with wealth, is not highly regarded, and the discovery of a woman's wealth readily led to a modification of the estimate of her looks or, more accurately, of her desirability in the marriage stakes.

The eighteenth-century English novelist and magistrate Henry Fielding was a great champion of love, but he shared the traditional equivocations and confusions over beauty. He has Squire Allworthy in *Tom Jones* speak up strongly in favour of marriage being founded on love, and against parental compulsion, avarice for a great fortune, snobbery for a title and lust for a beautiful person. In what Fielding, as author, disarmingly terms Allworthy's 'Sermon' there is some double-tracking Allworthy opens and – as we shall see – closes with the formal morality of the time:

> For surely we may call it a Profanation to convert this most sacred Institution into a wicked Sacrifice to Lust or Avarice: and what better can be said of those Matches to which men are induced merely by the Consideration of a beautiful Person, or a great Fortune?

However, Allworthy then immediately continues, matching morality against self-awareness: 'To deny that Beauty is an agreeable Object to the Eye, and even worthy of some Admiration, would be false and foolish', admitting that, 'It was my own good Fortune to marry a Woman whom the World thought handsome, and I can truly say I liked her better on that Account.' But then intemperate moralising takes over:

> To make this the sole Consideration of Marriage, to lust after it so violently as to overlook all Imperfections for its Sake, or to require it so absolutely as to reject and disdain Religion, Virtue and Sense, which are Qualities, in their Nature, of much higher Perfection, because an Elegance of Person is wanting; this is surely inconsistent with a wise Man or a good Christian. And it is perhaps being too charitable to conclude that such Persons mean anything more by their Marriage than to please their carnal Appetites, for the Satisfaction of which, we are taught, it was not ordained.[7]

The unwitting testimony here is that, whatever might be the intention of sermons, there were, as always, those with a sharp and determined eye for 'Elegance of Person'.

In Fielding's poem 'Advice to a friend on Choosing a Wife' there are some moving lines:

> A tender Heart, which while thy Soul it shares,
> Augments thy Joys, and lessens all thy Cares ...

Soon, however, the language becomes intemperate, and there is a gross confusion between beauty and artifice:

> Of Beauty's subtle Poisen well beware;
> Our hearts are taken e'er they dread the Snare:
> Our Eyes, soon dazzled by that Glare, grow blind,
> And see no imperfections in the Mind.

> Of this appriz'd, the Sex, with nicest Art,
> Insidiously adorn the outward Part.
> But Beauty, to a mind depraved and ill,
> Is a thin gilding to a nauseous Pill;
> A cheating Promise of a short-liv'd Joy,
> Time must this idol, Chance may soon destroy.

And then at the end we have the moralising:

> Fond of thy Person, may her Bosom glow
> With Passions thou hast taught her first to know.
> A warm Partaker of the genial Bed,
> Thither by Fondness, not by lewdness led.[8]

Nothing could speak louder than this reiteration of the equation of beauty with lewdness.

At the bottom of society, the struggle for existence continued to be so intense that there was little time for the contemplation of beauty on the part of either sex: 'you look at the money bag not at the face' was the folk wisdom of the peasants of Baden, in Germany.[9] In addition to their conviction that a beautiful wife was incompatible with the rearing of fine pigs, the peasants of the Franche-Comté had two other similar bits of folklore: 'You can't eat beauty with a spoon'; and, 'It is better to say: Ugly, let us have supper than to ask: Beauty, what do we have for supper?'[10] In England, the wise caution was a reminder that marriage was 'more than four legs in a bed'. In any case, as Professor Olwen Hufton reminds us about eighteenth-century France: 'a woman or man who was not pockmarked, who did not suffer from a vitamin-deficiency disease, or from a congenital defect was in a small minority'.[11]

For most of history, for most people, marriage always entailed personal inclination accommodating to economic and social reality. As we have seen, there is plenty of evidence that women have often been just as susceptible to a beautiful male face and form as men have generally been to the equivalent in women, and that women with the requisite freedom and power usually acted upon 'their humour and brutish passion', as, indeed, on occasion, did humble servant girls. As we move through the nineteenth century and into the twentieth, some women had greater opportunities to travel further and more frequently than ever before, and so had new opportunities to observe and respond to the

many varieties of male beauty, without necessarily having anything in
the way of matrimony in mind – something more than temporary excitation would be required for that.

In the nineteenth century, American women, as Charles Dickens
recorded in his *American Notes* (1842), travelled widely and unchaper-
oned. In several of her private letters the upper middle-class Mary
Hallock, who was quite accustomed to travelling alone by boat between
her home up the Hudson River and New York City, described the
people she observed. On one return journey:

> The boat was pervaded by lovers. They were very funny but there was
> besides something rather grand in their supreme and utter indifference to
> public opinion. But I found myself after the way of the world more inter-
> ested in the well-dressed and handsome lovers than the plain and awkward
> ones.[12]

It is characteristic of traditional ideals of beauty that they are largely
derived from fictional sources (or visual representations), while the
modern appraisal of beauty is based on actual living, moving people,
even if those are seen only on film or television. Mary Hallock refers her
friend to 'Clive's blond beauty' in *The Newcomes* by Thackeray:

> I confess to a weakness for the beauteous Clive; he is one of a series of
> ardent generous gallant youths of whom I have been very fond at various
> stages of my novel-reading career. Quentin Durward was about the first
> and had the least intellect of any of them but even he with his honest heart,
> strong arm and comely face was more satisfactory than our melancholy
> subtle modern Hamlets, old before their time and weary of the world.[13]

Mary Hallock married in 1875, and there are many references in her letters to her husband, whom she clearly loved deeply; was that reason
enough, perhaps, for never once commenting on his looks? Male
appearance did continue to fascinate her, and when, as Mary Hallock
Foote, she moved with her husband to California, she was greatly taken
by the powerful men she encountered in San Francisco:

> Mr Hague is very handsome and has great harmoniousness – he never jars
> – I fancy his calm philosophy conceals a gentle cynicism – but it is not evi-
> dent – Mr Ashburner is prematurely gray, with keen dark eyes which give
> distinction to the otherwise plain countenance – Mr Janin is dark and
> strong jawed – very black, troubled-looking eyes – I speak of the men first

because at the dinners and evenings they talked to me and because they were rather more remarkable than the women.[14]

Do women pay more attention to men's eyes than men, on the whole, pay to women's? It seems likely, as it also seems that women are more flexible in their appraisal of looks in men than men are in appraising women (a difference that can be of importance in matrimonial choices). Let us, anyway, consider how, at the beginning of the twentieth century, Katherine Mansfield (aged seventeen), travelling on an ocean liner between Britain and New Zealand, registered in her journal her reactions to the presence of one beautiful male:

> The first time I saw him I was lying back in my chair, and he walked past. I watched the complete rythmic movement, the absolute self-confidence, the beauty of his body, and that [the next word is marked as *illegible* in the version of the journal published much later by her husband, but presumably the word is 'longing', or 'desire' or 'excitement', or something similar, and sufficient to upset a husband] which is everlasting and eternal in youth and creation stirred in me. I heard him speaking. He has a low, full, strangely exciting voice, a habit of mimicking others, and a keen sense of humour. His face is clean cut, like the face of a statue, his mouth completely Grecian. Also he has seen much and lived much and his hand is perfectly strong and cool. He is certainly tall, and his clothes shape the lines of his figure. When I am with him a preposterous desire seizes me, I want to be badly hurt by him. I should like to be strangled by his firm hands.[15]

So much for secret observations and hidden desires. Let us examine an eighteenth-century marriage, and from the male point of view. What Thomas Turner, a prosperous shopkeeper in East Hoathly, near Lewes in Sussex, hoped from marriage was companionship and someone to run his household: his diary evidently served a useful function in enabling him to record his despair over the way in which his hopes were not being fulfilled. 'Oh!', he exclaimed in his entry for Saturday 30 August 1755, 'what a happiness must there be in a married state when there is sincere regard on both sides and each party truly satisfied with each other's merit.' But, he continued, 'it is impossible for tongue or pen to express the uneasiness that attends the contrary'. Miserably, he notes the many quarrels between himself and his wife, constantly agonising over where he had gone wrong. After another quarrel he stated, on the first day of the new year, his reasons for having married: 'I was neither instigated to marry by avarice, ambition, nor lust. No, nor was I prompted to it by anything; only the pure and desirable sake of friendship'.[16] Such motivation, obviously, coincides exactly with the sermonising of the time. It may be that a modicum of lust would actually have gone down rather well, and that the very rationality of the approach was what was ruining the marriage. At no time is there any reference to his wife's looks, yet in February 1756, after another quarrel, he describes her as 'so infinitely dear to me' and 'the charmer of my soul'. In October he states that given his chances over again he would still make the same choice.[17]

One cause of marital friction may have been his wife's poor health. In 1761 she died. There are many lamentations over her loss and tributes to her qualities as a wife, tributes very much in keeping with the notion of marriage as a rational partnership in which one certainly did not marry for 'lust'. First he declares that 'She was undoubtedly superior in wisdom, prudence and economy to most of her sex and I think the most neatest and cleanest woman in her person I ever beheld'.[18] Eighteen months later he is lamenting that he cannot find another woman to compare with her: 'I shall never have a more virtuous and prudent wife than I have already been possessed of '.[19] A year after that he declares that 'I have never spent hardly one agreeable hour in the company of a woman since I lost my wife, for really there seem very few whose education and way of thinking is agreeable and suitable with my own'.[20] The notion of the wife's role in the business of marriage comes through in the lament of 10 November 1763: 'No one but a servant to trust the care of my concerns to or the management of my household affairs, which are now all confusion. My affairs abroad are neglected by my confinement at home ...' Clearly this is all deeply felt, though in fact Turner's shop was continuing to prosper. But most significant of all is the latter part of the very first entry lamenting his wife's death:

> I think words can convey but a faint idea of the pleasure and happiness that a husband finds in the company of a virtuous, prudent and discreet woman, one whose love is not founded on the basis of sensual pleasures but on the more solid foundation of friendship and domestic happiness, whose chief delight is to render the partner of her bosom happy.[21]

When, at last, another woman did enter his life the first reference to her (Monday 19 March 1764) is utterly laconic 'I dined on the remains of yesterday's dinner. At home all day; posted my day book. Molly Hicks drank tea with me. In the even wrote my London letters. Very little to do all the day.' Five days later, however, the entry is much more enthusiastic and once again gives us an insight into the qualities Turner looked for in a wife:

> After tea my brother Richd and I took a walk (Molly Hicks, my favourite girl, being come to pay Mrs Atkins a visit in the even, went home to her father's, and I along with her, my brother going with her companion for company.) We came back about 8.10. This is a girl I have taken a great liking to, she seeming to all appearances to be a girl endued with a great deal of good nature and good sense, and withall so far as hitherto come to my knowledge is very discreet and prudent.[22]

Molly was in fact working as a servant to a local JP, not an unusual occupation for a girl from, say, the artisan or smallholding class, and one which was reckoned an excellent training for marriage. Only with the very last entry in the diary do we learn that she has excellent financial prospects: thus his earlier assertion that, along with lust, avarice and ambition were no part of his motivation in seeking a wife may not have been completely candid. On the evening of Good Friday, 5 April 1765, he met Molly by appointment and walked home with her; the weather being excessively bad he remained there with her till past five o'clock in the morning. One presumes that no sexual activity took place.

The comment next day, the comment of a man lacking confidence in himself and recalling the turbulence of his previous marriage, is: 'In the even very dull and sleepy; this courting does not well agree with my constitution, and perhaps it may be only taking pains to create more pain.'[23] There is no direct reference to an engagement, but an entry in the diary just over a week later, mentioning that after dinner on Sunday 14 April he set out to pay Molly Hicks a visit, refers to her as 'my intended wife'. He spent the afternoon 'with a great deal of pleasure, it being very fine weather and my companion very agreeable. I drank tea with her and came home about 9.30'.[24] Then, in a long entry, he considers how news of his intentions will be treated in the world, 'some likely condemning, others approving my choice'. But since the world cannot judge 'the secret intentions' of his mind and may censure him though not knowing his true motives, he decides he will set down 'what are really and truly my intentions and the only motives from which they spring', which, he adds, 'may be of some satisfaction to those who may happen to peruse my memoirs'. In his statement he refers first to the general role of marriage – he puts great emphasis, it should be noted, on marriage as a Christian duty – moving quickly to his own personal loneliness, and then to the qualities of his intended:

> as to the motives which spur me on to think of marriage, first I think it is a state agreeable to nature, reason and religion and in some manner the indispensable duty of Christians. For I think it is the duty of every Christian to serve God and perform his religious services in the most calm, serene and composed manner, which if it can be performed more so in a marriage state than a single one, it must be an indispensable duty. Now as to my present situation, my house is not at all regular, neither is there any family devotion performed in that serious manner as formerly in my wife's time, nor have I one friend in the world; that is, I have not anyone whom I can thoroughly rely upon or confide in. Neither have I anyone to trust the management of my affairs to that I can be assured in their management will be sustained no loss. I have not one agreeable companion to soften and alleviate the misfortunes incident to human nature. As to my choice I have only this to say: the girl I believe as far as I can discover is a very industrious, sober woman and seemingly indued with prudence and good nature, and seems to have a very serious and sedate turn of mind. She comes of reputable parents and may perhaps one time or other have some fortune.[25]

Now comes the only reference to her personal appearance (as also to his own): 'As to her person I know it's plain (so is my own), but she is cleanly in her person and dress (which I will say is something more than at first sight it may appear to be towards happiness)'. There follows a discreet comment on her figure, focusing, presumably, on her bosom, since the remainder would have remained fairly well concealed in her voluminous clothing: 'she is I think a well-made woman'. Immediately he passes on to other qualities, and finally back to his overall aims in marriage:

> As to her education, I own it is not liberal, neither do I think it equals my own, but she has good sense and a seeming desire to improve her mind, and, I must in justice say, has always behaved to me with the strictest

honour and good manners, her behaviour being far from the affected formality of the prude, nor on the other hand anything of that foolish
fondness too often found in the more light part of the sex.

This said, he comes to what he terms his 'real intentions'. They are:

> of marriage and of the strictest honour, having nothing else in view but to
> live in a more sober and regular manner, and to be better able to perform
> my duty to God and man in a more suitable and truly religious manner,
> and with the grace of the Supreme Being to live happy and a sincere union
> with the partner of my bosom.

It is important to comment that, though the diary from time to time,
with some regret, mentions bouts of drinking (from which, we have
seen, he hoped marriage would protect him), there is no suggestion that
Turner had sought sexual adventures during his years of loneliness.
Comment must also be made on his dislike of 'foolish fondness', that is
to say, manifest demonstrations of affection; this thoroughly eighteenth-
century element of would-be fastidious gentility may well have played a
part in his difficulties with his first wife. That there *is* affection on his
side is evident; a few days later he admits that in spending a 'delightful
evening', there was 'nothing wanting to make it so except the company
of my dear Molly'.[26] The following Sunday, 28 April 1765, he once more
stays the greater part of the night with her, coming home about 4.40
a.m. Then he seriously injures his leg, and the fondness issue comes up
again:

> At home all day; my leg very painful. In the even my intended wife and
> her sister called to see me and sat with me some time. This may possibly
> be imputed to the girl as fondness, but I must do her the justice to say I
> esteem it only as friendship and good manners. For I have never met with
> more civil and friendly usage from anyone of the fair sex than I have from
> this girl.[27]

As the wedding drew near, Turner succumbed to a fever (psychosomatic, one can't help suspecting), and for fourteen days after the
wedding (which took place on 19 June) he suffered intermittently. At
this point the diary ends, suggesting that Turner now felt himself settled. He declares that he is 'happy in my choice', continuing: 'I have,
it's true, not married a learned lady, nor is she a gay one, but I trust she
is good natured, and one that will use her utmost endeavours to make

me happy, which perhaps is as much as it is in the power of a wife to do.' His his last words, as I mentioned earlier, are, entirely in keeping with the ethic of the time, on her economic prospects: 'As to her fortune, I shall one day have something considerable, and there seems to be rather a flowing stream.'[28]

Turner's diary makes no mention of the procreative function of marriage, though this was probably due to personal reticence, particularly since his first marriage was childless (as also, it transpired, was his second). But the production of children to continue the family line, provide labour and ensure support in old age was, as we have seen, a very strong motive behind marriage, which often meant that, in a wife, robustness rather than beauty was what was sought. From roughly the same period, in France, the account (somewhat dramatised) given by the novelist Rétif de la Bretonne of the courtship of his father, a humble clerk, indicates sensitivity to beauty while overwhelmingly demonstrating the influence of employers and parents, and above all considerations of status and wealth, in marital choice.[29]

I make no apology for pointing out that with Turner beauty very much was not in the eye of the beholder: much as he esteemed Molly, he had no illusions that her many virtues added up to beauty. What is also striking is the emphasis on cleanliness, which really does remind us of the age we are dealing with; when such elementary considerations were so important, beauty for the many was something of an unreal luxury. Yet just once in a while we get glimpses of how looks do figure in personal preferences. Such a glimpse is afforded by the advertisement placed by a country gentleman, 'fifty-two years of age next July, but of a vigorous, strong and amorous constitution', in the *Daily Advertiser* (1750). He was looking for a wife:

> Tall and graceful in her person, more of the fine woman than the pretty one; good teeth, soft lips, sweet breath, with eyes no matter what colour, so they are but expressive; of a healthy complexion, rather inclined to fair rather than brown; neat in her person, her bosom full, plump, firm and white; good understanding without being a wit, but cheerful and lively in conversation, polite and delicate of speech, her temper humane and tender, and to look as if she could feel delight where she wishes to give it … She must consent to live entirely in the country, which, if she likes the man, she will not be unwilling to comply with; and it is to be hoped she

will have a heart above all mercenary views and honest enough not to be ashamed to own she loves the man whom she makes her choice. She must not be more than fourteen years, nor less than seven years, younger than the gentleman.[30]

The specified age range of thirty-eight to forty-five suggests that the breeding of children was not a consideration, but the woman had to be personable, and there is an agreeable, and tasteful, stress on sexual 'delight'.

Now it would be absurd to suggest that marriage was a guarantee, or a condition, of happiness for a woman in the eighteenth century. Repeated pregnancies and births were a dreadful burden, so that sometimes wives were pleased rather than otherwise when their husbands took mistresses and fathered children elsewhere. Nevertheless, all contemporary evidence indicates that, such were the attitudes, conventions and economic realities of the time, that to remain unmarried was a likely cause of unhappiness for a woman. It would be quite inaccurate to maintain that the plain were the ones that did not get married (we have Thomas Turner's testimony to the contrary), but there is evidence to support the common-sense guess that matters were stacked against the unprepossessing. The author of the *Tableau de Paris* commented sourly on the avarice for dowries which led, he alleged, to penniless women being condemned to the single state. Even more acid was his comment on the plight of the many young women who had neither a fortune nor an attractive appearance: those with beauty, he declared, should be auctioned off to provide dowries for those without.[31]

The knowledge of being physically unattractive could certainly bring bouts of misery to men. Dudley Ryder, a shopkeeper's son who, through the prosperity of his father's business, was already in 1715 moving in gentlemanly social circles, had a keen eye for female beauty, as well as a full measure of sensuality; drink could temper the former and increase the latter. Of one social occasion he remarked: 'There were some few pretty ladies enough but nothing very extraordinary'. After another social occasion he 'was very warm with drinking wine and had a mighty inclination to fill a whore's commodity'.[32] Joining in the social round at Bath, he was smitten by Sally Marshall, the 'most celebrated beauty' there. 'She had something so very agreeable in the cast of her countenance and features of her face as troubled me very sensibly when I first saw her.'[33] But in comparison with his handsome friend Samuel Powell, he saw himself as having no chance with Sally, remarking unhappily on: 'My littleness and want of beauty, ill complexion, not being merry company nor gay and diverting'.[34] Whatever personal unfulfilment there may have been, and Ryder remained single for another twenty years, his social ascent through the legal profession was not obstructed: eventually he became a peer and Lord Chancellor. In his forties, secure in status and riches, he married.

Throughout the nineteenth century and beyond, wealth and status continued to be important considerations; though under the impact of industrialisation and romanticism there was a decline in the institution of the arranged marriage and an increase in the freedom of young people to make their own personal choices. As we have seen, personal choice does not necessarily simply imply good looks; as in every age, individuals have to accommodate to their circumstances and opportunities, and to the implacable fact that, to repeat, although the beautiful are always with us, there are always far too few of them to go round. Beauty, and the lack of it, is noticed, commented upon, and is sometimes an obsession, with men and women. Other times it does not enter into the reckoning.

The unpublished 'Memorial of James Howard of Manchester (1738 to 1822)', written between 1853 and 1862 by his daughter Rachel Barrow (1789–1870), reveals, the calculation having been made that economic circumstances were right for the selection of a wife, that beauty, at first sight, made the vital initial impact; the follow-up 'enquiry' suggests standard prudence (though no 'avarice') in a serious business, and perhaps a slight touch of conventional sentimentality. Judge for yourself:

> Having thus disposed of his three sisters, he looked around for a partner for himself, having been in business some three or four years. – He was married to Hannah Gorse in the year 1777; he saw her at chapel and was struck by her beauty – I have been told by several of both sexes, that she was the handsomest woman in Manchester …
>
> My father used to say my mother's beauty alone would not have fixed him, if on enquiry her character had not proved to be all he could wish – her character was the subject of praise from everyone – she was blessed with such sweetness of temper that she was never known to shew any angry spirit but once …[35]

From the beginning of the century we have an account by a journey-man printer of his two courtships, one resulting in rejection, the other in marriage. In his journal, dated January 1809, he is looking back after nearly four years of a marriage in which he has allied himself to a deeply religious family and during which he has risen to become a partner in a printing firm. Evidently, within a very limited circle, he has acted from personal choice, but what he sees as really governing his actions is 'wise providence'. Beauty is not mentioned:

> About this time I fell in love, made an offer of marriage, but was rejected. This I have no doubt was overruled by a wise incalculable advantage, as had this match taken place, in all probability the person who had been more immediately the instrument in God's hand of awakening my drousy & languid conscience and consideration about eternity would have per-haps never have been brought within the circle of my acquaintance. When Annie Collie, with whom I had been long acquainted, & who had been the object of my choice in my younger years, though the thought of my own youth, and the danger of my affections leading to precipitancy, made me resolve, however reluctantly to check myself in time, & break off all inter-course at least for a time. This was done, – and after the interval of many months, if not years, it was again commenced and for the same reasons abandoned. – It was a considerable time after this second break off, that my affections were engaged to the other, & to whom I proposed marriage. – but my suit being rejected, in a few months, I resolved to attach myself to my first love which I did, & on the 25th day of October, 1805, we were married in her father's by the Rev James Struthers.[36]

A description of her engagement, seventy years later, by an upper middle-class young lady is even more phlegmatic. In the spring of 1875 Elizabeth Hardcastle was in Rome, seeing the sights. Her diary consists of brief, almost laconic entries, reminiscent of the formal minutes of a business meeting. Mostly they refer to the other Britons in Rome at that time. Miss Hardcastle is sensitive to human beauty: of one couple in the circle she notes, 'they are both so handsome'.[37] A trip to Ostia and Cas-tel Fusano was aborted because of rain: 'Graham was to have gone in our carriage so after breakfast he turned up and we sang a duet and then went to the Borghese Gallery where Mr Freeman joined us'. Four days later (Sunday, 11 April 1875) these two characters are mentioned again: 'church twice. Walked with Mr Freeman and Horace Thornton to

S. Peters to hear Vespers. Graham came to tea'. The entry for the next day consists of three sentences:

> Rode with the Miss Colvilles, Captain and Mr Bland, Horace Thornton and Graham to the Cook Valleys. Robert Graham asked me to be his wife, which after much consideration I consented to. Mr Freeman went away this morning.

The day following the proposal and acceptance merits two sentences, and the bridegroom-to-be, as previously, only his surname: 'Graham brought me over the sweetest letter from his mother. Afternoon we went to see the Vatican pictures together.' There is no other sign of family considerations or interest. Obviously bride and groom belonged to the same social set; within that (considerable!) restriction this was an authentic nineteenth-century individualistic, romantic engagement (even if described most unromantically by the bride). Pasted in beside the crucial entry there is a photograph of the intended: an agreeable, if not particularly striking, member of the gentry class. Nowhere has there been any comment on his looks, nor indeed on any of his other attributes. Yet Miss Hardcastle was a witty and highly literate young woman. The diary opens with a sparkling description of her sister's wedding, in which members of the bridal procession are termed 'the mourners'. The 'Cook Valleys' in the quotation above derive their name from the tourists ('Cookies' or 'Cookisti') delivered there by the pioneering Victorian travel firm Thomas Cook. The making public of the engagement nine days later is rendered thus: 'We divulged the awful secret to the Roman world causing thereby a great sensation'. The wedding is not described, nor the honeymoon, though there is a full description of the arrival at Skipness, the Graham home, the welcome by local farmers, the settling in, the rounds of visits; there is nothing at all which hints at physical attractiveness, let alone sexual feeling.[38]

The Anderson family papers at Stanford University, California, provide us with quite a full account of the courtship and first years of marriage, in the 1870s, of Melville Anderson and Charlena Van Vleeck, educated Americans; marvellously, they also contain photographs, so that we can see that both Melville and Charlena were pleasantly personable, but not specially good-looking. They were thrown together because Melville was a student in lodgings and Charlena was the landlady's daughter. Their courtship was an undemonstrative one, and in the early stages of marriage they happily accepted long separations in the interests of Melville's career as an academic. In the copious letters from both partners there is never any reference to the physical appearance of the other.[39] There are marriages, marriages which belong in the public sphere, where beauty, on the part of one or other or both partners is of critical importance; I shall return to a few such marriages, each of special interest, at the end of this chapter. What my cullings from a miscellany of letters and diaries have demonstrated is, that for the mass of humanity, marriage is too serious a matter for beauty, or to be ruthlessly realistic, the absence of it, to be a crucial factor. But we all know that, anyway, don't we? The trouble is, swamped in romantic fiction, film and television, where every lover and every loved one is beautiful, we don't always *want* to know it. This book simply seeks to record life as it actually is: some sorts of success (which may not be to everyone's taste anyway) depend on the entirely arbitrary chance of possessing good looks, but lack of good looks need not necessarily be a barrier to other types of success, and certainly not to a happy marriage. It may be that what most men throughout history have wanted in their dreams is to bed as many beautiful women as possible, but in the real world they (kings as well as commoners) have recognised the need to make as 'suitable' (agreeable, workable, sustainable, etc.) a marriage as possible.

The fascinating French publication of 1825, *The Secret of Conquering Women and Holding Their Affections* is not, as might be expected, a guide to the arts of seduction; its fundamental premise is that it is vital for a man to make a sensible marriage and thus it offers advice on how men may make themselves pleasing to women, and also on how to choose an appropriate wife. Discussing first 'The Art of Pleasing', the book begins with 'Physical Qualities', remarking that they are the ones that come into play almost immediately and the ones whose effects are the most involuntary. A tall stature, regular features, good proportions exercise from the start 'an almost irresistible power', which, the book continues, in an interesting anticipation of evolutionist theory on this subject, comes from 'an instinct natural to all beings to tend towards preserving the beauty of the species'. In love there is always an element of 'personal vanity': a woman is 'flattered to capture a man whom her rivals find beautiful'. Evidently anxious not to lose the custom of readers whose stature falls short of the desirable, the author then adds the reassurance typical of almost all guides to personal appearance and self-presentation: those who are short 'can often make up for this by their grace and vivacity'; if a man is 'well proportioned one can forget that he is small'. But it is not possible to console all customers: 'beauty is a matter of proportion, and a fat man is as disagreeable to the eye as an extremely thin one'; however (and perhaps this is a sop to the fat), 'thinness is less suited to love'.[40]

After these introductory opinions, the book settles down to practical advice on care of the hair, the mouth, the teeth, the eyes and the eyebrows. With regard to the mouth, it is recognised frankly that 'a man with a sweet-smelling mouth will be most likely to invite kisses'; furthermore, 'fine teeth are the finest ornament'. This highly rational section concludes with the admonition that an indispensable quality for pleasing women is 'cleanliness' and that in this area 'excess is quite permissible'.[41] Then we're back with the stock-in-trade of all such guides: 'The spirit is truly the man; without it the purely physical appearance has no charms ... with a sensitive spirit one is beautiful, with a dull one the most regular features will give birth only to the most ephemeral passions' ('ephemeral passions', of course, may be exactly what men 'with the most regular features' are counting on arousing, but then *The Secret of Conquering Women* is about the serious business of matrimony). The section on how to retain a woman's affections reveals a rather misogynous estimate of female aspirations and fidelity. All women 'desire a man of birth, fortune and beauty'; beauty in a woman is often destructive of the happiness of a husband – 'a lovely woman always has many admirers and it is rare for a beautiful woman not to succumb to temptation'. Beauty, then, is not a quality a man should look for in a wife; much more important is health, without which there will 'only be loathing and disgust, since physical attraction cannot exist without health'. Altogether a risky business marriage, it seems. 'A man who is much older than his wife, whatever his other qualities, must expect to be deceived.'[42] If he does marry he should marry someone 'of the same social status; otherwise he risks humiliation'. Guides such as this, directed solely at men, are very rare; this one is useful for reinforcing the general picture we have of marriage as a serious business where beauty, though it may well inspire 'ephemeral passions' (in both sexes) is not a highly-rated ingredient. Analogous guides for women, coun-selling them on how to make themselves pleasing to men were, inevitably, published by the bucket-load. I'll turn to them when, in the twentieth century, they begin to show a change in tone which is of great historical significance.

As travel increased and societies became more mobile, the chances of encountering beautiful persons of the opposite sex increased. To exem-plify that mobility, which enabled increasing comparison and appraisal of personal appearance, we have (despite the improbable name) the life of a German-American, Henry Theophilus Finck. Both his father and his mother came from near Stuttgart in Germany, but they did not actu-ally meet until they both found themselves part of a German-American settlement in Bethel, Missouri. He was an apothecary and a gifted ama-teur violinist. Henry was born in 1854; when his mother died a few years later his father moved the family to Oregon, travelling via the Panama Canal. In the predominantly German community of Aurora Mills, Henry nurtured his ambition to traverse the entire width of America in order to study at prestigious Harvard. There the young Finck supported himself on scholarships, and in 1876 he graduated with highest honours, having majored in philosophy and psychology, and also taken classes in music. On borrowed money he travelled to the first Bayreuth Festival, with commissions to do reports for two American journals. He wintered in Munich, returned briefly to the US, then spent three more years on a scholarship in Berlin, Vienna and Heidelberg. He changed his middle name, Gottlob, to its nearest Anglo-Saxon equivalent, Theophilus. Dis-appointed in his hopes of an academic career, he established himself as a music critic and popular lecturer. As can be seen from the photograph in his autobiography, Finck was a very good-looking young man, and it is clear that, no doubt with the decorum suited to the age, he took a lively interest in attractive young women.[43] Although he was subse-quently to bring out books on Chopin, Wagner, Grieg and Schubert, his first book was, in the language of the time, a 'philosophical work', *Romantic Love and Personal Beauty*, in which, among other things, he made the age-old error of laying down narrow rules about beauty in women – he declared brunettes superior to blondes (a view also pro-moted by English guru, John Ruskin). Published in two volumes in 1887, this tome was immensely successful in both the USA and Britain.

So successful in fact that Finck's thoughts turned towards marriage. Continuing his extensive travels (his appraisals of beauty in *Romantic Love and Personal Beauty* were based partly on his own travels and partly on the many travel and anthropological books pouring from the presses in the later nineteenth century), in Spain he met a certain Mr Curry, 'and his niece Virginia, a girl of dazzling beauty', who made such an impression on him that he decided to make her a present of the one copy of his book which he had with him. Virginia was a blonde: Finck's reaction to her blonde beauty demonstrates once again how feeble preconceptions about what constitutes beauty (in this case concerning the superiority of brunettes to blondes) are in face of living, breathing beauty of whatever type. Now that preconception was rather embarrassing, and most unlikely to endear him to the object of his passion. Thinking fast, he had a 'happy thought': 'I gave her the book after writing in it following her name: Please remember that the chapter on 'brunettes versus blondes' was written before I had seen you'. In the event he didn't marry Virginia, 'nor did I marry one of half-a-dozen other beauties who had temporarily dazed me'.[44] I think we can safely formulate the maxim that in marriage beauty plays the greatest part amongst those who have the widest choice, and practically no part with those like Thomas Turner or Charlena Anderson, whose choices are circumscribed by social circumstance and their own lack of strong physical attractiveness.

The woman he did marry was called Abbie Helen Cushman. His description of their first meeting both shows that the processes of getting acquainted with a beautiful woman don't change much and suggests that, whatever the conventional mode of expression, it is not so much beautiful eyes as the eyes of a beautiful woman which thrill. Abbie was at a concert in New York in the company of Nellie Learned, the managing editor of the *Evening Post*, who was known to Finck: 'One glance and I hastened to sit right behind them, casually as it were. I was introduced to Abbie and the first glance of her dark merry eyes stabbed my heart ...' Abbie was only seventeen and the marriage did not take place for another four years. His comments on Abbie at twenty-one, which I referred to in an earlier chapter, show (as we shall see later with the young Sarah Bernhardt) the absurdity of the notion that men in the nineteenth century could not appreciate beauty in women who were not buxom: 'She had no figure worth talking about at that time, being slight as a school girl, which makes it all the more remarkable that I, a born sensualist if ever there was one, should have fallen so madly in love with her'. Not remarkable at all when one looks at the slim beauty in the photographs reproduced in Finck's autobiography. It was, Finck continued, enumerating the conjunction of factors which can make for an enduring marriage – at least in male-centred nineteenth-century society:

> A genuine romantic love: eye love, face love, soul love. And she has a mind as well as a soul. Music was her passion, and her preferences were usually the same as mine. Soon she began to help me with my critical work and after a few years she could write so cleverly in my style that few could detect the author.[45]

To conclude this chapter I want to look at three marriages which have a strong public character but which also illustrate truths observable in private lives: first, the rather banal one of female beauty securing social promotion; secondly, the less familiar one of similar fruits reaped by male beauty; and, thirdly, that of marriage brought about by the insecurities and needs of the unprepossessing but professionally ruthless and rapidly upward-moving male, and the skill, poise and experience of the personable, though not beautiful female. First I go back to the mid eighteenth century, and the poor but honest Gunning sisters, Elizabeth and Maria. Despite the frequent attributions of their beauty to alleged Irish ancestry, they were actually born in England, though brought up in Ireland, where their father established himself as a member of the very minor gentry.[46] Unfortunately he was a spendthrift, so the family home had to be sold. But the Gunning status was sufficient, and the mother sufficiently knowledgeable and astute, for her to be able to wangle a small government pension for the family. She then brought the two sisters back to England and – it is as simple as that – put them on display. (Many of the better-known portraits of the two young ladies are stiff and formal, stressing status but lacking in allure; occasionally, as in the mezzotint of Elizabeth by Finlayson after Catherine Read, one gets a clear sense of what all the fuss was about: contemporaries are unanimous in their praises.) One could say that the sisters led *careers* as beauties, not after the style of Kitty Fisher and the celebrated courtesans, but with great care to keep reputation and everything else intact. One young aristocrat who took a connoisseur's interest in beautiful women was the handsome roué James, Duke of Hamilton, so great an interest in fact that, appreciating their rarity, he was prepared to marry one. He had first of all proposed to Elizabeth Chudleigh, whose fame as a beauty was only subsequently rivalled by the scandal she involved herself in as the bigamous Duchess of Kingston. Discovering that she was already secretly married, Hamilton turned towards her great rivals in the beauty ratings, the Gunning girls, who, wrote a contemporary, neatly summarising the business of marriage as transacted at this exalted level, 'had luckily brought their stock in trade to a market, where beauty frequently fetches an excellent price'.[47] The price won by Elizabeth Gunning was to become Duchess of Hamilton; a pamphlet of rhyming couplets produced by a young member of the Hamilton family celebrated the alliance between a peer of the realm and *virtuous* beauty:

> When *Beauty* spreads her Glories to View,
> Our wond'ring Eyes the radiant Blaze pursue;
> Enraptur'd we behold the pleasing Sight,
> And lose ourselves *in infinite Delight*
> *Unruly Passions* urge us to possess
> The richest Treasure of a Mortal's Bliss.
> But when *strict Virtue* guards the charming Fair
> With Prudence arm'd, and Chastity severe,
> We stand at Distance, and almost adore ...
> The gen'rous Peer, regardless of his Blood,
> Thinks it no *Stoop* to love the Fair and Good.
> Virtue, tho' e're so low, commands Respect,
> And Beauty never passes with Neglect ...[48]

Mrs Gunning had perfectly fulfilled a mother's duty. The 'poem' is saturated in the all-pervading power of social heirarchy – it specifies lower-class virtue and lower-class beauty; but it also resonates with the raw power of beauty (even if lower-class).

Hugh Smithson, the *DNB* boldly pronounces, 'was the handsomest man of his day',[49] and the Gainsborough portrait (exhibited in 1783) deliberately shows off his gorgeous legs, the perfect setting for his Order of the Garter. Silver spoons dropped by the dozen into the mouth of Smithson, yet it was surely his beauty (and, therefore, sex appeal) which swept him into the marriage (strongly opposed by the bride's family) which led to him becoming first Duke of Northumberland in the new creation. He was born in 1715 in Yorkshire. In 1729 he succeeded his grandfather, Sir Hugh Smithson, as fourth baronet of Stanwick, Yorkshire. Eleven years later he inherited property in Middlesex from another relative, Hugh Smithson, Esq., of Tottenham. He became High Sheriff of York in 1738 and MP for Middlesex in 1740. This was also the year in which he made his brilliant marriage. Elizabeth Seymour was daughter of Baron Percy and granddaughter of the sixth Duke of Somerset (who strenuously opposed the marriage). On the death of the sixth Duke, Lady Betty's father was created Earl of Northumberland, with the succession to Smithson and his heirs by Lady Betty. Smithson succeeded in 1750 and in the same year assumed, by Act of Parliament, the name and arms of the Percy family. 'For the next thirty years Northumberland and his wife figured prominently in social and political life.'[50] In 1766 Smithson (now Percy) was created Duke of Northumberland. He had the face, the figure and the legs for it.

One of the most famous of all marriages was that between Napoleon and Joséphine; a glance at the early life of the latter brings out some of the stranger facets of arranged, and re-arranged, marriages in eighteenth-century France. Marie-Josephe-Rose (later Joséphine) de Tascher de la Pagerie, the eldest of three daughters, was born in Martinique in June 1763. The family belonged to the ancient country gentry of France and still had excellent connections there, but had fallen on hard times – Joséphine's father was a struggling sugar planter. There was talk of a marriage alliance with Alexandre de Beauharnais, son of the powerful Marquis de Beauharnais. Although the Beauharnais had not actually seen any of the de Tascher de la Pagerie girls, the choice fell on the second daughter, Joséphine being considered, as the Marquis explained, too old:

> I would have very much desired that your eldest daughter were several years younger. She would certainly have had the preference, since I have been given an equally favourable picture of her, but must declare to you that my son, who is only seventeen and a half, finds that a young lady of fifteen is of an age too close to his own.[51]

The middle sister died, and Alexandre, who was anxious to lay hands on the inheritance which would become his on marriage, calmly agreed to the youngest, at this time eleven and a half; her father wrote of her that 'health and gaiety of character are combined with a figure that will soon be interesting'.[52] Mother and grandmother united in defence of the child, however, so that the choice at last passed to Joséphine. The Marquis had the banns published in Martinique, wisely leaving a blank where the name of the bride should have been specified. Joséphine sailed across the Atlantic and the engaged couple had their first meeting at Brest in October 1779. A long letter from Alexandre to the Marquis mentions many other matters before coming, courteously but unenthusiastically, to his intended: 'Mademoiselle de la Pagerie will perhaps seem less pretty to you than you expect, but I believe I can assure you that the honesty and sweetness of her character will surpass whatever people have been able to tell you about her'.[53] Alexandre got the marriage he needed and his inheritance, then happily continued his relationship with his mistress, Mme de Longpré. He and Joséphine were legally separated in 1785.

It was ten years later that Joséphine, now a widow of thirty-one, met Bonaparte, who was twenty-five. Joséphine had never been beautiful, but she now had great poise and self-confidence, and, as the Duchesse d'Abrantes later wrote, 'was still charming in this period ... Her teeth were frightfully bad, but when her mouth was shut she had the appearance, especially at a few paces distant, of a young and pretty woman'.[54] Several portraits of her 'in this period' (portentous words), among them one by Gros, show her as certainly personable. Napoleon was pale, thin and awkward-looking. He afterwards recalled:

> One day when I was sitting next to her at table, she began to pay me all manner of compliments on my military qualities. Her praise intoxicated me. From that moment I confined my conversation to her and never left her side. I was passionately in love with her, and our friends were aware of this long before I ever dared say a word about it.[55]

Two weeks after their first meeting Napoleon was appointed Commander-in-Chief of the Army of the Interior. They could well have drifted apart; it was Joséphine who took the initiative in writing to him. Even after they were married they were necessarily much apart; she may have had one extramarital affair, but she certainly became, and remained, an excellent wife as he became Emperor of France. But fate is unfair in many matters other than the distribution of beauty. Joséphine failed to produce a son, a necessity if Napoleon's dynastic ambitions were to be fulfilled. Napoleon divorced her in 1809. He was Emperor; she was an ageing woman, and – though still an international figure – died a lonely one in 1814.[56]

6

Grandes Horizontales

A rich and important public figure takes a beautiful lover. A son is born, but shortly afterwards the lover dies of consumption. Sometime later, the important person marries a gorgeous young thing ten years younger, who, however, the honeymoon over, is ditched. Earlier in the century an even more famous celebrity, whose beauty was much commented on, and who was in effect the first widely appreciated heart-throb, perhaps even the first pin-up, in history, had sought to maintain a much-admired elegance of figure through pioneering attempts at slimming. The rich public figure was Hortense Schneider, the original Belle Hélène (1864) in Offenbach's operetta of that name. The lover who died of consumption was the Duc de Gramont-Caderousse. The beautiful deserted young spouse was the feckless Italian Emile Brionne, who called himself the Comte de Brionne. Schneider was famous in her own right as undisputed leading lady in the highly successful Offenbach operettas, able to chose her lovers, who included the Khedive of Egypt and the Duc de Morny. Surviving into her eighties (until 1920, in fact), she lived out her later life graciously, devoting herself to her mentally challenged son.[1]

Born in 1833, Catherine Schneider was the daughter of a Bordeaux tailor. She was stage-struck at a very early age, but as a poor but beautiful girl she was, in the career structure I have already identified, set to work where she could display her looks, in a shop. This was her first step towards the career she desired. Energetic and dedicated, she spent her limited spare time at a rather rudimentary sort of drama school; even more important, she encountered an elderly musician, Nestor Schaffner, who was so captivated by her beauty that he committed himself to giving her singing lessons – also recommending the change of name to Hortense. She was now prepared for the second step, joining the theatre at Agen as an opera singer. Here she worked with fanatical zeal, her talent and looks attracting a number of devoted male admirers. They provided the funds to get her to Paris – step number three. In Paris her beauty won her an influential protector, who introduced her to Offenbach. To star in operetta she had to be beautiful; but it was because of her exceptional singing voice that the famous composer signed her up, projecting her into her illustrious career.

The famous celebrity from earlier in the century was Lord Byron, whose slimming campaign involved hot baths, copious drafts of vinegar, and violent exercise. He used curlers in his hair and sometimes adopted exotic costume. Reputed 'mad, bad, and dangerous to know', Byron was famous as a poet, traveller, lover, and for his looks. Those women who actually did meet him, I should add, commented also on the allure of his voice. 'The tones of Lord Byron's voice were always so fascinating, that I could not help attending to them', declared the novelist Amelia Opie, adding that it was 'such a voice as the devil tempted Eve with; you feared its fascination the moment you heard it'. At a small evening party, Jane Porter, author of a book on *The Scottish Chiefs*, was distracted 'by the most melodious Speaking Voice I had ever heard. It was gentle and beautifully modulated. I turned round to look for the Speaker and saw a Gentleman in black of an Elegant form ... and with a face I shall never forget.'[2] Distant admirers never heard the voice, but could, through engravings, swoon over the face ('so beautiful a face I scarcely ever saw', said another contemporary), while also swooning over the poems.

Despite my little game, I can't pretend to be demonstrating any real reversal in sex roles – we've already seen that a man could be admired for his looks while a woman could achieve some of the freedoms of a man through exploitation of her beauty. Byron's success was based primarily on his talents as a poet, though that was fortified by his sex appeal. Schneider's success was based on the vital conjunction of beauty *and* a willingness to trade sex for early advancement in her career; only *once launched*, did her exceptional musical talent and singing voice become critical. There was a whiff of admiration in the epithet applied to Schneider and the other rich and eminent women who made similar careers during the period from roughly 1840 to 1914, '*Grandes Horizontales*'; but there was also a demeaning odour of disrepute, of belonging to the not wholly respectable *demi-monde*. No such label was ever applied to a whole class of men (and, one may add, the deformed foot, which enhanced Byron's romantic appeal, would on a woman have sabotaged any claim to beauty). Schneider's connection with some of the most famous men of the day was recognised in a still more vulgar sobriquet, derived from the name of an alleyway near the rue de Richelieu: she was known as the *Passage des Princes*. Only when beautiful women (as well as beautiful men) are selling sex appeal, not sex, only when beautiful women are celebrities, not as courtesans, but solely as film stars, singers and fashion models, has the modern evaluation of beauty eclipsed the traditional one.

We are now well into the first era of industrialisation and of capitalistic entrepreneurship, of railways, steamships, and mechanical means of reproducing images, often images of beautiful people (engravings, then photographs). This period, the period of King Louis-Philippe (1830–48), President Louis Napoleon (1848–51), who established the Second Empire (1851–70), with himself as Emperor Napoleon III, and *La Belle Époque* (end of the nineteenth century, beginning of the twentieth), and also of that international phenomenon Victorianism, while one of gigantic material change, was, in attitudes to sex and to beauty, very much one of more of the same – much, much, more! But it was also the period of the last of the same, marking the culmination of the process whereby beautiful women, in order to achieve fame and fortune, had first to trade sex. There were more renowned courtesans than ever before, many also being famed for their association with show business, and some for running salons. These *grandes horizontales* were recruited from an ever-increasing range of nationalities and social classes. Of the twenty-six most celebrated beauties of the Parisian *demi-monde*, three were Italian, three British, one Spanish, one Austrian and one Russian; from Paris, one took her assets for a spell in Budapest, another for a spell in London, three for spells in St Petersburg. Lola Montez and La Belle Otero went to America, as, from Britain, did dance troupe 'The British Blondes' and courtesan and actress Lillie Langtry. Two were from the nobility, four from the respectable middle classes, twenty (including Schneider) from 'the popular classes'. The best way of giving meaning to that term, which, broadly, comprises the lower middle class, the urban and rural working class, and the yet lower class of itinerants and casual workers, the 'residuum' as it was called in Victorian Britain, is to look individually at some of them.[3]

Thérèse Jachmann (later Blanche and later still 'La Paiva'), born in 1819, was the daughter of a tailor in the Moscow ghetto. Apollonie Sabatier, christened Aglae-Joséphine, was born in 1822, the illegitimate daughter of a washerwoman in the Ardennes who shortly married a soldier called Savatier. Rose Alphonsine Plessis (Marie Duplessis, fictionalised as 'La Dame aux Camélias'), born in 1824, was the daughter of a pedlar in Normandy. Elisabeth-Céleste Vénard (the actress, 'Mogador'), also born in 1824, was illegitimate and brought up erratically by her mother, who for a time worked as a cashier in a hatters; at sixteen Céleste became a registered prostitute, being for a time confined 'for her own safety' to the women's prison at St-Lazare, and falling heavily into debt with her brothel keeper (just another occupational hazard for prostitutes). Eliza Emma Couch (Cora Pearl) was born around 1835 in Plymouth, the daughter of a music teacher of Irish origins, who shortly deserted her mother. Born in 1837 to a poor family in Reims, Jeanne Detourbey worked first as a wool picker in a factory, then as a bottle washer in a Reims champagne house. Anna Deslions, mistress of Louis Napoleon's cousin, Prince Napoleon, was a 'working-class girl of exceptional beauty'.[4] When Spanish troops invaded south-west France in 1841 they fathered a number of illegitimate children: one was Marie Colombier, later actress, courtesan and chronicler of the *demi-monde*.[5] The origins of Caroline Letessier (who after a sojourn in St Petersburg came back to rival Schneider as a singer and courtesan), 'Emilienne d'Alençon' (like many others she assumed the noble-sounding title) and Giulia Beneni ('La Barucci') are even more obscure, though it is possible that Letessier's foster-father was a butcher, while it is known that La Barucci was born in Rome; d'Alençon, at fifteen, ran off with a gypsy. Catherine Walters ('Skittles') was born in 1839, the daughter of a minor customs officer in Liverpool. Marie-Ernestine Antigny (who styled herself Blanche d'Antigny, and did so well in St Petersburg that she returned with a letter of introduction to the Palais Royale operetta), born in 1840, was the daughter of a carpenter in Martizay, near Bourges. Julie Leboeuf ('Marguerite Bellanger', eventually mistress to Emperor Napoleon III), also born in 1840, came from an agricultural worker's family near Saumur, and got a job as a hotel chambermaid, then as a circus acrobat and bareback rider. Leonide Leblanc, born in 1842, was the daughter of a stone breaker. All of these were courtesans of note under Louis-Philippe or during the Empire of Napoleon III. From among the famous courtesans of *la belle époque*, Louise Delabigne, who took the name Yolaine de la Bigne and, painted by Manet, was the inspiration for Zola's Nana, was born in 1848 to a Parisian laundress,[6] Caroline Otero came from a Spanish gypsy family, and Lina Cavalieri (born in Rome, 25 December 1874) from an unknown Italian one.

These bare details of birth and origins say no more than that it was *possible* for a woman of the humblest background to achieve the wealth and celebrity of the *demi-monde*, to a degree that, Nell Gwyn notwithstanding, had not been true of previous centuries. The same elements of ambition, determination, strategy and luck were required, as we shall see from looking further at some individual cases. Were all of the *grandes horizontales* beautiful, and was beauty the essential prerequisite? From both the visual and written evidence it is absolutely clear that twenty-five out of the twenty-six courtesans I am speaking of possessed a beauty which we would, most of us, recognise today, and which spirited men recognised at the time. With La Paiva, it is less clear.[7] From written testimony it is evident that she had a superb figure – womanly breasts and curves set within a slim, girlish figure: combined with her youthfulness (she was seventeen when – we don't know exactly how – she arrived in Paris). This made her devastatingly attractive enough for her to move rapidly out of common prostitution and into the realm of the kept woman. She had large, fiery eyes and sensuous lips, but there were many adverse comments on her face, particularly on the shape of her nose. It may be that she was thought to look too Jewish (and perhaps too openly sexy) for comfort, while actually having a type of beauty which many powerful men (including, during a profitable stay in London, the British Prime Minister, Lord Derby) found irresistible – her social ascent is indisputable as, through her professional services, she accumulated wealth and, through brilliant marriages, became successively Marquise de Paiva, then Countess Henschel von Donnersmarch. Or it may be that, along with Ninon de Lenclos, Mesdames de Pompadour and de Staël, she was one of those exceptions, who, personable rather than beautiful (though certainly not plain), captivated and exploited men through force of character. In an excellent and thorough book, Virginia Rounding is unable to do other than fall back upon those stock phrases we encounter so often, telling us that La Paiva 'was not conventionally beautiful' while possessing 'undeniable, but indefinable, sexual allure'.[8] There being no portraits, and the written evidence being in conflict, the question must remain an open one.

The looks of Cora Pearl – as well as her manners and speech – were also much criticised. Alphonse Daudet (author of *Lettres de mon moulin*) wrote of her 'hideous head', and that her 'lithe young body', grudgingly admitted in passing, was no compensation for the 'sewer of a mouth' and 'comic English accent'.[9] The Comte de Mugny, in his *Le Demi-Monde sous le Second Empire* (1892, published under the pseudonym 'Zed') recalled of her:

> English by birth, character and allure, she had the head of a factory worker, neither good nor bad, violent blonde, almost red, hair, and unbearably vulgar accent, a raucous voice, excessively course manners, and the behaviour of a stable-boy.[10]

Her colossal success with rich and powerful men, de Mugny complained, was beyond his comprehension. We are still in an era where judgements on a person's appearance could be heavily affected by snobbishness. In fact, Cora Pearl was enthusiastically bedded by every rich and powerful Frenchman who could get his hands on her. From her portraits we can see why: her face was perfectly proportioned, slightly boyish as is sometimes the way with the Irish, and, in sum, enticingly beautiful. Today's expert on courtesans, Kate Hickman, however, once again offers her own favourite explanation: Cora Pearl, 'like all successful courtesans had the gift of being able to make men think she was beautiful'[11] – for myself, I think it's simpler than that, and that the gift Cora Pearl had was beauty. A photograph of 'Skittles', the Liverpool girl, Catherine Walters, taken around 1860, shows her as very much the elegant, aristocratic-looking, seductive woman of the world, as beautiful (to the man without preconceptions or prejudices) as Cora Pearl, though an entirely different type. She fitted Zed's snobbish tastes:

> English like Cora Pearl, but as beautiful, elegant, distinguished, and graceful, as Cora Pearl was lacking in these qualities. She had blonde hair, a natural blonde, deep blue eyes, striking complexion, perfectly proportioned features, slim build, aristocratic curves: a real keepsake.[12]

Fashion will be fashion, and, naturally, hairstyles, costume, etc., changed over time, but beauty itself came to the fore in an increasing range of types. Generally, but not exclusively, beauties in the nineteenth century were plumper than those of the early twenty-first century. However, Marie Duplessis, Alice Ozy, Lola Montez, Caroline Letessier, Cléo de Mérode, and Emilienne d'Alençon, as also Sarah Bernhardt (when young) were notably slim (a contemporary noting – probably quite erroneously – that Duplessis would not have suited the Turks). Facial appearances varied enormously and were certainly not tied to particular sub-periods (Second Empire, or *Belle Époque*, say). La Barucci (Second Empire) was dark with strong, striking Italian features, while Blanche d'Antigny matched convention exactly with her sweet, slightly chubby face, dimpled chin and plump figure. Léonide Leblanc was a blonde with a plump face and a turned up nose. Cavalieri (*Belle Époque*), under dark hair, had delicate soulful features; but then *La Belle Otero* (also *Belle Époque*) had the heavy looks of the Spanish gypsy that she was.

The careers of these women involved an intelligent, calculating, exploitation of their looks, sometimes bringing in ancillary talents, such an ability to sing, act, dance or ride. The exploiter might be solely the woman herself, or, in the early stages at least, an 'agent' (usually male, but possibly female). In conversation with the actress Judith Bernat, Marie Duplessis seemed to be assuming total responsibility for her own destiny: 'Why did I sell myself? Because honest work would never have brought me the luxury I craved for, irresistibly ... I wanted to know the refinements and pleasures of artistic trade, the joy of living in elegant and cultivated society'.[13] In fact the first to perceive the commercial value of her beauty had been her own father, who, in effect, sold her for a year to a wealthy septuagenarian in Normandy.[14] Rose Alphonsine (as she still was) then took herself off to Paris, her looks securing her the jobs (still relatively menial) which at least kept her clear of the registered brothels while she was also working on her own account as a prostitute. We have portraits, including the one by Edouard Viénot (*c.* 1845), and the later description (1888) by Romain Vienne already alluded to:

> She was tall, slender, fresh as a spring flower; the beauty of her body was perhaps lacking in that fullness so appreciated by the Turks, in that richness of shapely curves without which there is no perfection. A painter would have chosen her as a model, a sculptor never. But she was deliciously pretty. Her long, thick, black hair was magnificent, and she

arranged it with inimitable skill. Her oval face with its regular features, slightly pale and melancholy when calm and in repose, would suddenly come to life at the sound of a friendly voice ... She had the head of a child. Her mouth, sweet and sensual, was ornamented with dazzlingly white teeth.[15]

A widower named Nollet, also spotting her dazzling potential, encouraged her to change her name to the grander sounding Marie Duplessis. Her plunge into the society to which she aspired was achieved when she became the mistress of the Duc de Guche-Gramont. Thereafter she had merely to *appear*, at the theatre, at a dance, in a salon, to attract the attention of the rich, or the celebrated, such as the novelist Alexandre Dumas *fils*, who based his later *La Dame aux Camélias* on the Duplessis who had set herself up in a lavish suite on the Boulevarde de la Madeleine, and with whom he had a passionate and ill-starred affair. The real Rose Alphonsine Plessis was only twenty-three when, on 3 February 1847, she, like La Dame aux Camélias ('Marguerite Gautier'), died of consumption; beauty had taken her out of a squalid social background, but it could not overcome the disease which was probably also the legacy of that background. Giuseppe Verdi transformed Dumas' tale into the opera *La Traviata*, with the tragic heroine renamed Violetta: in Act Two Violetta has forsaken her former luxurious life to live simply in the country with her young admirer, Alfredo. In a heart-rending episode at the end of the act Alfredo's father persuades Violetta to give up Alfredo since his association with her is ruining his sister's chance of marrying. Less noticed is the father's use of the clinching argument that, living unmarried and in poverty with Alfredo, she will be utterly helpless once age destroys her beauty and with it Alfredo's love. 'E vero!', exclaims Violetta, whose former life has schooled her in the way of the world.

Céleste Vénard recounted what it was like to be a registered prostitute:

> What torture we suffered! To have to laugh when you wanted to weep, to be dependent and humiliated when you pay so dearly for the little you possess! If someone killed the wretched creatures who expose themselves to this, they would do them a service ... Love takes a cruel revenge on the women who profane its image.[16]

She explained how she hoped, through prostitution, to transmute looks into wealth: 'I saw myself rich, and covered with lace and jewels. I looked at myself in my little bit of mirror; I was really pretty ...'[17] Only because of her beauty did she escape; one of her clients – apparently also impressed by her desire to become an actress – buying out her debts to the brothel. Of her career, Vénard wrote: 'Fortunately for me, I had understood from the first that a love affair is like a war, and that tactics help you to win it.'[18] After her release from the brothel, modest success came, not in acting, but as a dancer, first at the Bal Mabille on the Champs Elysées, where it was her partner Brididi who gave her the compelling name of Mogador, after the fortress in Morocco just captured by French toops, and then at the Théâtre Beaumarchais. An affair with the leading circus impresario Laurnet Franconi led to an engagement (brief, as it transpired) as an equestrienne; a further one with the Duke of Ossuna established her as a *grande horizontale*. Dancing and horse-womanship had been excellent ways of displaying an adorable figure.

There are two slightly unusual aspects to the career of Apollonie Sabatier (she modified her stepfather's name, then became known as La Présidente) which engage our attention. First, she is one of the few great beauties whose physical allure is best known through a work of sculpture, *La Femme piquée par un serpent* of 1847, in which Auguste Clesinger represents a nude Apollonie, obviously in the final throes of sexual ecstasy. Secondly, she comes over as much less calculating than most of the other women being discussed here, never suppressing the fascination (generally impecunious) artists and bohemians had for her; indeed she worked for a time as an artists' model in Paris. Even when, in 1846, she moved into the fairly comfortable, settled life (she was never totally financially secure) as the mistress of the wealthy industrialist Alfred Mosselman, the noteworthy point is that he was a great patron of the arts. The title 'La Présidente' recognised her eminent position in the salon established by Mosselman; the all-consuming love affair which gives her something of the historical significance of a Ninon de Lenclos or Mme de Staël was that with the poet Charles Baudelaire.

Like many another comely woman in poor circumstances, Blanche d'Antigny had begun as a shop girl, attracting the attention of a visiting gentleman who took her with him to his native Bucharest, where the single compensating circumstance was that she learned to ride.[19] Quickly back in Paris, she got a job as a rider at the Cirque d'hiver which led, two years later, to an engagement as the 'living statue' of La Belle Hélène in *Faust* at the Théâtre de la Porte Saint-Martin. Within a couple of weeks she was launched as a courtesan. Skill in horseriding, which she somehow acquired when her family moved out from Liverpool to the nearby Wirral peninsula, was also an important factor in the rise of Catherine Walters to eminence as the *grande horizontale* Skittles.[20] Her first important employment when she went to London in search of fame and fortune was in showing off horses (and, concomitantly, herself). Her first truly important lover in London was Lord Hartington; but prospects were steadier in the Paris of Louis Napoleon, whither she betook herself.

Marie Dolores Eliza Rosanna Gilbert ('Lola Montez'), born in Limerick, Ireland, in 1818, reared in India, educated at Montrose in Scotland and at Bath, in England, came of a respectable English middle-class family. To escape an arranged marriage with an elderly, though very rich supreme court judge in India, she eloped with, and married, a young officer, who subsequently deserted her.[21] She was beautiful (see especially the portrait by Joseph Carl Stieler), but she had to earn her living – so she took lessons in Spanish dancing. Though she had no great talent for it, it was upon dancing that, as Lola Montez, she founded her career as a European lover (she had a much-publicised affair with the great romantic composer and pianist Franz Liszt), courtesan (she was a celebrity in the Paris of the 1840s, and inherited considerable wealth from the newspaper proprietor Henri Dujarier), and adventuress (supremely confident in her looks, she forced herself on King Ludwig I of Bavaria). Nicknamed 'the new Du Barry', she was, until the Revolution of 1848, effectively the uncrowned Queen of Bavaria.

Dance was the first career of Cléo de Mérode, and dance or mime the main second string and means of self-display for such contemporaries as Caroline Otero (who visited the United States in 1890) and Anne-Marie Chassaigne ('Liane de Pougy' – one of those who took her assets for a spell in Russia, and to whom Sarah Bernhardt gave the advice: 'Display your beauty, but once on the stage you had better keep your pretty mouth shut').[22] A nice variation was practised by Emilienne d'Alençon, who began attracting attention, and rich lovers, by performing an act with trained rabbits at the Cirque d'été (and so may have been an inspiration for the fictional Zuleika Dobson, whose forte was per-

forming conjuring tricks on stage); later d'Alençon kept herself on display by doing her act at the Folies Bergère. Lina Cavalieri had more
orthodox talents as an actress and opera singer.

Have I taken it too much for granted that these women were well
rewarded for their skilful deployment of their double-edged sword, one
edge beauty, the other sex? Duplessis, we saw, died at twenty-three. La
Barucci, risen also from poverty, at around thirty-three, and also from
consumption. From her late thirties till her death in her fifties Cora
Pearl led a sad, neglected existence. Blanche d'Antigny died at thirty-
four. For those who lived out their allotted span there was, of course,
no avoiding the ravages and pains of age. Consorting at one time with
the King of Belgium, Emilienne d'Alençon, after the First World War,
became a drug addict and ended her life in misery. But most amassed
considerable fortunes, and some acquired genuine titles. Alice Ozy
(born Julie-Justine Pilloy, in 1820), whose foster mother had exploited
her charms by having her serve in the family jeweller's shop, accumulated enough lovers as an actress to be able to retire early from the stage,
and made so much out of them that, even when all her looks had gone,
she could afford a succession of young lovers.[23] Lola Montez, back in
England, married a rich officer ten years her junior, but, accused of
bigamy, had to flee to the USA, where she had a prosperous career as a
lecturer and writer on women's rights, and on 'beauty'.[24]

Anne-Marie Chassaigne came from a respectable middle-class family,
making a sound marriage to a naval officer. She, however, made the
decision to leave him and their child, believing, rightly, that her great
beauty could be turned to good account in the Parisian *demi-monde*.
Fellow *horizontales* christened her Liane, and from her first important
client she borrowed the name de Pougy. After a long career as reputedly
'the most beautiful courtesan of the century' (not really a statement of
absolute value – Cavalieri was reputedly 'the most beautiful woman in
the world'),[25] she married the Roumanian Prince Georges Ghika, many
years younger than herself, and lived for twenty-seven years as part of
the international set – then entered a convent.[26] That Jeanne Detourbey
was genuinely beautiful is attested by verbal accounts, by the reactions
she aroused,[27] and by the 1862 portrait in the Louvre by Amaury-Duval.
Her early rise from her proletarian origins was that of any other fledg-
ling courtesan, attributable, in the words of Cornelia Otis Skinner, to 'an

inborn intelligence and a calculating evaluation of her own beauty and God-given charm'.[28] She came, naturally, to Paris, where one of her first noteworthy lovers was Marc Fournier, director of the Théâtre de la Porte Saint-Martin. That an acting career sometimes required talent as well as beauty is suggested by the fact that Detourbey did not persevere with a career on the stage. She moved on to a more prestigious lover, celebrated in both *monde* and *demi-monde*, Emile de Girardin, owner of *La Presse*, founder of *La Liberté*, and a practising politician, through whom she encountered, and had a brief liaison with, 'Plon-Plon', Prince Napoleon. After an affair with the unavoidable Alexandre Dumas *fils* she succeeded in marrying the Comte de Loynes. Although the outraged family were able secure the annulment of the marriage, Jeanne clung onto the title and a substantial inheritance. She perhaps more than any-one had the last laugh, using her well-gotten gains to support the celebrated salon that she ran from 1870 to 1908.

One famous, or perhaps infamous, figure from *La Belle Époque* I have not yet mentioned. Margarethe Zelle ('Mata Hari') came from a solid Dutch family, but her father went bankrupt. She answered a Dutch army captain's advertisement for a wife, and went to Java with him. Then, in 1902, aged twenty-six, she turned up in Paris. No buxom Dutch blonde, she was tall (five foot ten inches) and willowy with a dark, almost oriental beauty. The glory days of celebrated *Grandes Horizontales* were coming to an end – France of *La Belle Époque* was also France of the worthy Third Republic. Accordingly Zelle never had the easy success of an Otero or a Cavalieri, and so drew upon her experiences in Java, and her sensual looks, to create the character of Mata Hari, making her way by doing exotic, nearly nude, 'oriental' dances. She was also, as a Dutch national who spoke French, German, Spanish and English, something of an *Horizontale Internationale*. Unfortunately the international order was breaking up, Europe hastening towards the greatest, most horrific, most bitter war ever. Margarethe had always (as she cheerfully admitted) been susceptible to the sex appeal of a mil-itary uniform. She was a woman of many talents and a strong personality; but she had no understanding of the intense hatreds being generated at that time between, above all, the French and the Germans, and of the suspicions aroused by her, so to speak, international con-nections. Fundamentally her way of life was to maintain her high, though precarious, standard of living by performing whatever services men asked of her. When war broke out in July 1914, she happened to be performing in Berlin: she had a dance engagement, while among her lovers were a naval officer, an army officer and the Berlin Chief of Police. British suspicions were aroused, although partly, at least, because there was confusion with another woman who definitely was a German spy. Mata Hari returned to the Netherlands, a neutral country, but dull and uncomfortable to live in, despite the fact that she was funded by the rich Baron Van der Capellen. She was approached by a German consul, Cramer, and accepted 20,000 French francs to seek out French military secrets (which she always said she had no intention of doing). The lure of Paris was intense. In a Dutch ship she went first to Britain, where she was arrested on espionage charges, then released on the understanding that she went on to Spain and not back to the Netherlands. In Spain she consorted with the German authorities, and may (or may not) have had the official designation 'Agent H–21'. Paris, however, was her intended destination (she had some notion of meeting up with the then dominant genius in the world of dance, Diaghilev). In Paris, spymaster Captain Ladoix, who had been warned about Mata Hari by the British, asked her to spy for France; she expressed willingness and demanded a million francs (it was not forthcoming, but Ladoix was confirmed in his suspicions as to her true nature). Meantime she was receiving sums of money, particularly from Van der Capellen, which to austere French intelligence officers seemed excessive for a mere kept woman. On the morning of 13 February 1917 she was arrested in the Elysée Palace Hotel on the Champs Elysées. From then till 21 June she was, in the Saint Lazare prison, subjected to intense interrogation. As part of her equipment as a courtesan she carried a liquid spermicide which she used as a postcoital spray; her interlocutors were convinced of its use as invisible ink. Never in any way a dedicated professional spy, and never in any way responsible for the terrible military disasters which in 1917 were corroding all French reason and all French judgements, Mata Hari had undoubtedly been monumentally indiscreet, and she now, as the leading upholder of her innocence, Sam Waagenaar puts it, 'talked herself into death'.[29] Sitting for less than two days, on 24 and 25 July 1917, her military tribunal found her guilty on eight charges of spying for the Germans and condemned her to be shot by firing squad. On 15 October she was rushed by car from central Paris out to the military complex at Vincennes, where the sentence was promptly carried out. Mata Hari died with exemplary courage, refusing to be tied to the execution post or to be blindfolded.

Some courtesans actually started out from quite elevated social circles. Cléo de Mérode had a real entitlement to her *particule* (she was from the Austrian branch of the family) and was certainly born into quite a substantial lifestyle. The Countess of Castiglione, included in my count of three Italians, was a courtesan more in the old courtly style than in that of the brash nineteenth-century *demi-monde*. Having been the mistress of the brilliant Piedmontese politician (and architect of Italian unification) Count Cavour, she was sent by him to the court of Louis Napoleon to influence the Emperor in favour of Piedmont. Castiglione was scarcely successful in her mission, but she clearly enjoyed her status as imperial mistress and much-desired lady of the court.[30]

Such ambition and intrigues were alien to the puritan, republican culture of the United States, where, however, the printing presses had got moving early in the reproduction of images of beautiful women. In her authoritative and scholarly study, *American Beauty* (confined, of course, to women), Lois W. Banner argued that in the United States what was considered beautiful in women changed every twenty years or so: before the Civil War the frail, willowy woman, described by Banner as the 'steel-engraving lady', dominated the fashion magazines; in the decades after the Civil War favour switched to the heavy, buxom model of beauty, termed by Dr Banner the 'voluptuous woman'; in the 1890s the vogue was for tall, athletic, 'natural' women, this image crystallizing in the 'Gibson Girl' of the satirical drawings of Charles Gibson.[31] The notion of changing fashions in beauty has been central to all standard (and female-originated) histories of the subject; given the meticulous documentation which supports Banner's impressive monograph, it is impossible to doubt that she produces an accurate representation of changing emphasis in the fashion magazines, and perhaps even in types of actresses and chorus girls involved in popular entertainments. In any case, Banner does acknowledge that no one type ever really completely dominated popular taste.[32] Actually what made a woman prized for her beauty, in the USA as well as everywhere else in the West, was not her

conformity to a particular fashion, but her being the most perfect spec-
imen of her particular type of beauty. The two best-known American
beauties of the late nineteenth century were the actresses Lillian Russell
and Marie Doro: they are very different, Russell the blonde doll, appeal-
ingly innocent looking, Doro brunette with a cheeky up-turned nose.

Banner identifies Lillian Russell, leading star of the popular musical
stage from the late 1870s onwards, as personifying the 'voluptuous
woman'. Yet, Banner's own scrupulous account of Lillian Russell's
appeal scarcely supports this generalisation: she had a 'lithe figure' and
was known as 'airy fairy Lillian'.[33] Slightly oddly, in my view, Banner
then continues:

> As Russell grew older, her originally lithe figure grew heavier, as though
> she felt herself obliged to modify her appearance to conform to a standard
> that the British Blondes, among others, had originally established. More
> than this, she loved to eat ...[34]

The British Blondes, a troupe of, for the time, shockingly sexy dancers,
had first hit New York in 1868, and had had their 'triumphant march'
through the United States in 1869 and again in 1872. If the voluptuous
model which they allegedly established was so important, why was Lillian Russell with her lithe figure and 'airy, fairy' appearance so successful
in the late 1870s and early 1880s? It seems likely that she grew heavier as
she grew older because, in the normal course of events, people do,
unless they exercise special care with their diet, which evidently Lillian
did not do. That she became a byword for beauty through to 1890 is not
to be doubted: 'For two decades she was the most photographed woman
in America, and people went to see her plays to see more than the productions.'[35] Nor can there be any doubting the testimony of the late
1880s: 'She was a voluptuous beauty, and there was plenty of her to see.
We liked that. Our tastes were not thin or ethereal.'[36] Yet the well-
known photograph of her dating from 1889 shows not so much the
'avoirdupois' identified by Banner in commenting on this portrait,[37] as
a lovely fresh face and elegant figure. Of Banner's conclusion that 'she
incarnated the voluptuous woman and brought elegance to the ideal',[38]
the latter part seems to me more to the point than the former. Russell
had established her popularity before filling out to voluptuous contours;
once established, her enormous celebrity was not affected by the scarcely

abnormal or contrived fact that she subsequently put on weight. In any one decade or generation different tastes and proclivities coexist; women of different ages will be competing for the limelight, older ones with the advantage of popularity, triumphs, and status already achieved, younger ones with the advantage of youth and perhaps novelty, but a shape acceptable in the one may not be in the other.

The most important development in the United States with respect to the growth of a modern evaluation of beauty, and enhanced life chances for the beautiful, was the invention of the *commercial* beauty contest. The 'commercial' must be stressed because forms of beauty contest went far back into the past, with the crowning of a queen at May Day or other local festivals, and were part of the traditional vision of women as inherently the beautiful sex. The modern, American element was the attempt to capitalise commercially on the appeal of beauty. The great pioneer entertainments entrepreneur Phineas T. Barnum had attempted to organise a live beauty competition in the 1850s, but had fallen foul of the opposition of respectable citizens to the notion of women displaying themselves. Such objections were eventually circumvented with the help of the technology (the half-tone plate) which from the late 1880s permitted the reproduction of photographs in newspapers and periodicals. The first properly organised beauty competition (conducted on the basis of photographs) was set up by another great entrepreneur of the circus, Adam Forepaugh, in 1888: 11,000 women submitted photographs for a prize of $10,000 and a starring role in one of Forepaugh's productions; the winner was an actress, Louise Montagne.[39] In working-class areas it was possible to ignore the shibboleths of conventional respectability and hold parades of beautiful women in 'dime museums'. Lois Banner claims that such 'beauty contests were significant means of transmitting to immigrant men and women American standards of physical appearance'.[40] More likely, they were significant means of turning the universal appeal of female beauty into fast dimes for the owners of the museums. Above all, beauty competitions, and the display of photographs in the press, made personal beauty a matter of consuming interest to the masses.

According to Banner, when in 1882 English actress Lillie Langtry (then in her late twenties) first toured the United States, 'many Americans did not find her attractive', since she was 'athletic' and 'English' in appearance, rather than rounded and 'voluptuous'.[41] Apparently there were reservations too about her strongly marked mouth and nose, though opinion on the latter seems to have been, as one might expect, somewhat confused. Banner's argument is that eventually there was a swing in favour of Lillie's type of looks.[42] Whether the arguments were those of high fashion, or simply of crude jingoism – a Chicago newspaper declared that Lillie 'could not compare with scores of American ladies in every city where she is on exhibition'[43] – the critical fact is the emergence of beauty as a topic for popular discussion (and no one pretended that the discussion was about beauty as truth or godliness).

Whether American perceptions of Lillie really did change is not terribly important. What is important is the strategy by which Lillie Langtry had, well before coming to the United States, established herself in England as a renowned beauty. With Langtry it was not a matter of having had any kind of success on the stage; quite simply, from a very early age, she set out in a most single-minded way to exploit her personal appearance, which, as a plentiful choice of paintings and photographs demonstrate, was so devastating as to make any discussion of conventions of beauty practically irrelevant. Born Emilie Charlotte Le Breton, she came from a well-connected family in Jersey, where her father was an Anglican rector. In order to reach the fringes of London society, her major target, she made a reasonably good marriage to an undistinguished member of the gentry class. In London artists were keen to paint her, and she saw clearly the advantage of encouraging them. *Jersey Lily* by Millais became one of the most famous ever renderings of female beauty; a lesser artist, Frank Miles, did sketches of her which were both sold as originals and (critical development) reproduced as postcards.[44] Lillie could not afford to dress other than plainly, but she made an impact at all the social occasions she attended, displaying boldness and independence of spirit (her husband was a man without grace or style) which attracted still further attention. Lillie sought no other career than to promote herself as a society beauty, and as such she came to the attention of the Prince of Wales. Their first assignation was arranged by an intermediary, much practised in such matters; it took place in 1877 when Lillie was twenty-three, the Prince of Wales thirty-six. Public recognition (by word of mouth in high society, more widely through the scandal sheets) as a mistress of the Prince of Wales brought to a climax the career of Lillie Langtry as a professional beauty, whose likeness circulated in Britain, across the Atlantic and even the Channel.

Unlike the mistresses of Charles II, Lillie gained no direct material reward from her liaison with royalty. With or without the embraces of 'Bertie', she was an acknowledged beauty, that beauty underwritten by Sir John Everett Millais, James McNeil Whistler and Oscar Wilde; but the royal connection was a final seal of approval which accelerated still further the circulation of reproductions and postcards. Lillie preferred the dashing young Prince Louis of Battenberg, and became pregnant by him. Not unexpectedly, she was discarded by the Prince of Wales. Needing to find a more active means of cashing in on her assets, she now (and only now) took to the stage. As a beauty and a celebrity, she was able to do reasonably well in her new career. But the important extrapolation is the sequence of events: status as a beauty first, career as an actress subsequently.

As a publicly recognised beauty in the United Kingdom in the seventies and eighties, Lillie Langtry had only two rivals, the very English Ellen Terry and the notably French Sarah Bernhardt. Compared with Lillie, Ellen Terry was a different kind of beauty and from a different social background.[45] Indeed, for a considerable time her career seemed to demonstrate the hazards, rather than the advantages, of beauty. That she ultimately became a celebrity owed most to her acting talent and her determination to rebuild her own life and find a means of supporting her children; but, inevitably, it depended also on her beauty. Ellen Terry came from an acting family; her direct physical appeal shines out from the famous painting of her, aged sixteen, by G. F. Watts (*Secrets*, 1864). In that very year she was married to the ageing artist. Watts's claim, rather like that of some of the Pre-Raphaelite painters around the same time, was that he wished to educate and elevate his young model. He may possibly have been impotent: anyway, life with him was grim and gloomy, and Ellen shortly fled to live in poverty with an architect, by whom she had two children. Although, before her marriage, she had shown outstanding talent on the stage, she had cheerfully put all theatrical ambitions behind her. Desperate to find a means of supporting herself and her children, she returned to the stage and was fortunate to the extent that the greatest male actor and theatrical figure of the day had not yet found an ideal leading lady.

John Henry Brodribb, nine years older than Ellen Terry, was born in 1838 into a poor Cornish family; he did, however, inherit £100 from an uncle. He was not particularly good looking, was, as an adolescent, called 'spindle-shanks', and he had a stutter; nevertheless he was determined to become an actor, and the £100 helped.[46] Under his stage name of Henry Irving he was already enjoying considerable success when Terry teamed up with him. His appearance did seem to improve slightly as he matured and Ellen herself recorded later, 'I doted on his looks'. As a highly popular actress, Terry, in common with other actresses, had her likeness featured on the postcards of the 1870s and onwards.

Sarah Bernhardt (born Henriette Rosine Bernard) did not conform at all to the convention of the voluptuous woman. She was thin, with a profoundly appealing, dark, Jewish beauty, including the faintest suspicion of a too long (though highly enticing) nose. Fortunately her looks at the time of her debut at the Comédie Française in 1862, when she was eighteen, were recorded by the great pioneer photographer Felix Nadar. In career terms, and in exploitation of her sexuality, Bernhardt was nearer to Langtry than Terry, and nearest of all to the courtesans discussed earlier. Although both she and her mother (a Dutch Jew) were illegitimate, they lived in fairly comfortable circumstances, since her father settled money on her, and their circle included such luminaries as Alexandre Dumas *père*, the composer Rossini and the Duc de Morny. She got an early start at the Comédie Française, but had to leave after insulting the leading lady there. For a time she lived quite openly, and apparently happily, as a kept woman; she had a son, probably by the Prince de Ligne, though later she was reported as saying, with deliberately mischievous humour, that she could never remember whether the father was Victor Hugo, Gambetta, or General Boulanger.[47]

She resumed her acting career at the Odéon in 1866. While there can be no gainsaying her supreme talent in voice, expression and sheer daring and originality, it is true that, uniquely in Paris, the Odéon, the left-bank theatre of the radical young, provided the right ambience for Bernhardt's particular abilities. A true actress, and not simply a star, she took an enormous range of parts including several that called for concealment, not projection, of her looks. By 1869 she was being lauded as a great, if not the greatest, actress of the day. Her personal bravery, a notable characteristic to the very end of her long life, showed itself in her refusal to leave Paris during the events of 1870 (Franco-Prussian war, Prussian siege, and the Commune). In 1872 she returned to the Comédie Française. But she was not a woman to be fitted into any compartment, however elevated, and in 1880 (at the age of thirty-six) she again broke with France's premier theatre and set out on a series of foreign tours which established the basis of her international (and British) reputation – as both actress and beauty. A grandmother in 1889, she now had the statuesque looks which are familiar from the photographs of her in various dramatic roles, taken by Nadar's less gifted son, Paul; yet the air of youthful appeal was remarkably well preserved. From 1893 she directed her own company at La Renaissance and in 1899 the Théâtre Sarah Bernhardt was established at Châtelet. Along the way she had contracted one not very successful marriage, and had had many lovers. As well as directing, and playing an incredible range of parts (including male ones), she channelled her formidable creative energies into painting and sculpture. All that, and beauty too! Given such talents, would she not have made her mark in the world without great beauty? In some spheres, possibly; though had she been plain she could not have succeeded on the stage. But for the life of Sarah Bernhardt as it actually unfolded, as with the other real lives we have studied, personal beauty was crucial at a number of precisely identifiable stages. Without it she would not have got started at all in 1862. It enabled her to live comfortably as a kept woman when ejected from the Comédie Française, and while subsequently establishing herself at the Odéon (these periods did not last long enough, nor was she prominent enough in them, nor sufficiently closely linked with famous male names, for her usually to be numbered among the grand horizontals, and, anyway, all else was obliterated by her sublime ascendancy in the theatre). Her beauty was vital in getting her a fresh start at the Odeon. Along with her dramatic talents it was instrumental in winning the acclaim and devotion which swept her back to the Comédie Française and on to international fame. And, finally, her acknowledged position as a great international beauty (as well as actress) in the last decades of the century depended on the remarkable, unfading quality of her striking looks.

In 1896 the director of *L'Illustration* in Paris put on a form of beauty competition. Like those already being organised in the United States, it depended on photographs of the competitors, but unlike them it was

not open to the general public, being confined to actresses. Sarah Bernhardt, her great theatrical rival Rejane, and even Otero, were only
runners-up. The winner (not really surprisingly) was someone much
younger, Cléo de Mérode, still in her teens – there is, ultimately, no
denying the devastating additional bonus of youthful beauty.[48] The
major consideration here, however, is that the French competition constituted a further milestone in the march of female beauty out of the
boudoir, and the world of the personal and purely sexual transaction,
into the wide public world where it is gawped at, and *paid for*, not by
princes and bankers but by the masses. And for this particular epoch I
shall not overstate the value of youthfulness. Women who had established themselves many years before (Bernhardt, Russell, Terry)
maintained their appeal, their following – and the *value* of their personal
appearance. In 1897, for example, a photograph of Ellen Terry in one
of her last great roles, as the laundress Madame Sans-Gêne in Sardou's
play of that title, was used as an advertisement for the washing additive
'Nixey's Blue'. A famous beautiful face, in a relevant context, was a
great advertising *coup*; but advertisers were now appreciating the value
of associating even an unknown face with their products – provided, of
course, it was a beautiful face.

The lines dividing *horizontales* ('*moyennes*', and '*petites*', as it were, as
well as *grandes*), mistresses, prostitutes and artists' models (we noted the
example of Apollonie Sabatier) were constantly fluctuating and seldom
rigid. However, a new, entirely respectable calling did begin to emerge,
that of mannequin. By the middle of the nineteenth century, the more
beautiful salesgirls (often recruited in the first instance, as we have seen,
for their looks) began to take on the extra roles of showing off shawls,
mantles and cloaks to customers. Englishman Charles Worth (born
1825), the epitome of the gorgeous salesman of ladies' fashions, easily
gained employment at the Paris shop of Gagelin et Opigez at 93 rue de
Richelieu. Within months he had married a fellow salesgirl, Marie Ver-
net, also gorgeous (photographs exist of both). Soon he was designing
clothes for her to model, so that we may call her the first fully professional mannequin in history. Shortly Worth began the special
recruitment of attractive young women, several of them English. The
first photographs of mannequins did not appear till 1910 – though they
certainly helped to sell clothes, they remained anonymous. In the first

half of the twentieth century the role of mannequin in the fashion mag-azines was taken on by aristocratic celebrities and distinguished actresses; the model as we know her today was a product of the Cultural Revolution of the Long Sixties, the subject of Chapter 9.

The artists' models many of us (think we) know best are those 'lus-cious ladies' appearing in the Pre-Raphaelite paintings of the second half of the nineteenth century, particularly those of Dante Gabriel Rossetti. Taking the position that 'the concept of female beauty is entirely a social construct', Jan Marsh, in her brilliant *Pre-Raphaelite Sisterhood* (1985), maintained that two of the models, Lizzie Siddall and Jane Burden were, in reality, plain, while Alexa Wilding (whose stunning beauty, like that of Fanny Cornforth, Emma Hill, Annie Miller and Georgie Macdonald, simply cannot be gainsayed) is dismissed as having 'an expressionless face'.[49] Lizzie was thin and red-haired and so violated two of the sillier Victorian regulations for beauty; some contemporaries criticised her looks, some praised them; using, in particular, her own self-portrait of *c.* 1853–54 and two drawings of her by Rossetti (1854 and 1855), I con-clude that she was highly personable (and certainly not plain). Photographs of Jane Burden show her as having a strong nose and chin – some might describe her as 'masculine', others as 'sexy', as of course she certainly appears, for example, in *La Belle Iseult* by William Morris, or *La Pia de' Tolemei* by Rossetti; plain she, too, quite definitely wasn't.[50] The original Pre-Raphaelites went out deliberately looking for what they referred to as 'stunners'; there can be no doubt that the women they chose as models were chosen for their looks – plain women simply would not have been considered. All came from the rural or urban working class, save for Georgie Macdonald, who was the daughter of a Methodist minister. Initially both Jane Burden and Alexa Wilding failed to show up for their first sittings: posing was not fully respectable and carried the danger of sexual impropriety. The reward was a somewhat erratic one shilling an hour. Alexa (real name, Alice) preserved her hon-our, and secured a regular retainer of 30 shillings a week as Rossetti's most painted model. The others all definitely advanced in social status: Emma Hill married Ford Madox Brown; Jane Burden married William Morris, later becoming Rossetti's mistress; Georgie Macdonald married Edward Burne-Jones; Lizzie Siddall married Rossetti; Fanny Cornforth made a good marriage outside the artistic circle, then later became yet another of the lovely Rossetti's mistresses – her social promotion was actually the greatest of all since, alone of the models, she (born an impoverished country girl) had been a prostitute before joining the circle. But, as with so many of the women in this book, the notion of 'success' has to be very carefully considered: Lizzie Siddall (who, when discovered, had been working in a milliner's shop), being increasingly neglected by the ever-priapic Rossetti, took to drugs and died in her early thirties.

As a beauty, Fanny Cornforth had actually made a good living as a prostitute, as was by no means impossible. That indefatigable observer of Victorian womenkind, A. J. Munby recorded in his diary:

> Saturday, 30 July ... Going to the Opera, I met in the Strand one Sarah Tanner, who in 1854 or 5 was a maid of all work to a tradesman in Oxford Street: a lively honest rosyfaced girl, virtuous & self possessed. A year or so after, I met her in Regent St. arrayed in gorgeous apparel. How is this? said I. Why she had got tired of service, wanted to see life and be independent; & so she had become a prostitute, of her own accord & without being seduced. She saw no harm in it: enjoyed it very much, thought it might raise her & perhaps be profitable ...[51]

It was, and three years later Sarah was able to set herself up as the proprietor of a coffee house. Journalist Henry Mayhew found a beautiful twenty-seven-year-old prostitute earning anything from four to ten pounds a week, when an artisan would be earning only two.[52] William Booth, founder of the Salvation Army, lamented that 'there is no industrial career in which for a short time a beautiful girl can make so much money with so little trouble as the profession of courtesan'.[53] B. Pierce Egan's *Life in London*, published at the end of the 1860s, makes it clear that in the higher-class brothels the women did rather well, but they had to be beautiful.[54]

We are back with the oldest profession and the most basic transmutation of beauty into cash. But we have also seen hints of, as I put it, the march of female beauty out of the boudoir and into the public world, to be admired (and paid for) by the masses. During the twentieth century the way in which the beauty of actual people (famous or unknown) was publicised and, in diverse ways, turned in for a cash price, was to have a profound effect on the general evaluation of beauty. Human beings would continue to want to believe in beauty as connoting moral excellence; but the evidence was multiplying that it possessed an entirely independent value (separate, that is, from other personal qualities). That evidence, certainly, related almost exclusively to women; but already by 1900 the first movie cameras were rolling – commercial fiction film would bring the evaluation of male beauty also into the centre of contention. The large, but logical, stride from *La Belle Époque* to the era of film was personified by the fascinating Lina Cavalieri. At the age of thirty-nine she entered the world of American movies, playing opposite her husband Lucien Muratore in *Manon Lescaut* (1914). She returned to make films in France and Italy; but *La Rose de Grenade* (1919) was no great success and really marked the end of this brief autumnal career.[55] Cavalieri had done well in her day, but for this lovely *horizontale* the cinematograph had arrived just too late.

7

The Tallest Wins

Up at least till the end of the First World War, national politics in the major western countries was a masculine occupation: women did not stand for election, nor did they vote. Many plain and gross men attained high office. Even where wide electorates existed (and this is still true today), there was no such thing as the untrammelled choice of the people. To be put before the electorate a person has to have been the choice of a tiny cell, the ruling oligarchy, the party bosses or, at the very least, a local committee. In some cases, and this is the main point relevant to our study, consideration *might* be given to any personal qualities possessed by a prospective candidate which have special appeal for the electorate. Presidents (in the United States), and the Emperor Napoleon III (in France) were intended as replacements (representing the will of the people) for the monarchs of the past. As with former kings, appearance, once the presidential office or the imperial crown was attained, would be commented on, and a good appearance could be useful in maintaining support – this was also true of certain British Prime Ministers. Beauty is not a totally negligible factor – and there are some intriguing aspects to be noted – but it only becomes a substantive topic with the arrival of complete universal suffrage electorates and, more crucially, television.

The one successful political leader who stands out in eighteenth-century Britain as having something in the way of a genuine popular following is William Pitt the Elder, subsequently the Earl of Chatham, known to contemporaries as 'The Great Commoner', and described a century later by the *Dictionary of National Biography* as 'pre-eminently the most striking figure on the English political stage during the eighteenth century'. All *DNB* biographies of leading political figures, drawing upon contemporary testimony and portraits, conclude with a formal section on the subject's personal appearance. With Pitt the Elder, the first emphasis is placed on his voice, the biographer quoting from Butler's *Reminiscences* of 1824: 'his voice was both full and clear, his lowest whisper was distinctly heard; his middle tones were sweet, rich, and beautifully varied; when he elevated his voice to its highest pitch, the house was completely filled with the volume of sound'. As the evidence consistently indicates, a good voice and an imposing presence were the most important personal qualities for a politician, and for some time to come far outweighed considerations of mere beauty. The same biographer tells us that 'Chatham's figure was tall and imposing, with the eyes of a hawk, a little head, a thin face, and a long aquiline nose. He was scrupulously exact in his dress ...' We also learn that 'his vanity was excessive, and he delighted in pomp and ostentation'.[1]

Pitt, then, was personable, tall (this, as my chapter title hints, does emerge as a specially noteworthy personal attribute for politicians), but far from good-looking. One of the other great popular figures of the eighteenth century, John Wilkes – a Radical where Chatham was a super-patriotic Tory – was quite definitely ugly. Sir Joshua Reynolds put it thus: 'his forehead low and short, his nose shorter and lower, his upper lip long and projecting, his eyes sunken and horribly squinting'.[2] The cartoon by Hogarth is one of the best known in eighteenth-century political caricature. Of it, Wilkes himself said: 'It must be allowed to be an excellent caricature of what nature has already caricatured'.[3] Alexander Carlyle, in his *Autobiography*, spoke of Wilkes's 'ugly countenance', but added that he was 'a sprightly and entertaining fellow'.[4] Wilkes did in fact take pains, through walking and riding, to preserve his good figure. He was dynamic, eloquent and, though direct in expressing his sexual interest in the women he desired, impeccable in manners. As a great and courageous campaigner against Lord North and George III, he attracted attention and won much favour. Politically he was successful, winning one of his most important battles against the government when the judiciary declared general warrants (by which 'all the usual suspects' could be scooped up without details being specified) illegal; he was also extremely successful with women, it being said that his other qualities very quickly obliterated his misbegotten face.

Let us never fall into the error of thinking that looks in men were not noticed. The very sobriquet of Prince Charles Edward Stuart, leader of the Jacobite Rebellion of 1745, should alert us against that. Looks gave him something of the popularity which attended upon Monmouth, but whereas Monmouth's looks may actually have affected events, birth and cause would undoubtedly have made 'Bonnie Prince Charlie' an active and plausible claimant to the throne even if he had been born a hunchback. Just exactly how good-looking the Prince really was is, as so often, a matter on which the sources are not entirely clear. As Donald Nicholas showed in his classic study, *The Portraits of Bonnie Prince Charlie* (1973), many of the best-known representations are incompetent copies of copies, and many that are reproduced show him as a boy rather than a young adult. It was Nicholas's considered judgement that 'except perhaps for the portrait of him by La Tour, the Prince could not be called handsome'. For myself, I am prepared to back the accuracy and talent of Maurice Quentin de la Tour, as demonstrated in the pastel exhibited in the Paris Salon of 1747, and find Charlie indeed bonnie. For a few months, after his victory over General Cope at the Battle of Prestonpans, Charles lorded it in Edinburgh as the heroic cynosure. Looks, I am sure, were very much part of the overall image, though they were really rather wasted since the Prince, poor fellow, had no taste for beautiful women, even though they threw themselves at him.[5]

In seeking elements of a modern appraisal of beauty, let us turn to what was in most repects the most open and democratic of western societies, the United States of America, surveying the twenty-five men who attained presidential office prior to the First World War (excluding Jefferson Davis, who headed the secessionist Confederacy while Abraham Lincoln was President of the Union). There are portraits of some sort for all of the Presidents, and, naturally, vast amounts of biographical information. The *Dictionary of American Biography* (1928–) for the entire period, and *Appleton's Cyclopaedia of American Biography* (1888–89), for most of it, like the *Dictionary of National Biography*, always comment if the subjects are felt to be particularly good-looking, or, alternatively, distinctly ill-favoured, and *Appleton's Cyclopaedia*, in addition, carries engravings. Particularly lavishly illustrated are *Pictorial History of American Presidents* (1958), by John and Alice Durant, and *'To the Best of My Ability': The American Presidents* (2000), edited by James M. McPherson. Herbert Agar, in his *The American Presidents from Washington to Harding* (1935), has a usefully old-fashioned determination to characterise the personal appearance of each President (save on the few occasions when words fail him!) You the reader may recall the 1546 Venetian report on King Francis I of France: 'His appearance is completely royal, so that, without ever having seen his face or his portrait, on seeing him one would say instantly: it's the King'. The equivalent comment in presidential biographies, particularly popular ones, is: 'He looked like a President'. Alas, as is faithfully recorded, a large number of the twenty-five (apart from any other deficiencies) did not. The popular aphorism, 'The tallest wins', seems to have originated at the time of Abraham Lincoln, but it did not come into wide currency until well into the twentieth century, and achieved prominence with the disastrous candidature of Michael Dukakis, who was not only short, but rather odd-looking; yet fully eleven of the first twenty-five Presidents were 'tall', 'large' or 'over six feet', the apparent relevance of height being driven home by the many references to others as 'short and pudgy', 'stocky', 'small in stature' or 'stumpy'. I have noted how female writers discussing the appearance of female celebrities tend to fall back on such clichés as 'unconventional beauty' and 'indefinable sex appeal'. Male writers describing male Presidents have their own clichés: 'his appearance was in keeping with his nature', or 'mirrored his character', or some such phrase, more appropriate to a gothic novel than to rigorous historical analysis.

The American political system evolved very rapidly. All white males had the vote, but, in presidential elections they, at best (five states out of sixteen in 1800), voted for 'electors' whose responsibility it was to elect the President and, in the early days, Vice-President – whoever was second choice; in the other states a smaller body, usually the state legislature, chose the 'electors'. The country grew, popular participation increased, parties (with their party conventions) formed and re-formed. The first presidential election was won by (a reluctant) George Washington, beating John Adams into a poor second place (and thus the vice-presidency). Together these two enemies served two terms, then, with Washington retiring, Adams secured election to the presidency. It is a commonplace of American history that Adams was miserably conscious of the contrast in his appearance with that of Washington, who was a commanding figure, six foot two inches tall, lean, muscular, and with a square massive jaw and strong hands. His features were large, his lips usually firmly closed, giving his face a stern expression.[6] In fact he had false teeth, as American historian Robert Darnton delights in telling us, but then, as Darnton also keeps insisting, eighteenth-century people were obsessed with their dental problems.[7] He bore some of the marks from the smallpox he had caught at the age of nineteen, but not too distressingly in an age when few had perfect complexions. If not beautiful, Washington was highly impressive in figure and countenance. His accession, manifestly, depended on achievement, as vanquisher of the British and founding father of the Republic, but, as with a European king, it was a valuable bonus that he looked the part. Such was not the case with Adams (known to senators as 'His Rotundity'),[8] whose self-consciousness about his own appearance was further embittered when at his inauguration he was completely eclipsed by the retiring Washington.

> The contrast in personal appearance between the two men added to the cruel effect of inauguration upon Adams's mind. Washington was tall and lean, Adams short and pudgy; Washington was dignified, Adams pompous; Washington looked like a great man, Adams like a fussy short-tempered professor. As we know from his embarrassingly self-critical diary, Adams had ever since boyhood been awkwardly self-conscious about his appearance ... the public ignored him in favour of his more handsome and more famous rival ...[9]

Let me first single out the presidents who, indisputably, were tall. Thomas Jefferson (1801–09) was, however, 'loose-jointed, and ungraceful', giving an instant impression of 'awkwardness',[10] and definitely 'not prepossessing in appearance'.[11] James Monroe (1817–25) was 'a little ungainly', being 'inclined to stoop', this general appearance, apparently, 'mirroring' his 'unsensational competence'.[12] Andrew Jackson (1829–37) was 'a tall, lank, uncouth-looking personage' according to fellow politician Alfred Gallatin,[13] with 'a long stern face and lantern jaw', 'deep-set wild blue eyes', 'high cheek-bones and a strong mouth', 'the whole face crowned by a great shock of intractable hair', an appearance, Agar assures us, 'in keeping with his nature'.[14] William Harrison (1841; he died in office before the year was up) who 'made an impressive figure in the saddle', being 'tall, slim and erect'.[15] John Tyler (1841–45), apart from being 'tall and thin' was unremarkable.[16] Millard Fillmore (1850–53), however, was 'impressively handsome', as well as being 'erect of carriage' and 'always faultlessly groomed',[17] qualities which rendered him 'a good type for the public platform'.[18] James Buchanan (1857–61) was 'stately', 'his outward casing' being 'most impressive',[19] but with funny eyes, one near-sighted, one far-sighted. Chester Arthur (1881–85) was 'courtly' with an 'air of breeding and intelligence', and 'looked', in the lapidary words of the Durants, 'like a President'.[20] Finally, William Howard Taft (1909–13), identified by the Durants as 'our largest president',[21] six foot two inches tall, weighing over three hundred pounds, who was in fact gross and unprepossessing, his consuming passion gluttony. (Byron, early in the previous century, had sought strenuously to control his tendency to plumpness. Towards the end of the twentieth century, New Zealand's overweight prime minister David Lange underwent a dangerous stomach bypass operation in order to reduce himself to a more acceptable shape; most nineteenth-century politicians were not greatly troubled by such considerations.)

Among the Presidents who were not tall, James Madison (1809–17) incidentally draws our attention to the question of the personal looks of a politician's wife (and, perhaps, other womenfolk). Actually, it is only with the gathering twentieth-century preoccupation with beauty that the appearance of the wife (and potential consort) becomes a matter for overt discussion, just, ironically, as women were starting on political careers of their own. Literary essayist Washington Irving set down his impressions of the Madison entourage:

> Mrs Madison is a fine, portly, buxom dame, who has a smile and a pleasant word for everybody. Her sisters, Mrs Coutts and Mrs Washington, are like the two Merry Wives of Windsor; but as to Jemmy Madison – Ah! Poor Jemmy! – he is a withered little apple-John.[22]

Madison was supremely impressive in print, but, it has been widely accepted, not at all so in person. As for John Quincy Adams (1825–29), his 'personal characteristics' were not 'ingratiating'; he was short and stocky and by the time he became President he was suffering from an unfortunate male affliction, which, as the recent experiences in Britain of William Hague and Iain Duncan Smith have suggested, generally does a public figure no great favours: 'his very large head was almost completely bald'.[23] On the other hand, Martin Van Buren (1837–41), the 'little magician' (also known as 'the careful Dutchman from New York') did have a certain charisma to go with his 'long curly yellow hair' and

9. Sarah Bernhardt. Most portraits show Bernhardt in statuesque middle age, but when she exploited her beauty to launch her stage career she was certainly enticingly slim with delicious Jewish features. Photograph, Félix Nadar, 1862.

10. Ellen Terry (1847–1928). Famous as an actress and beauty, she was one of the first to appear on picture postcards, then in advertisements for washing products. Painted on strawboard by her elderly husband, George Frederic Watts, *c.* 1864. (*National Portrait Gallery*)

11. La Belle Otero. Coming from many nations and all classes, *grandes horizontales* exemplified all types of beauty. Looking the Spanish gypsy she was, Caroline Otero (birth date unknown) used stage dancing as her launch-pad, danced in America in 1890, and in 1896 took part in France's first beauty competition, organised by a popular illustrated magazine. Photograph, *c.* 1890.

12. Franklin Pearce is universally reputed the most beautiful of American Presidents, at least until Kennedy, Reagan and Clinton. He owed his job almost entirely to looks, charm and family connections. Engraving, *c.* 1840.

13. Abraham Lincoln was variously described as 'striking' and 'ugly', but he was 6 foot 4 inches tall, whereas his principal pro-Union opponent, Stephen Douglas, was precisely one foot shorter. Photograph by Alexander Heller, 1860.

14. Rudolph Valentino. Film, according to a French movie guide of 1921, imposed 'a general and absolute rule that heroes must be beautiful'. Rudolfo Guglielmi, born in 1895 in Italy, beginning as a male taxi-dancer and gigolo in New York, before (and after!) his early death from appendicitis became the greatest heart-throb ever. Publicity photograph, *c.* 1923.

15. Mary Pickford. Born Gladys Smith in Toronto, she was the diametric opposite of Garbo in being able to look much younger than she really was. Appealing to millions through the magic of film, she could make millions without even having to contemplate selling sex in the way concubines and courtesans had had to do. Studio photo for advertising purposes, *c.* 1920.

DAM-HATTAR

från de enklaste till de mest eleganta

Mod. ›CLARY›
Damhatt av filt i
beige, marin, svart,
brunt, fraise el. röd=
brunt   Kr. 28.—

Mod. ›ETHEL›
Damhatt av sammet
i cerise, ljusblått,
mörkblått,   brunt,
mullvad, lilas eller
beige   Kr. 25.—

Mod. ›JANE›
Damhatt   av
sammet i grönt,
marin, brunt el.
mörk lilas
Kr. 48.—

Mod. ›HELNY›
Damhatt av filt i beige, mullvad, brunt,
neger, jade, vinrött el. marin Kr. 28.—

Mod. ›SOLVEIG›
Damhatt av filt i brunt, svart, grönt,
marin el. mullvad   Kr. 35.—

16. Greta Garbo, modelling hats for a Stockholm department store catalogue, 1920. Born Greta Gustafson in 1905 to a Stockholm street sweeper, she would never have escaped to films, via being a shop assistant and part-time model, had it not been for her striking, and strangely mature, beauty.

'large blue eyes'.[24] 'His appearance', we are assured by the always pre-
dictable Agar, 'mirrored his character' – Van Buren was a shrewd
political schemer but no statesman. James Polk (1845–49) was 'stiff and
angular' with 'a face lean of outline and almost morose in expression'.[25]
Zachary Taylor (1849–50; he died in office) was short and fat.[26] At five
foot nine inches, Andrew Johnson (1865–69) was 'solidly built'.[27] Many
of those who made it to the presidency had service as soldiers behind
them (there were wars against the British – twice; the Indians – most of
the time; the Mexicans; the Spanish and themselves). The most famous
of the soldiers, and also one of the most intriguing in respect of personal
appearance, was Ulysses S. Grant (1869–77), the victorious, and ruthless,
general in the Civil War. Described by the Durants as a 'shy, stumpy little man' (he was five foot eight inches), he was, when young, rather
effeminate in appearance. Fellow soldiers called him 'Little Beauty' and,
in an army show in Texas, he played the part of Desdemona. He would
never allow himself to be seen in a state of total undress (quite difficult
in the army): was he perhaps embarrassed by undersized genitals?[28]
James Garfield, though a 'blue-eyed blond', was not a very striking one,
while Grover Cleveland (1886–89), short, fat and bull-necked, was
notably lacking in physical appeal.[29] Smallest of the lot was Benjamin
Harrison (1889–93), at five foot six inches a 'bland nonentity', 'a cau-
tious, frigid, unimaginative little man'.[30] Theodore Roosevelt (1901–9),
although energetic and full of infectious zeal, was a martyr to asthma
and defective vision, and not at all good-looking.

Among those I have not so far discussed are, first, America's most
famous nineteenth-century President, Abraham Lincoln (1861–65; re-
elected for another term, he was assassinated soon afterwards), and,
secondly, the one truly beautiful man (all accounts are agreed) to reach
the presidency, Franklin Pierce (1853–57). There was almost the same
sort of contrast between Lincoln, ugly, gnarled, unkempt, and Jefferson
Davis, President of the Confederacy (also 1861–65), who 'looked an aristocrat' with his 'clear-cut, beautiful features',[31] as there was between
John Adams and Washington, save that, at six foot four inches, Lincoln
was the tallest of all the nineteenth-century Presidents.

Lincoln's own father said of his son that his body 'looked like he
needed a carpenter's plane put to him',[32] and Lincoln himself was conscious that his face could reasonably be termed 'ugly', though also

'rugged' and 'striking'. Practitioners of the new art of photography posed and lighted him in many dramatic ways, but the physical essence of the man comes through in the relatively straightforward photographic portrait of 1860 by Alexander Heller.[33] Both of the major biographical dictionaries have much to say on Lincoln's physical appearance. First the *Cyclopaedia.*

> Mr Lincoln was as unusual in personal appearance as in character. His stature was almost gigantic, six feet and four inches; he was muscular but spare of frame, weighing about 180 pounds. His hair was strong and luxuriant in growth, and stood straight out from his head; it began to be touched with gray in his last years. His eyes, grayish brown, were deeply set, and were filled, in repose, with an expression of profound melancholy, which easily changed to one of uproarious mirth at the provocation of a humorous anecdote told by himself or another. His nose was long and slightly curved, his mouth large and singularly mobile. Up to the time of his election he was clean-shaven, but during his presidency the fine outline of his face was marred by a thin and straggling beard.

The twentieth-century account is more extensive:

> The Lincoln of the Prairies was a man of marked individuality. Standing six feet four, with uncommon length of arms and legs, his figure loomed in any crowd, while the rugged face bespoke a pioneer origin and early life of toil and poverty. In a head not over large each feature was rough and prominent. In contrast to the round full-cheeked Douglas [Lincoln's main rival in the presidential election], Lincoln's face showed deep hollows and heavy shadows. The craggy brow, tousled hair, drooping eyelids, melancholy gray eyes, large nose and chin, heavy lips, and sunken, wrinkled cheeks produced an effect not easily forgotten. A wide variety of qualities is revealed in his portraits, which give the impression of a character whose depth is not really sounded – a personality in which conflicting hereditary strains were peculiarly blended. Those who have described him from life dwell upon the contrast between the seeming listlessness of the face in repose and the warmth of the countenance when animated with conversation or public speech. The trappings of the man intensified the effect of crudeness. In a day of grandiose adornment Lincoln's habiliments departed as far from the Godey fashion plate as did his mid-western speech from the sophisticated accents of the East. The battered stove-pipe hat stuffed with papers, the rusty ill-fitting coat, the ready-made trousers too short for the legs, the unpolished boots, the soiled stock at the neck,

the circular cloak in winter or linen duster in summer, the bulging umbrella and hard-used carpet-bag, gave an entirely unpremeditated effect of oddity, the man's appearance being apparently of no more concern to him than the food which he seemed to eat without tasting.[34]

Lincoln's very carelessness of dress may suggest that he felt his features and form simply not worth the attention of good grooming. He referred in public to his 'poor lean, lank face', and there was one story about his appearance he particularly liked to tell – apocryphal, no doubt, but highly revealing of his image of himself. Splitting rails one day, he claimed, he was yelled at by a passing stranger. Looking up, Lincoln found the stranger aiming a gun at him, declaring that he had promised to shoot the first man he met who was uglier than himself. After scrutinising the stranger's face closely, Lincoln declared, 'If I am uglier than you, then blaze away.'[35]

Lincoln made a socially advantageous but, from the point of view of personal happiness, disastrous marriage. He was not successful with women, possibly because of self-consciousness over his appearance, and led what must be accounted an unfulfilled sex life.[36] Yet a young Southern woman is reported as saying:

His face is certainly ugly, but not repulsive; on the contrary, the good humor, generosity and intellect beaming from it, make the eye love to linger there until you almost find him good-looking.[37]

What comes through most strongly in the written testimony is the way in which his appearance was transformed once he began speaking and became animated. According to Horace White, editor of the *Chicago Tribune:*

The dull, listless features dropped like a mask. The eyes began to sparkle, the mouth to smile, the whole countenance was wreathed in animation, so that a stranger would have said, 'Why, this man, so angular and somber a moment ago, is really handsome'.

Another male contemporary declared Lincoln 'the homeliest man I ever saw'; yet, Lincoln's face, he said, 'brightened, like a lit lantern, when animated'. In action, Lincoln had enormous appeal; he had charisma. That apart, he was always striking. After seeing him for the first time, William Howard Russell, correspondent of the London *Times,* wrote: 'it would not be possible for the most indifferent observer to pass him in the street without notice'.[38] Lincoln made his way 'from log cabin to White House' by energy, dedication and considerable talent (he was a highly respected and successful lawyer); in the electoral arena his striking appearance and charisma were undoubtedly positive, if far from critical assets. But he was not beautiful, nor, apparently, sexually very appealing. This is the case of an ugly man with other personal qualities, including even physical ones (such as great height), having enormous success in public life, though, it may be surmised, suffering a deprived private life.

How exactly did he win the crucial presidential election of 1860? As newspapers, pamphlets, and speeches at (often well-attended) political meetings made clear, resentment was gathering in the Southern states over the possibility of Federal interference in Southern property rights (including slave-holding) with threats being made of secession from the Union, while many leading politicians regarded total maintenance of the Union and federal powers as non-negotiable.[39] The Republicans acted positively in selecting Lincoln, as against the rather better-known William H. Seward. The Democrats were disastrously divided: their leading figure, Stephen A. Douglas, like Lincoln a mid-Westerner and strong supporter of the Union, was opposed by incumbent President, James Buchanan, who favoured his Vice-President, John Breckenridge. In the event Breckenridge stood as well as Douglas. The fourth candidate was a former Democrat, a slave-owner, John Bell, who had become leader of the Whigs in Tennessee, and now stood as 'Constitutional Union party' candidate. Douglas disconcerted party oligarchs by going out on the stump, directly addressing voters in the different states (in keeping with the original monarchical image, Presidents and would-be Presidents were still expected to maintain a certain detachment). Douglas was for maintaining the Union, but also for conciliating the Southerners; in the course of his electioneering he quickly reached the conclusion that, in the North at least, the uncompromising Lincoln was bound to win. In the South he had the challenges of Breckenridge and Bell to face. These are points I had to make before coming to Douglas's physical appearance. His height was five foot four inches. He had, his biographer Robert W. Johanssen tells us, a 'massive head, broad shoulders, full chest and short stubby legs'. 'His eye was quick and penetrating under a large projecting brow and thick masses of dark brown hair, his visage stern and heavy.'[40] In the photograph Johanssen reproduces, the heavy, projecting forehead appears to squash together the remaining features of Douglas's face. As Johanssen concludes, 'His was an appearance not easily forgotten'. In remarking on the truth of that statement, one must recall that by 1860 Douglas was possibly the leading figure in American politics.[41] In the direct confrontation with Lincoln, the advantages as I've indicated were, in any case, with Lincoln, but the contrast between the tallest and the smallest was undoubtedly a cruel one. Douglas's setting out on his unconventional electioneering tour provided the occasion for his enemies to circulate a satirical sheet entitled ' "Boy" Lost': 'He is about five feet nothing in height, and about the same diameter the other way. He has a red face, short legs, and a large belly'.[42] Nevertheless, Douglas did very creditably in the popular vote, polling well over a million and a quarter to just over a million and three quarters for Lincoln, with Breckenridge somewhat under a million and Bell just over half a million. However, where it counted, Douglas was piling up votes uselessly, consistently coming behind Lincoln in the election of presidential electors. That vote Lincoln won 173 to 12 against Douglas, with Breckenridge and Bell (both strong in the South) on 72 and 39, respectively. 'The tallest wins' was a not unreasonable deduction.

My researches, though feminist critics have always failed to understand this, are as much concerned with scrutinising the looks of men as with, in traditional fashion, scrutinising the looks of women. In this lengthy discussion of Abraham Lincoln I have concentrated on what the various sources, primary and secondary, say about his looks. Clearly no nineteenth-century woman would ever have had the sorts of comments I have quoted here written about her. A question to ponder now is whether any woman in the twenty-first century, however distinguished, however famous, would have such comments made about *her* – while it is still quite normal for famous males to be discussed in exactly the way Lincoln was discussed. Major conclusions to which this book is tending are: growing equality between men and women with respect to their roles in society and the way in which they are treated by society; and the emergence of a situation in which, with regard to looks men are increasingly evaluated in the way in which women have always been evaluated. However differences do persist. We have just lighted on one of them – and, having studied the remarks made about Lincoln, we should perhaps just pass on with a muttered '*Vive la différence!*'

Last of the American presidents to be discussed is one we can, at least in part, treat in the way in which women had always been treated. 'Perhaps the handsomest president', reads the rubric under the portrait of Franklin Pierce in McPherson's illustrated biographical dictionary.[43] Tributes to his beauty are everywhere, though he was, it may be noted, of only medium height. How did a man get to be President? The first presidents were all Virginian patricians who, in one way or another, had been leaders in the Revolution. What all had in common were Protestant British, or (in two cases) Dutch names and origins (families long established in America, we may note, tended to produced taller progeny than families in the rest of the world; immigrants from southern and eastern Europe tended to be short in stature). Soldiering, we saw, was one road to advancement – Franklin Pierce served in the Mexican War; the law was another. As everywhere, and in all walks of life, family connections could be useful. Pierce's father had been a general in the Revolutionary War; he then served for two terms as Governor of New Hampshire. Franklin Pierce studied at Bowdoin College before becoming a lawyer, then at the early age of twenty-eight secured election to the New Hampshire House of Representatives where, we learn from Larry Gara's standard work on the Pierce presidency, 'his charm and family connections' helped him become Speaker. Positions in national politics followed as smoothly: first, two terms in Congress, then, in 1837, election to the Senate. 'Handsome and well-groomed', Gara continues, Pierce 'influenced others by a pleasing habit of appearing to agree with whomever he was conversing.'

> He became a party leader with very little effort of his own. His main assets were family background, total loyalty to the Democratic party, a willingness to be a party hatchet-man, and, above all, his charm and striking appearance. More than any of the others, he looked like a president.[44]

By a stroke of luck the Democratic convention was in a state of deadlock between other abler, more energetic, and better-known candidates, so that Pierce emerged as the rather unexpected compromise choice. Pierce's good looks had played an important part in getting him, just, into the reckoning. They were important in these particular circumstances when a candidate without any strong signs of intellect or political commitment, but with a certain bland appeal, was required;[45] fittingly, his wife was as attractive as he was, and this may be an early case where that too weighed with the party bosses. Beautiful Pierce undoubtedly was, but he can by no means be accounted fortunate overall: he had to struggle against alcoholism when that condition was not understood, and apart from his appalling failings as President, he suffered the trauma of seeing his only son killed in a railway accident.

Beauty of face and form may be a source of appeal to a wider public, or it may simply win over a small oligarchy or a powerful patron. In British politics for the major part of the nineteenth century the latter was a more important consideration than the former. The most renowned for looks among Victorian ministers was Henry John Temple, Viscount Palmerston, the dominant figure in British politics from 1850 to 1865. In the main body of the entry, the *Dictionary of National Biography* speaks of the young Palmerston as having had 'the advantage of a strikingly handsome face and figure', which, the writer continues, 'afterwards procured for him the name of "Cupid" among his intimates'.[46] The basic reasons for Palmerston's success was that he was an aristocrat, groomed for office from very early years. His way was smoothed for him by his guardian, Lord Malmesbury, and there is no reason to believe that this had anything to do with Palmerston's looks or sex appeal. As an aristocrat, Palmerston was able to take his MA 'by right of birth' (that is without the inconvenience of any kind of examination), then, entirely through patronage and influence, was returned to Parliament for a pocket borough; already the influence of his guardian had secured him a post as a Lord of the Admiralty. (America now really does begin to seem a beacon of democracy!) Soon after, Palmerston was appointed Secretary at War, a post in which he remained for nineteen years. His career had got off to an early start: he was in a post he liked; he could afford to relax and enjoy life. During his early years at the War Office he became a member at Almack's, the exclusive club run by a group of aristocratic ladies who were very particular about the men they admitted to membership; several of these ladies were Palmerston's mistresses (how very civilised, compared with the French *demi-monde* of the same era!). 'On first acquaintance,' commented Lord Shaftesbury, 'I could see nothing in him of the states-man, but a good deal of the dandy.'[47]

Palmerston's most recent biographer describes him as: 'tall, dark and handsome ... about five feet ten, with a fresh complexion, dark hair and magnificent blue eyes (though lacking a few teeth from hunting acci-dents, occasionally inclining to overweight, and with a definitely reced-ing hairline)'. His appearance can be confirmed from his portraits, particularly the dashing early one by Heaphy, and from the later state-ment of the painter Benjamin Haydon that 'his nose is small, forehead fine, and he is handsome'.[48] In 1839, at the age of fifty-five, Palmerston married one of his mistresses, now fifty-two, the Countess Cowper, whose late husband had himself been reputed one of the handsomest men in London. The marriage was a happy one, which did not prevent Palmerston continuing his amorous adventures. As Victorian Britain reached its highpoint in confidence and optimism, Palmerston's brand of assertive patriotism endeared him to politicians and public. It is not surprising that, in a time of fragmented party politics and shifting align-ments, this still-handsome figure should assume supremacy. Palmerston was born into his opportunities; his good looks simply facilitated the nonchalance with which he let them fall into his lap. They enabled him to lead a particularly full social and sexual life and contributed to the relaxed attitude which moved a nineteenth-century biographer to comment on 'the tardiness with which Lord Palmerston reached politi-cal prominence'.[49] But then, in fact, everything, including the prime ministership, fell into place for him.

For an early nineteenth-century aristocratic insider like Palmerston, good looks were simply a highly desirable optional extra. For Benjamin Disraeli, son of a Jewish man of letters and accordingly something of an outsider in the Tory party, they were rather more important. Speaking of an early speech (1837, when Disraeli was thirty-three) in the House of Commons, the *Dictionary of National Biography* refers to 'the thin, pale, dark-complexioned young man, with long black ringlets and dandified costume'.[50] Twice further on the same page the impression made by Disraeli's appearance is remarked upon; it was, if not beautiful, certainly personable and, partly through dint of dress, striking. Commenting on Disraeli's later unwillingness to take up votes for women (though he was not unfriendly in principle to the idea), a recent authoritative biographer has said that Disraeli himself stood most to gain by such an extension of the franchise.[51] Disraeli was certainly attractive enough, as well as distinguished and dynamic enough in both his literary and political careers, to marry in 1839 an extremely wealthy widow, Mrs Windham Lewis. It was with her fortune that he was able to set himself up as the country gentleman, quite definitely the single most crucial stage in his career towards the prime ministership, entailing (eventually) a helpful special relationship with Queen Victoria, and an earldom. Had Disraeli been manifestly ugly, a John Wilkes, say, it is unlikely that his in many ways remarkable career would have evolved as it did. But Disraeli's personal charm was exerted over a relatively small circle and, for all his sponsorship of the concept of Tory democracy, we cannot cast him into the same category as the present-day politician anxious to cut the best possible figure on television.

Looks were an added grace for Palmerston, an important blessing for Disraeli; they could have been ruinous for a handsome, lower-class would-be politician late in the century. David Lloyd George was born in 1863, the son of a schoolmaster who returned to his farming roots in north Wales, dying while David was still very young, so that he was brought up by his uncle, a master shoemaker. His brother described him as 'a good-looking youth with a vivacious manner and a ready wit', and his nephew added that 'he had realised early in life how attractive he was to women'. The entry in the *Dictionary of National Biography* (by top civil servant Thomas Jones) is more circumspect, stating simply, 'his charm was irresistible'.[52] On the matter of sheer looks, the photographic evidence is utterly conclusive. The small north Wales town of Criccieth in which Lloyd George grew up was dominated by nonconformist morality, and an ambitious young man eager to make his way upwards in the world had to observe constraints unknown to Lord Palmerston. Rebuked by his sister for his amorous forays, the young Lloyd George recorded in his diary (17 June 1880) his own intention to exert self-discipline:

> I am rather seriously disposed to give up these dealings; this I know, that the realisation of my prospects, my dreams, my longings for success, are very scant indeed unless I am determined to give up what, without mistake, are germs of the 'fast life'. Be staunch and bold and play the man. What is life good for unless some success, some reputable notoriety be obtained.

But the risks of disreputable notoriety were considerable. 'Blast these malicious gossips', is an entry of a few years later.[53] To his further irritation his uncle took to spying on his evening activities. Treading a careful path, the young Lloyd George showed himself a man of distinct promise in the solicitor's office in which he worked, while establishing a reputation as a fiery and effective public speaker in the Liberal cause. He paid court to Maggy Owen, the only daughter of a well-off and rather superior family, whose members saw themselves as gentlemen farmers rather than mere working farmers; eventually, against the initial resistance of the family, he married her on 24 January 1888. For the time being solid respectability was fully established. Just over two years later David Lloyd George was elected Liberal member of parliament for the Caernarvon Boroughs. Safely based in London (which his wife hated, and from which she subsequently departed for long periods in Wales), and steadily rising in political reputation, or to use his own word 'notoriety', he found discretion more to his taste than abstinence. In 1910 began a long relationship with Frances Stevenson, a beautiful secretary less than half his age, whom eventually, after the death of his wife, he married. Though at all times Lloyd George had many enemies, not a word of this relationship was ever referred to in the press. These were indeed the days of discretion and deference. Lloyd George had made it to the safety of high politics, but he could easily have been sunk before ever he got there; he now cannily steered clear of divorce, which would also have been disastrous. Status and looks, in a man, were a devastating combination; but the latter without the former could still be an ambivalent gift. Lloyd George's recent and justly celebrated biographer John Grigg contents himself with the verdict: 'Lloyd George was attractive to women, and they to him. His sexual impulses were abnormally strong …' He concludes that the sexual 'dealings' which Lloyd George had mentioned in his diary 'remained a distinctive, though unimportant, feature of his life from adolescence to old age.'[54] 'Unimportant'? – I'm not so sure.

What of beauty and public life in France? Revolutionaries, it would seem, do not need to be beautiful – no more so, anyway, than ordinary run-of-the-mill politicians. Louis Blanc, the leading socialist figure of 1848, was undersized and unimpressive in appearance. For charisma we have to turn to Louis Napoleon, elected President of the new republic in 1848, who declared himself Prince President in his coup d'état of 1851 and was subsequently ratified as Emperor in a national plebiscite. Napoleon III's greatest asset was carrying the name, and being a nephew, of the great Napoleon. He was also a man of considerable personal courage, with a certain animal magnetism, and cut a dashing figure on a horse. Beaky-faced, he was certainly far from good-looking. The narrative which follows gives a nice insight into the relative values of status and beauty in nineteenth-century Europe. Louis Napoleon was desperately anxious to underpin his position and establish himself as a true monarch by contracting a marriage alliance with one of the European royal families, in particular with that of the most powerful nation of the day: his plan was to marry Queen Victoria's niece, Princess Adelaide. But since the British Queen scarcely concealed her view of Napoleon as a contemptible upstart, the Emperor was forced to turn from royalty to beauty, going against the advice of his most trusted advisers.[55] The woman who, at the age of twenty-six, became the Empress Eugénie had been born in Granada in Spain. Tutored by her mother, she had just enough in the way of resources and connections to have established herself as an international beauty, at home in Parisian high society, as well as in the company of the British aristocracy (at a reception given by Lady Palmerston in the spring of 1849, she was described as 'a vision of youth and beauty'),[56] and among the prodigiously wealthy Rothschilds, through whom she had been introduced to Louis Napoleon. She had indeed used the greatest skill and the greatest self-discipline to ensure that her beauty (not shown off to advantage in the well-known Winterhalter portraits, which make her look dumpy in the regal style of Queen Victoria, but perceivable in the 1850 portrait bust by Jean-Baptiste Carpeaux) brought her the highest possible social status.

And so we return, as is only fitting in a study of nineteenth-century politics, to female beauty. Antonia Fraser's aphorism that queens (or imperial consorts) were not expected to be beautiful may still have been true – Louis Napoleon would certainly have preferred royalty to beauty – but generally the most successful women on public display in the spheres open to them, the courtesans and the actresses, had to be beautiful. Men on public display in their sphere, politics, generally did not, though there could be special rewards for those who were. However, as audiences, thanks largely to mass communications and the arrival of something like true democracy, became wider and wider, politicians, and their party managers, became increasingly concerned about personal appearance.

8

Movies

In the twentieth century the rapidity of technological innovation was dazzling, the challenges to established ideas and conventional ways of doing things deafening. Within the first half-century two cataclysmic total wars took place each with enormous social and cultural repercussions. During the second half-century there followed the further upheavals of 'The International Cultural Revolution of the Long Sixties, c. 1958 to c. 1974'.[1] Across the entire hundred years, and on into the twenty-first century, there were transformations in lifestyles, living standards and fashions, and, above all in the status of women, and in how they lived their lives. Traditional attitudes to beauty were under attack as never before, though it was not till the sixties that the modern attitude began to assume ascendancy, with, of course, many people continuing to cling to the old conventions and subterfuges. The single most important agent of change was film, which reached its biggest audiences worldwide in the 1940s, after which it was, to a considerable degree replaced by television. By the time it became fully organised and capitalised in the 1920s, the film industry was already the greatest single source for the employment of beautiful people. With the movies came a whole new literature, preserving images of the stars in a form which could be pored over and pinned to bedroom walls. Publishing guides to both female and male stars, a French firm, in *Les Grandes Vedettes du cinéma: beauté masculine* (1929), claimed, accurately, that cinema had 'overturned all the old conventions about the unimportance of male appearance, imposing a general and absolute rule that heroes must be beautiful'.[2]

The way in which old norms were being replaced by new ones is clearly demonstrated by the revolutionary changes in fashion and in the advice, and assistance, offered with respect to improving one's personal appearance. In the world of high fashion the first portentous innovations were those of the radical Parisian dress designer Paul Poiret when he made a deliberate attempt to herald the first decade of the new century by echoing the less trammelled, more 'natural' styles of Napoleon Bonaparte's First Empire, exactly one hundred years before, beginning the rejection of the voluminous, trailing skirts which concealed, or exaggerated the contours of, the lower half of the female form. However, the unique influence of the Great War (1914–18) is neatly encapsulated in the twofold circumstance that it was the compulsory enlistment of Poiret in the French army that left the way clear for 'Coco' Chanel, with her inborn instinct for simplicity, to establish her ascendancy on the home front – where, in any case, and in all countries, the need for women to be dressed fittingly for the arduous war work they were undertaking combined with difficulties in obtaining the required materials, led to shorter and simpler skirts.[3] Much nonsense is talked about the female fashions of the early twenties. Boring old farts of both sexes may have complained about the 'boyish' look (short hair, flattened breasts, skirts shorter than had ever been seen before), but young men, as Robert Roberts testifies in his account of young manhood in working-class Salford, were not confused:

> What undoubtedly attracted young men of the period was legs! Far from looking male, girls, with that daring length of limbs on show, appeared not less but more delightfully feminine than ever. Young men in dance halls, talked 'legs' – ankles, calves, shapes.[4]

In the 1960s, analogous old fogeys complained of boys looking like girls: girls then were no more fooled than boys had been in the 1920s. Fashions do change (soon hair and skirts lengthened, breasts re-emerged), but their effects on human perceptions and human behaviour are generally overestimated. However, the changes of the war period and immediately after did have mighty and irreversible consequences. Henceforth, whether thighs and knees were concealed or not, whether breasts were flattened or uplifted, whether hair was worn short or long, a basic concept of physical beauty, always known but always subject to ambivalences and confusions, had been exposed in the 1920s as never before; there would be no more cover-ups.

In pre-industrial times, 'beauty' guides, while often inflected by the prevailing moral tone of beauty being a snare and a delusion, generally accepted that women (and, it was occasionally recognised, also men) naturally wished to put the best front possible upon their appearance. Steadily the great flood of nineteenth-century works began to accept that the aspiration after a pleasing appearance was a perfectly respectable one; indeed they became quite stern in insisting that a woman had a *duty* to work on improving her appearance. The sense of the superiority of nineteenth-century attitudes over those of a more superstitious age come over strongly in a substantial volume published in New York at the very end of the century, *The Woman Beautiful,* by Ella Adelia Fletcher:

> It is not so very long ago that there existed a certain prejudice ... against the endowment of physical beauty, it being looked at askance as a dangerous gift. And neither girl nor woman could have devoted the thought and time to personal care which is now thought necessary without being charged with the heinous faults of vanity.[5]

Addressed to the 'thoroughbred daughter of the nineteenth century',[6] *Harriet Hubbard Ayers's Book* (also 1899) expressed contempt for the 'old-fashioned', 'demoralizing' and 'absurd' idea that a woman should resign herself to the decrees of Providence and take no care of her personal appearance. There is much moral exhortation: 'She must not give herself up as hopeless, as many a plain girl does'.[7] The woman 'who wilfully neglects her personal appearance is deserving of the severest censure';[8] 'the sin of dowdiness is castigated'.[9] It would seem that the Victorian work ethic applied to women as much as to any aspiring office boy: hard work, as well as willpower, were frequently cited as essential factors in the cause of beauty, the French sources being particularly explicit, with one making it clear that working girls must be prepared to rise an hour earlier each morning.[10] The stern moral tone did not entirely disappear from beauty manuals in the first sixty years of the twentieth century, but was softened with suggestions that, in making-up and dressing-up, a woman will be giving expression to her own personality, giving pleasure to herself, and indeed will be indulging in activity that she really rather enjoys. There is a greater emphasis than ever before on health and naturalness, and, for the first time, though in a very discreet way, a few hints point to the connections between looking good and arousing sexual desire. A standard French beauty guide first published in the 1920s declared that, whatever her condition in life, a woman 'must never neglect the cultivation of her beauty'. But it continued:

> It is not only to be happy in love that you must, dear readers, offer to the sight of your fellow creatures an agreeable appearance, it is also for you yourself, for your moral health, so that you do not become more and more sad behind your despondent face.[11]

Though the preface to this book contains a token inclusion of male readers as well as female ones, it is obvious that the work is intended entirely for the latter. Indeed, despite the new interest in male looks brought about largely by films, there is no suggestion anywhere that men should ever dream of going beyond routine health and teeth care, shaving, having regular haircuts, and taking some care over their dress, to actual use of cosmetics. In an autobiography primarily concerned with the achievement of business and social success, Mrs Hortense Odlum, the prospering owner of a women's fashion shop in New York, set out what were widely seen to be the essential differences between men and women in this respect:

> While it is true that women demand comfort today in their clothes – we've come to look upon corsets that bind our bodies ... as expressions of decadence – there is an additional requirement in clothes of women. We use them as a means of expressing our personalities and as a way of enhancing our attractiveness. Masculine attractiveness stems much less from physical beauty than feminine. A fine and honest mind, a kind and sensitive heart and spirit are the first essentials of true beauty for either man or women, but physical beauty in a woman is much more emphasized. When we catalogue a man's good points we are apt to comment on his physical attributes last of all. But the first thing we usually say about a woman is that either she is or she is not attractive looking ...
> Women paint their finger nails garnet, their lips flaming red and their eyelids blue, green or brown, not in an attempt to simulate nature, not even to improve upon nature, but to add a quality which is otherwise lacking. It's a kind of extension to their physical bodies of the gaiety and picturesqueness of their clothes ...
> Makeup to women does not mean artificiality as it does to men.[12]

No sign of the influence of male movie stars in this upper-class document, certainly; and, though open and clear-headed about the prime importance of physical beauty in women, Mrs Odlum none the less felt the need to include a measure of the old comforting pap about 'beauty' of heart, mind and spirit. But there is rich unwitting testimony to the heightened preoccupation in the 1920s with female self-presentation, and its more ludic aspects, as compared with previous eras.

Such preoccupation called for more outside assistance than ever before. As an American War Department Manual published during the Second World War pointed out, 'women couldn't cut their own hair and they soon discovered that, once cut, it required special care to look well'. At first, as bobbed hair gained in popularity, many women went into men's barber shops for cutting and trimming. But 'they soon wanted additional services not offered by barbers. They turned to available beauty shops and the increasing demand for service brought new shops.'[13] The most important service offered by the beautician at this time was permanent waving. The first machine had appeared in 1910, but permanent waving only became widely acceptable and popular in the 1920s. The manual summed up the situation at the end of the inter-war period, giving due weight to the importance of film:

> Certainly a tremendous aid to the growth of cosmetology has been the attention given to hair and skin care, make-up, and good grooming in general by magazines, newspapers, and the radio. Advertisers of the many beautifying and cleansing products also have played a big part in sending more and more women to beauty shops. And possibly the greatest influence of all has been the motion picture, setting fashions in hair arrangement and make-up.[14]

A French publication of 1930, *The Beauty Industry*, celebrated the achievements made by Institutes of Beauty since the first one had been founded in 1895. The book pointed out that the success of feminism had increased, rather than destroyed, demand: women competing for jobs with men had to look their best.[15] The great expansion, in the late nineteenth century, of the advertising of beauty lotions and beauty aids continued, almost exponentially, in the twentieth. More critically, an increasing number of advertisements aimed at men began to appear, advertisements for hair creams, after-shave lotions and treatments for pimples, baldness and greying hair, suggesting that Mrs Odlum's view that men were still required only to be neat and well groomed was not universally valid.[16] With such evidence it is difficult to determine how far there was genuine demand – whether stimulated by a desire to emulate male movie stars, an ambition to cut a dash at the local *palais de danse*, a belief that somewhere there was a world of sex accessible to the beautiful and youthful looking, or fear of unemployment – and how far skilled entrepreneurs, aware of the power of carefully conceived advertising, themselves created such demand as there was. Most striking is the evident fact that a new form of nose machine which became available in the twenties was directed at least as much at men as at women. 'M. Trilety's Newest Nose Shaper' was a vicious-looking metal object, held over the nose by straps buckled round the head, and fitted with an array of screws which could be tightened to apply pressure to the offending width, length, bump or crookedness. A ghastly little gadget of this sort existed, not to create a particular fashionable image, as perhaps hair cream did, but to mitigate ugliness – 'The Successful Correction of Ill-Shaped Noses', in the words of 'M. Trilety's' advertisement.[17]

That the object now is to remain young, rather than to grow old gracefully is argued in the French work *Beauty for All Ages*, which, while making the case for 'how to please and remain young', remarked that women of forty, considered past it quarter of a century previously, now dressed like young people. *Beauty for Every Woman* (British) is straightforward about the mood of the times:

> The beauty which comes from discomfort is not what we seek today. No modern girl would dream of shutting her body in corsets so tight that she might faint at any time, whereas girls of fifty years ago would have been horrified at the thought of using powder, rouge, and lipstick.[18]

Everywhere there was a new emphasis on exercise. Explicit attention was paid to breasts, rump and thighs, and their sexual connotations: 'a breast is beautiful if it is firm and of medium size'; 'a fine leg gives elegance and sets desire on fire'. 'It is beauty', we are told, 'which gives so much spice to love, for a man never forgets the delicious minutes he has passed in the arms of a beautiful woman swooning and palpitating.'[19] What the books were saying was matched by what the younger women were wearing:

> The sexual provocation of shortened skirts was further increased by wearing open lace work stockings and rolled hose that often bared flesh as well as contour. Silk stockings had become a necessity for the new-fashioned

women and an object of gift-giving and male attention, and sheerer models were overwhelmingly favoured by the young whatever the increased expense. Surely mere utility would not have dictated silk rather than lisle nor made the sheerer models more desirable. An enormous variety of colors, patterns, and degrees of opacity were displayed for the young woman's market – all helped to draw attention to the leg.[20]

Old prejudices about beauty and sexuality persisted – there were many denunciations of the blatant sensuality of twenties fashions. A more solid block to the full emergence of a fully modern appraisal of beauty was widespread poverty and deprivation, both of which hit even the United States in the 1930s. A series of articles on 'beauty' in *Le Petit Parisien*, a newspaper produced of course by wealthy proprietors, but aimed at a lower class readership, provoked this angry and bitter response from 'a woman of the people':

> We, those who set out every day for the office or the workshop, we don't have the time (or the money) to go to the institute of beauty; but the spouse, and the children who see us return in the evening, most certainly find in us the greatest beauty. Tell me, sir, what little child would swop his mother for a lady with well tended cheeks, but without a smile, without caresses (that would destroy her make-up!).
>
> To disperse the cares which preoccupy the flighty, they would only need other cares, those of the household, those of bringing up children; it would be enough for them to find ways of making their husband happy, in raising in a healthy and decent fashion the children given to them by the Good God. Sure, that gives one wrinkles, as crying in front of a cradle suddenly empty dulls the sparkle of the eyes; these wrinkles are the wrinkles of faithful grandmothers, who, when they arrive in front of the Judge, will not notice that they are no longer beautiful.[21]

A universal cry, one might say, and one which was to be repeated many times in different forms; in its very intensity it is arguing for a moral view of beauty now beginning to fall out of favour.

Such sentiments can be set against some striking portents of things to come. The most brash and unsubtle of these was the Miss America competition, launched in Atlantic City in 1921 and based on the simple premise of the dollar value of beauty – specifically that beautiful girls parading in bathing costumes would pull in the tourists. Despite the best efforts of the organisers to stress the wholesomeness of the contest and to play down its sexual connotations, the unambiguous significance of the latter was strong enough for the promoters to be pressured in 1928 into abandoning the contest – not because it was held to be degrading for women but because it was immodest. The relative potency of the different forces, preserving public modesty versus appearing in the vanguard of modernity and versus making a fast buck, can be gauged from the way in which uninterrupted presentation of the contest was resumed in 1935. No one out of the several types of beauty was specially favoured. Sharing in the widely held misapprehension that each age has its own standard of beauty, Lois Banner found it 'curious' that the second winner in 1922 'differed considerably in face and figure' from the first winner, Margaret Gorman. There was nothing curious about it at all (save for those who hold stubbornly to their theories in defiance of the evidence); we should, however, remind ourselves that at this level any decision as to one contestant being more beautiful than another was quite unreal; the one true line of demarcation is that between those who can, without manifest absurdity, enter a beauty contest and those who cannot.

Very few politicians, so far, we have already seen, could have entered beauty competitions. We are still a long way from mass exposure before the democratic electorate, still further from exposure within the intimacy of the home; in fact, for the next thirty years sound radio was probably as potent a medium in politics as film, putting a premium on qualities of voice rather than physical appearance. None the less, an important hint of what a visual medium of mass communication might achieve did appear in the very last year of the Great War when Screen Advertising Inc. ('Your Product Shown in Miniature Photoplays to Six Million People') began writing to congressmen with the following proposition:

> At a trifling cost to you, we will take a few hundred feet of motion pictures, showing you in your Committee Room, at your desk or anywhere else that you may select and, with appropriate titles, drive home to the voters the excellent work which you are accomplishing. From the original negative can be made a sufficient number of positive prints to serve the motion picture theatres in your District. If you wish us to, we will also arrange for the exhibition of these films. Why not count on every possible vote in your District?[22]

The shape of things to come indeed! Two caveats, however: first, not a great deal came of this particular scheme; secondly, displaying a politician at work, making speeches, etc., does not automatically and immediately mean a concern for their physical appearance – after all politicians had for generations happily shown off their (often) ugly mugs on election literature. Nevertheless, in the United States of the inter-war years *some* attention to the beauty or otherwise of politicians is discernible.

Traditional sentiments are as strong as modern ones in the account the distinguished journalist Mark Sullivan gave of the session of Congress which met to hear President Coolidge's address in December 1923, traditional in the song of praise for the ladies, modern in the singling out of the appearance of the politicians – dowdy:

> The House galleries filled up first and remained throughout the one part of the picture that was most pleasing to the eye during the joint session of Congress which heard the President's message today. The galleries were mainly filled by women who in their bearing, their choice of colors for their dresses and the alert intelligence of their countenances seemed rather the superiors and certainly more distinguished looking than the men of the two chambers who filled the floor.
>
> As you looked at the Representatives and the Senators you were convinced that for such achievement as comes out of them we must rely on the capacities inherent in average men. In clothes and countenance they were conspicuous, so to speak, in their averageness. There was hardly an outstanding head or face among them. As to clothes, the ordinary sack suit was universal ... To the eye it was like a meeting of the Farmers' Cooperative Association of Des Moines, Iowa, or a session of the male members of any small-town church.[23]

Woodrow Wilson, United States President at the end of the war, was a distinguished enough, if not particularly pleasing-looking man. The Republicans had no very brilliant figure to put up against him, nor did they have any very positive policies on which to fight the 1920 election. It is in such circumstances (as I suggested with regard to Franklin Pierce) that the factor of personal physical appeal may come into play. At any rate, Professor Edward Pessen has observed that the undoubtedly good-looking Warren Harding gained the Republican presidential nomination in part because of his looks, at a time when calm reassurance was required rather than vigorous policy initiatives,[24] going on to take the presidency in the 1920 election. Professor W. E. Leuchtenberg developed the point in words with which we have become familiar, declaring that Harding 'had no qualification for being President except that he looked like one'.[25] Harding died in office – because, according to one insider, he felt that as President of an avowedly prohibitionist nation, he ought to give up alcohol himself; within a fortnight of this grave decision he was dead.[26] Harding's Vice-President, and automatic successor, Calvin Coolidge, scarcely looked like a President; indeed the epithet 'funny looking' might have been coined for him, though Sullivan made quite an issue of the 'ingratiating appeal' of Coolidge's 'boyish features', 'blue eyes' and 'very blond head'. His appearance, Sullivan maintained, 'seems to say: "I am only a young fellow here, and I am new on this job, and I hope you will give me a kindly hand"'.[27] Having slipped into the presidency, Coolidge retained it in his successful campaign of 1924 on the slogan 'Keeping Cool With Coolidge'. Coolidge did not stand for re-election in 1928, the Republican mantle being inherited by the highly energetic and, in many respects, public-spirited Herbert Hoover, who had behind him a distinguished record as organiser of American relief operations at the end of the Great War; there was no call for distinction of appearance, and Hoover did not provide it.

Let us move on to Franklin D. Roosevelt's first campaign for the presidency, that of 1932 against the incumbent Herbert Hoover. One undisputed quality possessed by Roosevelt was that of extreme good looks; one undisputed feature of this campaign was that Roosevelt was 'on display' (in the words of the *Kansas City Journal Post*) as no candidate had ever been before – he undertook a daunting cross-nation campaign addressing vast open-air meetings.[28] Roosevelt, a member of an upper-class New York family and relative of the former President Theodore Roosevelt, was undoubtedly one of those whose birth was blessed by that 'good fairy' of whom the beauty guides often liked to speak. Family connections and good looks had given him an early start in politics: he was Assistant Secretary of the Navy during the Great War, and Democratic vice-presidential candidate in 1920. Then, at the age of thirty-nine, he was struck down by polio. Ambition and courage united in a fight-back which brought him the governership of New York. There was much opposition to him within the Democratic party, and his eventual nomination as presidential candidate was no soft, or compromise, choice.

The choice made, the question remained: was the Democratic candidate physically fit for office? Was he not still a hopeless cripple (to use the brutal language of the day)? One reason for the exhausting whistle-stop tour, 'tacit rather than expressed' as the *New York Times* put it, was 'to demonstrate to the people' that Roosevelt was indeed 'a man of fine physical stamina and rude health'.[29] Comments there were on this issue in plenty; but very, very little directly on Roosevelt's personal appearance, a matter still obviously considered not to be one for open discussion. Roosevelt did, in fact, dress in a manner calculated to attract attention to his looks, and his campaign photos showed him without his spectacles, eyes brightly shining, features highly lit to give a clean-cut appearance, the thickening jaw subtly lightened. Journalists used a surrogate language in referring to his looks (rather as good taste decreed that a man compliment a woman on her hat rather than on her own physical appearance). He was 'dapper in a dark suit and dark overcoat'; he gave 'his white dotted blue necktie a final tug'; 'his features' widened 'into a warm smile which is positively infectious'. A woman journalist recalled that when she first saw him in 1920 'he was a handsome and radiant figure', but in respect of the forty-eight-year-old Roosevelt of 1932 contented herself with referring to 'a physical disaster so valorously surmounted and lightly borne that it has become almost an asset'. Otherwise, she added, his luck has held, 'the luck of being a well-born and comfortably circumstanced American, happily following a chosen career'.[30] In an interesting twist, highly typical of certain attitudes which lasted till the sixties, the Democrats insisted that it was Republican enemies who 'love to emphasize his good looks and "personal charm", subtly suggesting that nothing lies behind it'.[31] This was not wholly accurate: what the Republicans paraded was Roosevelt's image as a slightly effete aristocrat, out of touch with the ordinary American – good looks could be used to a candidate's disadvantage.

Unquestionably Roosevelt's striking appearance did generate excitement at the meetings he addressed, though, of course, beautiful clean-cut features cannot mean much to vast audiences of thirty to fifty thousand. A writer in *World Telegram* pinned down how the current state of communications technology determined which personal quality was really Roosevelt's winner:

Governor Franklin D. Roosevelt may not win the election, but he has already won a championship. He is the best radio broadcaster among all recent Presidential candidates. Nor is this an unimportant title. Within eight years political parties may hold auditions rather than conventions [that didn't happen, but they would, *eventually*, hold televised conventions] ... The voice of the democratic nominee falls with such a pleasant cadence on the ear that on certain occasions the soothing sound of the man dims any sharp criticism of the sense.[32]

In a vast stadium the voice was again the major asset. In Chicago, reported that city's *Sunday Tribune*, 'The stadium had been wired for loud speakers and the Governor's deep resonant voice floated through every nook and corner of the big green field'. For those close up, Roosevelt's appearance did register: 'there were whispers of admiration from those near the speakers' stand'; ' "He looks like an athlete," remarked an eager woman'.[33] Beauty has to be *seen* to be recognised; it has *only* to be seen to be recognised.

Roosevelt did win the election, and he won it because, at a time when the country was devastated by economic depression, he offered hope. Through his formidable political talents and powerful personality he secured three further terms of office (advancing polio ultimately confined him to his wheelchair, a fact which was successfully concealed from the public), up to his death in 1945. He acted like a President; and he also 'looked like a President'. But no fashion was established. Roosevelt was succeeded by the incumbent Vice-President Harry Truman, whose appearance recalls Mark Sullivan's scornful description of the 1923 Congress.

There is little evidence of looks significantly affecting political choices in early twentieth-century Britain or France. Of characteristics apart from political talent, social background was by far the most important, to the extent, indeed, that it really outweighed talent, except in so far as 'talent' was in any case equated with having the correct manners, assumptions and prejudices. In the Labour Party, struggling in the 1920s to eclipse the Liberals, one way of securing a parliamentary nomination and thus the possibility of a launch into a political career, was to have sufficient private funds to spare impecunious constituency parties the burden of meeting electoral expenses. It is true that Labour's leader until 1931, Ramsay MacDonald, was strikingly handsome,[34] and remained so throughout his later years. Contrary to what has often been written about him, he did distinguish himself from his colleagues by qualities of industry, intellect and political sensitivity. He had emerged as leader before the First World War, and really there was no viable alternative when he was re-elected leader in 1922.[35] The image he presented was a complex one, yet it is abundantly clear that in giving him charm and personal magnetism, good looks did play a part in the favourable impact he made.[36]

Nobody, as I noted, referred openly to the good looks of President Roosevelt. Far other was the case with Anthony Eden (1897–1977), British Foreign Secretary at the early age of thirty-seven, and, eventually (1955–57) Prime Minister, an upper-class figure just as Roosevelt was. Roosevelt must be accounted one of the great successful statesmen of the twentieth century, always decisive, perpetually in action, as even his enemies recognised. Roosevelt looked like a handsome President, Eden like a beautiful film star. In conventional terms his career, right to the collapse of his Prime Ministership, seemed very successful; yet from the start there were those who used his outstanding looks to mock him.[37] It does seem, as I've remarked from time to time, that where other considerations are finely balanced, looks in a man can play a positive part. Eden had many other advantages and attributes, but it may be that looks helped him into his first post as Under-Secretary at the Foreign Office during the National Government of Ramsay MacDonald, when that post might easily have gone to the Prime Minister's son, Malcolm MacDonald. That first rung led to the second one, the Foreign Secretaryship itself. One of the themes of this book has been that women who are beautiful handle their beauty much more intelligently that do men similarly blessed; it also has to be recognised that, while beauty in women pleases men, beauty in men, particularly prior to the advent of television and the growing role of women in deciding popular choices, could simply annoy other less well-favoured men.

Before taking further the intriguing case of Anthony Eden, let us pause on the evidence, both verbal and photographic, as to exactly what his appearance was, and what impression it created. He was, his rather hostile biographer David Carlton tells us, 'the handsomest and best-dressed politician of his era'. The very hat he wore (a Homburg) was, from the thirties onwards, called an 'Eden' – you have to have the distinction of personal appearance Carlton identifies to have a hat named after you. He was constantly likened to the film star Ronald Coleman. Let me again quote the *DNB*:

> At thirty-eight he was the youngest foreign secretary since Lord Granville. He was also the best looking since Palmerston. Slim, debonair, well dressed, wearing the hat named after him, and talking with the clipped yet languid accents of the Eton and Christ Church of his day, he might have stepped out of a play by Noël Coward. He seemed more like a man of fashion than a serious public figure.[38]

Two scarcely veiled insults there, two suggestions of weakness: a matinee idol, a man of fashion. Later he was called after another film star 'Robert Taylor', and, with both topicality and evil intent, 'Miss England'. From his first appearance on the diplomatic stage, the Italians had named him 'Lord Eyelashes'.[39]

Let there be no doubt, however, that Eden possessed many outstanding qualities. During the First World War, when he was awarded the Military Cross for rescuing his own sergeant from certain death, he demonstrated quite exceptional personal courage. He worked hard at the task in hand, and at the end of the war took a First in Oriental Languages at Oxford, his intention being to enter the diplomatic service. He was a patient negotiator, though, unknown to the public, he had an appalling temper, which some affected to associate with what they perceived as his effeminate appearance. Eden resigned as Foreign Secretary in 1938 because he opposed the appeasement of the Italian Fascist Dictator Mussolini. This was a brave and principled act, whose impact was greatly lessened by Eden's failure to keep up a consistent and forceful opposition to appeasement, particularly, of course, that of Hitler. On the outbreak of war in 1939 he returned to government as Foreign Secretary in Chamberlain's Conservative government, continuing in that position in the Churchill National Government formed in May 1940. Both during the war and when Churchill came back as Conservative Prime Minister in 1951, Eden was very much second man to Churchill. Had Eden, his way smoothed by his looks, got ahead too quickly, only to be kept hanging around as Churchill's sidekick? As Churchill, in the early 1950s, kept his heir-apparent waiting, a tougher, less deferential man might have faced up to the ageing figure clinging on to office. Churchill did not let go till 1955. At last Prime Minister, Eden performed effectively in the general election which quickly followed, giving a consummate display of how to exploit his good looks on that new-fangled device, television. But then almost immediately (1956) he plunged into the disastrous Suez affair; perhaps trying to rekindle the image of the man who opposed the appeasement of aggressors, and, mistakenly perceiving Egypt's dedicated nationalist leader Colonel Nasser as another Hitler, he colluded with France and Israel in attacking Egypt, subsequently trying desperately to cover up this action.[40]

A seriously sick man, very shortly he was forced to resign, his once charmed career now in ruins. Eden, it is often said, would have made a good diplomat, but did not have the flexibility, the energy, the decisiveness to be a consistently successful politician. His looks served him well while he was on the way up, but made him a vulnerable target when his weaknesses began to show. He also lived up to his image as an empty tailor's dummy by, in conversation and discussion, depending heavily on platitudes, making him a notorious bore. He liked to be surrounded by people (who had to work hard to conceal their boredom), but he had no close friends. He did, in later life, marry a very beautiful woman, twenty years younger than himself, who was devoted to him. In his personal life, one can conclude, he did handle the gift of beauty adroitly; but in his public life he permitted it ultimately to become more a liability than an advantage. To attribute the folly of Suez to vanity induced by exceptional good looks would be going to far. What one can say is that, as with all beautiful people, Eden attracted special attention, special and sometimes hostile scrutiny, and led, sometimes to his disadvantage, a life different from that of the standard dowdy politician. The final conclusion must be that, in part due to the times in which he lived and to the class he was born in to, Eden did not know how to handle his good looks: instead of exuding a relaxed friendliness and grace as Tony Blair (admittedly in a very different era) was to do, he was aloof and stiff, confining himself to a very restricted circle.

Behind success in the higher echelons of the French civil service lay the interlinked factors of wealth, social status and education. In the United States the permanent government service was not nearly as highly rated as in Europe and was expected to be, and largely was, staffed by the relatively mediocre in talent, and often also in deportment and appearance.[41] In Britain, while there was recruitment from the middle class as well as the upper class, the qualities sought, and certainly admired, were those of poise, breeding, manners and good appearance (which is not necessarily the same thing as striking beauty). The head of the British civil service throughout the inter-war years, Sir Warren Fisher, was, however, noted also for his handsome good looks. That supreme upper-class standard setter of the inter-war years, Sir Francis Newbold, gave this advice in his *Handbook* for those making appointments to the colonial service: the candidate's

> physical appearance will, of course, have been noted at once, the cut of his face and the extent, if any, to which he has the indefinable quality of 'presence'. Colouring, build, movement, poise will have come under review, and even such superficialities as style of dress and hair, health of skin and fingers.[42]

For the upper civil service as a whole, as the 1931 Royal Commission on the Civil Service freely admitted, indeed boasted, great weight was placed on the 'interview test', it being denied, utterly unconvincingly, that this interview 'offered scope for a display of class prejudice';[43] it did obviously offer scope for the assessment of personal demeanour, if not simply good looks. Within the British upper class and governing circles (practically coterminous at this time),[44] imbued with the ideals and inclinations of ancient Athens, there was already a disposition towards giving a high evaluation to male good looks. This can be seen very clearly in the ascendancy which the gorgeous poet Rupert Brooke established over his immediate associates at Cambridge just before the First World War, or in a rather similar ascendancy established a little earlier by the novelist and barrister John Galsworthy, who was:

> Born among the wealthy classes, supplied from boyhood with every comfort and advantage, at a Public School and Oxford, intimately acquainted with horses and dogs, an experienced traveller for sport and pleasure, a welcome guest in Society, *handsome*, strong, a good athlete, married to a lady of remarkable *beauty*, charm and intelligence. [My italics][45]

As Ben Pimlott, biographer of Labour politician Hugh Dalton, has recorded, on his very first day at Cambridge 'Dalton met Rupert Brooke, and immediately fell under his spell.' Almost forty years later Dalton recorded that, 'no Cambridge friendship of mine meant more to me than this, and the radiance of his memory still lights my path'.[46] Dalton himself was nearly always something of an outsider in his political career (he was one of those whose money came in useful in securing a Labour seat in the 1920s):[47] he was a difficult man by nature, but in that, and in his lack of popularity with those of his own class, his unattractive appearance undoubtedly played a part.[48] From all this, it is evident that in the masculine power game in Britain in the early twentieth century beauty was certainly not particularly important, especially when compared with class position, but that it was nevertheless useful to be personable and that there was the possibility of discrimination against men who were not at least that. The prodigy at the end of the thirties, who became personal secretary to Churchill during the Second World War, John Colville, had the special good looks which could serve so nicely to underwrite precocity.[49]

In America the admiration denied to government servants was directed with full flourish towards entrepreneurs and business executives. Admiration for the truly self-made man was completely genuine; and it was certainly possible to have an ugly face and make a fortune. But recruitment into positions with high prospects within established businesses very largely came from the well-educated upper sectors of American society. At Yale two or three outsiders might be invited to join the exclusive Skull and Bones Club, an excellent moving staircase to high status in American business; looks might help, but the selected students would need to have shown concrete achievement, say as football captain, editor of the *Yale Daily News*, brilliant scholar or, perhaps, charismatic student politician. At Princeton, looks were one of a dozen or so headings on which students rated their classmates.[50] Detailed study has shown that in rating among classmates and, therefore, in election to the influential fraternities, involving in turn the high road to good jobs, looks did count; but what mattered above looks was the right social background or, at the very least, complete conformity to the attitudes and manners associated with that background.[51] Again, the conclusion is that beauty was far from a necessity, but that not being at least personable could be a disadvantage.

From those moving in the power circles of society, let us turn to those who served them. In general, the trends continued, and indeed accelerated, whereby high-status servants were usually good-looking servants, and shop assistants in high-class shops usually had a good appearance. Some details may be gleaned from the recollections of Gordon Grimmet, who from being coachboy (or 'tiger', as they were called) during the First World War rose to being a footman to Lady Astor. 'Tigers', who sat on the box of the carriage, were, Grimmet noted, 'preferably small and sweet faced.'[52] Grimmet moved to a job as lampboy to the Marquis of Bath at Longleat, then, while the war was still on, to the post of third footman.

> We were chiefly there as ornaments, for after we had dinner we were lined up in the beautifully dim-lit corridor and just stood there for the rest of the evening. It wasn't easy because we weren't expected to move, and powder as it hardens on the head seems to drag the hair by the roots and this caused the scalp to itch!! Nevertheless there's something artistically satisfying in wearing full livery and carrying it well. It encourages graceful movement and gesture and adds a bit of theatre and glamour to the occasion.[53]

Grimmet also served at Bath's London house in Grosvenor Square. He 'enjoyed walking in the nearby Hyde Park':

> I'd parade there in my waistcoat, with my starched shirt, white bow and livery trousers and the girls would all turn their heads and say, 'There's a footman' and I'd feel no end of a dog. I was a gayer bird than the soldiers in their khaki and a rarer one.[54]

Appearance evidently counted for much in his appointment by Lady Astor: 'He looks a big strong boy, Lee,' she commented to the butler. As an attractive male and a good dancer, Grimmet also made a good marriage: though only a second footman, he married the head gardener's daughter, who enjoyed some status as a floral arranger inside the Astor household.[55] The butler, Lee, was reared in poverty and when his father died and the family farm was sold up he seems to have gained his early appointment in domestic service almost entirely on the basis of appearance alone. He was appointed first footman to the Astors in 1912, the appointment being made by Parr the steward who commented, 'her Ladyship doesn't like pigmies'. At his first meeting with Lady Astor she remarked: 'I hope you stay. Look after him Parr, he seems a nice boy.'[56]

Although by this time good looks in female servants were often highly prized, the story could still be rather different for them. While the association between beauty and sexuality was more openly recognised than ever before, and fashion was more directly sexual – or perhaps because of these developments – manifestations of sexuality were very much discouraged. Speaking of himself and a female servant at Longleat, Grimmet recounted that: 'It was a rule of the house of course that we should never be in a bedroom together. For a man and a woman to see a bed in company would, in the eyes of our employers, only excite evil thoughts.' He further remarked that: 'There were some establishments that, as the sons reached adolescence, made a sort of tally of their maids' attractions. Those girls that came high on the list were gradually phased out and replaced by plain ones.'[57]

As I have repeatedly stressed, the social promotion of a beautiful woman in earlier ages, usually achieved by a stage-by-stage process of careful exploitation of her charms, almost invariably involved the conceding of sexual services; though, as we saw, the professional beauty, admired by the masses, was emerging at the end of the nineteenth century. The paradox of the modern evaluation of beauty as a quality of inherent independent value is that, although the value is intimately associated with sex appeal, it is not dependent on the actual occurrence of sexual activity. If I try to establish the point from the career of one of the most famous of all twentieth-century women, I do so from her early career which was far from untypical, rather than from her later elevation to the very pinnacle of celebrity.

Greta Gustafsson was born in Stockholm in 1905. Her father was a street sweeper. When he died, she, at the age of fourteen, had to seek work. Her first job was lathering faces in a local barber's shop. Her beauty was already striking, and here she was spotted by the son of the founder of Sweden's largest department store, PUB, where, like so many other beautiful girls, she got a job as a shop assistant. There was, however, a special quality to her looks: while some beauties in their thirties look twenty-one, Greta at fifteen, as she was in 1920 when she was asked to model hats for the store, looked twenty. Today we can still enjoy the fascination of the PUB spring catalogue, distributed in 50,000 copies, with pictures of her kitted out in some quintessential hats of the early twenties.[58] Unsurprisingly, she immediately got work as a part-time fashion model, a role in which a little dramatic talent is useful. At the same time she deliberately sought roles as an extra in the Stockhom film studios. The following year she appeared first in a film promoting PUB, then in a genuine feature, *Luffar-Petter (Peter the Tramp)*. 'Her voice,' the director commented, 'did not impress me, but her appearance did.'[59] Movies were just at the beginning of their worldwide dominion. PUB would not give Greta leave to take larger roles, so she made the calculated, but courageous, decision to break with them. Even if we had heard no more of her, she had still done pretty well for the daughter of a street sweeper. However, as with other beautiful women who got right to the top, she clearly did have talent, for she won a scholarship to the Academy of Dramatic Theatre in Stockholm. With an international film career now firmly in her sights (silent film was *the* international medium of communication), she changed her surname to one that could be pronounced easily in any language: Garbo. She was all of eighteen. At nineteen she went to Hollywood; the rest is legend. She had not, the evidence indicates, had to grant any sexual favours. Her Swedish director, who went with her to Hollywood, was gay. Garbo never married, though she had celebrated affairs with the great musician Stokowsky (who was twenty-three years older than her), the film star John Gilbert, Gayelord Hauser, George Schler and Cecil Beaton.

Other stars had already made it to the Hollywood that welcomed, though never knew quite how to treat, Garbo. Gladys Smith was born into a lower middle-class Toronto family in 1893. Her father died when she was not yet five; at five and a half she was appearing on stage. By the age of eight she had quite a reputation on the Toronto theatrical scene. At ten she made her New York debut and was now supporting the family. Even at this tender age she set out seriously to study other actors. Dedication and talent, clearly these were vital factors. She was also a very good-looking little girl; had she been plain it is impossible to believe that she would have been accepted on to the stage in the way that she was. She was also very determined, and she quite deliberately forced herself on the leasing Broadway impresario, Belasco. He it was who gave her the name Mary Pickford. She did well, but at the end of the season found herself without a part. Reluctantly she took herself to the film company Biograph, where there was just one film director, D. W. Griffith. He cast Mary, now sixteen, with a small part as a ten year old in *Her First Biscuits*:

> whatever it is that makes one person in a million so photogenic that the
> rest of us look at her with fascination, reflecting emotions from love to

hate – whatever that is, Mary Pickford had it. You can see it there on the screen, just the way the camera recorded it on April 20, 1909.[60]

Personally I think 'what it is' is great natural beauty, together with complete ease before the camera – quite a rare talent certainly, though 'one in a million' is sheer hype. Undoubtedly in the harsh film light a youthful complexion such as Mary possessed was a great advantage. She worked for various directors before joining with Adolph Zukor, who decided to forsake the short film for four-reelers: *Tess of the Storm Country*, released on 30 March 1914 was enthusiastically received. In the middle of the war, a few weeks after the American entry into it, the Mary Pickford Motion Picture Company was formed; at twenty-three she was earning over half a million dollars a year. Five years earlier, in January 1911, she had married a fellow actor, Owen Moore, a very beautiful creature, but with little talent and no great strength of character. Moore might perhaps have had a great career as a footman or a gigolo; as it was, he is yet another beautiful man to end up in the dustbin of history.

The film which brought to cinema serious recognition by the middle and upper classes was Griffith's *The Birth of a Nation*, released in June 1915. This was seen by a prospering actor, then thirty, who had previously been contemptuous of the medium. He now signed a contract stipulating that he must be directed by Griffith himself. This actor had been born in Denver, in May 1885, the illegitimate son of Ella Fairbanks and Charles Ulman, who was Jewish. It was from his father that Douglas Fairbanks inherited his dark skin, which was much resented by his mother. He was good-looking, and exuded virility, energy and self-assurance. As with any beautiful woman, there were winnings to be made in the sexual stakes. In June 1907 he married Beth Sully, daughter of an upper-class cotton trader. Fairbanks had to promise to forsake the theatre for business. But soon he was back on stage, the marriage remaining (for the time being) a secure and happy one. As a film actor Fairbanks achieved fame with *His Picture in the Papers*. In November 1915 he and Mary Pickford, who had admired his stage performances, met for the first time. In the post-war years they were to be, respectively, 'the most popular man in the world' and 'America's sweetheart'.[61] A celebrated triumvirate was completed by Charlie Chaplin. Chaplin was certainly a personable enough fellow, but there there is no question that talent (genius, even), rather than looks, was the crucial ingredient in his eminence in the film world.

Rodolfo Guglielmi, born in May 1895, came from a solidly prosperous middle-class family in Castellenata in Italy. There was no pressing need for him to emigrate to the United States at the end of the war, but when he did he found himself facing starvation. As with a Jeanne Bécu or a Lillie Langtry, a calm assessment of his assets and their potential was called for. Principally, his assets were romantic good looks and Italian grace. He became a 'taxi-dancer', a partner for hire in a public dance hall and, on the side, a gigolo. As his first boss recognised: 'With your looks and manner, you're going to spend a lot more time in bed with your partners than on the dance floor', adding: 'Make sure you do it in your own time and not in mine.'[62] And, indeed, Guglielmi habitually took what he called his 'love break' between the tea dance and the evening session. He worked hard on his dancing so that he could win a star position at the elegant Maxim's, for which post he delved back deep into family history in renaming himself di Valentina.

He was doing well, rather in the manner of a nineteenth-century *grande horizontale*, drawing heavy financial support from his rich mistress, when he fell foul of the sort of risk almost all those who live by their sexuality must run: his mistress shot her husband. Guglielmi, therefore, fled to San Francisco. Here he fell in with film people who had travelled up from Hollywood. His dishy looks made a considerable impression, but he had no immediate success in film and was forced to go back to dancing. It might have ended there: an everyday story of a beautiful male. However, he caught the eye of the established star May Murray, who insisted on having him as her leading man. On the strength of this, Guglielmi (or di Valentina), who certainly had no shortage of sexual partners, got married, unfortunately to the frigid Jean Acker. On marriage, he stabilised his name as Rudolph Valentino. It was the top-ranking script writer June Mathis (another female!) who picked out Valentino for *The Four Horsemen of the Apocalypse*. The rest, if I may dare to repeat the phrase, is legend. His life was stormy, and very short; we are all familiar with newsreel of the massive crowd scenes after Valentino's death, which cannot, of course, have been any consolation to Valentino. But to see his death as some inevitable retribution (reminiscent of La Dame aux Camélias) for living by sex alone is to underestimate the force of contingency in history and the unexpected lethality of the most harmless-seeming attack of appendicitis.

In the past, it had not been desperately important for male actors to be beautiful if they had talent. Now, movies made it the basic rule that film actors must be beautiful, as most stage actresses had always had to be. There were to be male stars, usually taking specialised roles as character actors or tough guys, who were not beautiful. There are no exact analogues among female stars, but one or two, while still filling traditional glamorous roles, did fall short of the standards set by the likes of Clara Bow (who from an impoverished Brooklyn background won the 1921 'Most Beautiful Girl in the World' competition, based on photographs), Gloria Swanson, Greta Garbo or, at the end of the thirties, Vivien Leigh. Even without a horrible accident at the age of eleven, when the Christmas tree candles burned all the skin off her face, Bette Davis was never going to be a beauty, but that accident certainly didn't help. Her sympathetic biographer Charles Higham makes the point by omission:

> She never thought of herself as attractive, yet she was: her infectious laugh, her stylish swinging walk, the trick of balancing herself on her heels and turning unexpectedly, her quick wit, and her wide blue eyes started to draw the attention of young bloods.[63]

She had a date with Henry Fonda: 'She was very attracted to him, but he says he was not attracted to her.'[64] What she did have was a driving will, backed up by that of her mother, to become a successful actress. She did.

When it came to casting the film of Margaret Mitchell's prodigiously best-selling novel *Gone with the Wind*, Bette Davis seemed to many the best-qualified actress for the role of Scarlett O'Hara, who, according to Mitchell, was not beautiful, though loaded with sex appeal. But in film a sex symbol had to be gorgeous. The part was won, against such candidates as Paulette Godard, Jean Arthur and Joan Crawford, by an actress whose looks truly were stunning; looks assisted, it should be added, by the mastering (on the part of an English girl) of the difficult Southern accent and a piece of luck. The young English actor Laurence Olivier (as a boy, a classic case of the dangers of good looks – he was brutalised at his posh boarding school, where he was jeered at as 'the school tart')[65] was just beginning to make his career in Hollywood, where his agent happened to be the brother of *Gone with the Wind* producer David O. Selnick; through this contact Olivier was able to recommend his own wife Vivien Leigh. Olivier recorded: 'I looked back at Vivien, her hair giving the perfect impression of Scarlett's, her cheeks prettily flushed, her lips adorably parted, her green eyes dancing and shining with excitement in the firelight; I said to myself, "David won't be able to resist that."'[66] He wasn't.

Movies gobbled up beautiful women, and in movies heroines were always beautiful. What if, according to the screenplay, she was not? Even in the 1950s that was a hard nut to crack, as was shown by the Academy Award-winning film *Marty* (1955).[67] This honourable film offers a penetrating insight into the manners and morals of sections of working-class and lower middle-class New York. Young males seek sexual partners at the Stardust Ballroom which, we learn, is 'loaded with [to attempt phonetic spelling] "tomaytoes"'. An even more vulgar word was used for the accessible young women (nurses apparently) some of the younger men are fortunate enough to get off with: 'squirrels'. Marty, however, misses out on all this. As he cries out when his mother once again raises the question of marriage (he is thirty-four): 'I am just a fat little man. Fat ugly man. I'm ugly. I'm ugly'. Ernest Borgnine, already an established star in tough masculine character parts, no handsome pin-up for sure, carried conviction in this part, letting his stomach sag and exuding a general air of defeat. Persuaded to go to the Stardust Ballroom, he meets a young woman, brought on a blind date by a young doctor, then callously dropped. She describes how on her last visit to the ballroom she had sat for an hour and a half: guys who approached her for a dance would suddenly have a change of mind at the last moment. Dancing with her, Marty consoles her in her self-doubt and loneliness with words of consummate charm: 'You see you're not such a dog as you think you are', followed by, 'Guess I'm not such a dog as I think I am'.

Clara, 'the dog', is twenty-nine. She and Marty get on well together, but Marty's friend Angie, his peer group of male chauvinist bachelors, and, most strikingly, his mother, are utterly contemptuous: Clara is 'scrawny', 'a dog', and 'looks at least fifty years old'. The revealing irony in all this is that the actress who plays Clara, Betsy Blair, was in fact

notably beautiful, with no attempt being made by the make-up department to render her otherwise.[68] Her alleged unattractiveness is merely
symbolised by her dress which is very formal, by the fact that she's a
chemistry teacher, by her reticent shyness, and, above all, by contrasting
her with the 'squirrels'. Thus the entirely false equation is made: that
plainness equals failure to project immediate availability (no doubt
bringing much false comfort to dozens of unhappy young film-goers).
Any normally-functioning male meeting Betsy Blair would, in the lapidary words of another of these philosophical experts on beauty, Clifford
Bax, 'find his aesthetic delight dangerously confused with his sexual
interest'[69] (the two, as this book has, I hope, by now demonstrated are
inextricably intertwined). The sad fact is that it was still quite impossible for Hollywood in the 1950s to put a genuinely plain woman on
screen, at least in a contemporary drama with which audiences were
expected to identify: the trick to reassure (and fool) mass audiences was
to *assert* someone's unattractiveness and then show that (by a hundred
miles!) she was not so unattractive after all, and indeed could find love
and marriage. Verbally the old comforting convention that beauty is
more than skin deep was being restated, though the visuals, in fact, were
demonstrating the opposite. (I don't think the point is invalidated by
William Wyler's *The Heiress* (1948), a classic costume drama, based on
the nineteenth-century Henry James novel *Washington Square*, in which
Olivia de Havilland is made up to look fairly plain, or, at least, severe; it
is intriguing that Betsy Blair also had plain girl roles in two European art
movies, the Spanish *Calle Major* and the Italian *Il Grido*, but scarcely
relevant to a discussion of mainstream ideas in the America of the 1950s.)

No discussion of beauty in the forties and fifties could fail to refer to
Marilyn Monroe, whose life epitomises both the power and the tragic
fragility of beauty Her career points up old truths about a beautiful
young woman getting her start in the world by offering sex to powerful,
predatory and, often, ugly males, and yet also points ahead to the liberation brought about by the cultural revolution of the 'swinging sixties'
whereby a woman could exploit the power of her beauty on her own
terms. Norma Jean Monroe (her mother's maiden name, though she
was sometimes also known as Norma Jean Baker), who was born on
1 June 1926 in Los Angeles General Hospital, had an appalling childhood, pushed from foster home to foster home, then into an orphanage.

She was kept going only by her conviction that, in this city of the world's most immense dream factory, she would herself escape into film stardom.[70] At fifteen, her erratic, legally-appointed guardian 'Aunt Grace' presented her with the alternatives of marrying a local aircraft fitter, Jim Dougherty, or returning to the orphanage. With the coming of war, Jim was sent abroad, Norma Jean herself went into an aircraft factory. There was no sign of a break in this working-class career pattern till the appearance at the factory in late 1944 of an army photographer charged with taking morale boosting shorts of attractive women doing war work. He spotted Norma Jean at once and was responsible for launching her on a career, the quintessential one for the dumb beauty, as a photographic pin-up.

Norma Jean was not in fact dumb, but she was certainly beautiful – we have the films, we have photographs of her as a devastatingly natural nineteen year old, we have the reactions of those around her (after she had her first, false, break into movies, Darryl Zanuck, head of Twentieth Century-Fox let her go because he did not find her attractive, and she was also spurned by Howard Hawks – in Hollywood where there were dozens of gorgeous eager girls, studio bosses who had them at their feet and on their backs could exercise highly individual choices). It has been suggested that her beauty (in the eyes of *almost* everyone – no woman, I have said right from the start, can expect more) was constructed, through cosmetic surgery. Certainly she was an expert in the application of make-up, and her hair (no surprise here), was bleached. She was to be well ahead of her time in going jogging to preserve her shapely, though buxom, figure. The first cosmetic surgery she had, also a few years later, was of a very minor kind: first to straighten her teeth, then to remove to tiny moles from her chin. Anyway, the next stage in the Norma Jean story was her meeting with Andre di Dienes, a photographer of rather more ambitious cast than the man from the army. Before discarding her, Twentieth Century-Fox gave her the name Marilyn Monroe; she divorced Dougherty. She began a primary, and for a time parallel, career as a pulp magazines pin-up, becoming 'Miss Cheesecake of 1951' for the troops in Germany. (Whatever the legions of adoring males might be doing with themselves, they were not, obviously, having sexual congress with Marilyn.) Meantime, however, she had joined the ranks of the *petites horizontales* attending the house parties of Hollywood moguls, constantly available, constantly hoping to barter sex for the right part in the right film. 'House girl' at home of producer Sam Spiegel, she was, on New Year's Eve 1948, spotted by agent Johnny Hyde, who really did have an eye for beauty. Falling in love with her, and wanting – a little runt, he had no hope – to marry her, he was instrumental in getting her the roles in *The Asphalt Jungle* (released in June 1950) and *All About Eve* (released in October 1950) which conclusively demonstrated her star quality. It now became known that the delicious nude in an immensely popular calendar series was Marilyn Monroe, in a pose taken in 1949. In the pinched and prissy morality of the time this revelation might have destroyed Monroe's film career; however, she was able to turn it to her immense advantage, having the story put about that she had only posed out of dire need for money to pay the rent. Added to the image she was already establishing, this sent her hurtling into orbit as the greatest sex symbol of all time (symbol, note, not necessarily practitioner). She received massive publicity, including the high-status accolade of a feature in *Life*, which declared 'the genuine article is here at last – a sensational glamor girl, guaranteed to entice people from all lands to the box office'.[71] 'Box office', that was the key, for, in the future, a woman who was 'box office' for millions had no need to sell sex to the powerful few. While all this was going on, Marilyn was devoting prodigious efforts to learning how to develop to the fullest her original, though wayward, talents as an actress – the fruits, as everyone knows, were a series of classic films.

At the age of thirty-six Marilyn Monroe died from an overdose of drugs, her death being surrounded by strange circumstances. It does seem clear that the announcement was held up for several hours, probably in order to cover up her association with Robert Kennedy. That she was actually murdered seems highly improbable; it is, however, quite likely that she did not consciously intend suicide.[72] Here these are not central matters: the point is that a great screen goddess, with an unprecedented reputation, met a tragic death. But we do have to ask here, how would Norma Jean have fared had she been plain? We don't know, of course, but to have had plainness added to everything else could well have meant an even unhappier life and perhaps an earlier tragedy. As to happiness, that is always hard to calculate. Marilyn Monroe did enjoy the fulfilment of relationships which, for short periods at least, went well, as with Arthur Miller and Joe DiMaggio; she enjoyed beautiful men in her earlier life and famous ones in her later one; above all she had the fulfilment of resounding and acknowledged success in her chosen career. Personal beauty was the essential ingredient.

I have already included Rudolph Valentino among the sexy, beautiful stars of the twentieth century. As we move through the fifties it becomes more and more easy to compare male stars and female stars on something like level ground. Opinions will differ, but there would be a fair case for arguing that the male analogue of Marilyn Monroe was Elvis Presley. Both were exceptionally beautiful, and both were stunningly sexy – Monroe because of the use of her voice, her eyes, her entire body language, Presley because of the profoundly suggestive gyrations of his lower body as he sang with his rich, seductive voice. Monroe bleached her hair, Presley dyed his black. Monroe was a serious actress who worked hard to improve her technique; Presley was a gifted musician, with a wonderful voice, who, intentionally or not, played a key role in the transformation of popular music from the boring ballads and swing of the forties and early fifties to the rock music of the sixties. Both died young, and in distress, Monroe in 1962, aged thirty-six, Presley in 1977, aged forty-two. Monroe remained in good condition, curvaceous, but shapely to the extent that she had always been; Presley became gross, his looks disappearing under layer upon layer of fat. Monroe continued to receive critical acclaim, giving her greatest performances in her last films; Presley gathered much criticism, particularly for abandoning rock for sentimental ballads, but the fact remains he was the single most popular singer in the first era of pop music. From her earliest years, Monroe, so clear have ideas of women as the beautiful sex always been, was recognised as beautiful, even though she came from a desperately impoverished background. Presley, however, was no Anthony Eden, no Rudolph Valentino: his looks, to Americans of his day, had no 'class', he was simply a gorgeous working-class hunk, whose beauty nakedly, directly and threateningly communicated sexuality. Thus, in contrast to the experiences of Monroe, his first middle-class friends actually found his appearance, as Peter Guralnick, one of his best biographers put it, 'a bit off-putting',[73] continuing that he 'needed a haircut', the rather greasy attempt at a duck's arse coiffure signalling vulgarity and the very opposite of beauty. Guralnick insists that it was Elvis's ingratiating quality rather than perceived physical beauty which got him started. I'm not sure about that since people do pretend not to see beauty (think of Cora Pearl), when it is really beauty which is affecting them most deeply. What is certain is that by the later fifties Elvis had triumphantly emerged as the prototype of the beautiful male icon, so important in our contemporary world.

9

The Swinging Sixties

At all times beauty has been recognised as having a special potency of its own, but the implications of this have usually been severely limited by the persistence of traditional conventions and shibboleths. With technological innovation, the weakening of religious faith, the growth of mass society, these conventions and shibboleths met with increasing challenges, yet the traditional approach to human beauty has proved extremely resilient. The greatest challenges of all came during that unique convergence of economic, technological, social, cultural, ideological and political forces, that blossoming of youth culture, civil rights and women's liberation which came about between the late 1950s and the early 1970s, known to historians as the 'International Cultural Revolution of the Long Sixties', and to others as 'the Swinging Sixties'.[1] Entailed within this 'revolution' was the triumph of the modern view of beauty, of physical, 'surface' beauty as possessing an independent value in itself – not, of course, in the hearts and minds of every single individual, but in society at large, in its public mores, its newspapers, its advertisements, its television programmes, its social, cultural and political behaviour. In the traditional view, the prized qualities were social position and wealth; beauty, apart from being an enticement to the sin of lust, was seen as a menace to both of these. Now beauty was universally praised and sought after; it had achieved a kind of parity with class and wealth, and was certainly no enemy to either.

While the response to beauty is a deep sexual instinct (sometimes experienced vicariously, as among those admiring pin-ups, the masses attending theatres or cinemas or men – as well as women – registering the sex appeal of handsome male celebrities), it requires reasonable living standards and real opportunities for comparison, contrast and choice (as provided, for example, through living in a major urban centre, or through travel, or through cultural exchange, or through all three) for a full appreciation of human beauty in all its varieties. Hence the importance of the point that the cultural transformations of the 1960s were *international*. For most of the 1950s western Europe was still very different from the United States, while America itself was in many ways inward-looking and parochial. But in the 1960s, European life-styles and fashion penetrated even the American Midwest. International pop culture, with important components from black America and working-class Britain, became all-pervasive. On the screens of cinemas and of domestic television sets, there appeared film stars and models drawn from a great array of geographical and national backgrounds. One was the working-class Scot, Sean Connery (the first 'James Bond'), whose slow, deliberate Edinburgh accent had the perfect mid-Atlantic nuances and comprehensibility for the new international culture: he, as *Paris Match* pointed out in April 1963, exuded sexuality, as did the actresses from many countries who appeared with him.[2] In the same year, an American fashion writer, remarking that 'all the girls copy one another', admitted that 'the trend-setters among them copy French and Italian film actresses as Hollywood stars seem rather behindhand nowa-days'.[3]

In an international culture there was a boom in international love affairs, all publicised by the press, again drawing attention to beauty in all its glamorous variety. One multiple entanglement brought together the lives of French film director Roger Vadim, his first numi-nous protégée, Brigitte Bardot, the stars and singers Annette Stroyberg, Sacha Distel, Yves Montand, Marilyn Monroe, and Montand's wife, Simone Signoret; a simpler one involved British photographer David Bailey, the British model Jean Shrimpton and the French star, Cather-ine Deneuve. Most resonant is the soppy little story of two middle-class unknowns carried by *Paris Match* in September 1965: 'The One Who Has Conquered the Most Beautiful Girl in the World: A French Student':

> Ingrid, the beautiful fiancée from Nuremberg, cries out in French: 'How suntanned you are!' Roland, the French student replies to her in German: 'Ich wusste dass du die Schönste warst!' [I knew very well that you were the most beautiful!] And Roland takes in his arms the girl whom he will marry in two years time, Ingrid Finger, twenty years old, whom a jury in

Palm Beach has just consecrated 'Miss International Beauty 1965'. Their story is one of the happy results of the extensive interchange between young people of the two countries: this year 150,000 young people aged twenty visited Germany. Three years ago Roland ... was on holiday near Sete. The Finger family happened to be passing through ... looking for a camping ground ...
And, beneath the sun of Hérault, the lightning struck. Ingrid and Roland together spent four weeks of bliss ... Ingrid entered the Studio Suzanne, the school for models in Nuremberg. Her file contains her measurements: height 1.7 metres, weight 55 kilogrammes, bust 91 centimetres, waist 58 centimetres, hips 91 centimetres. And these perfect proportions contributed to her successive elections in 1965 as Miss Munich, Miss Bavaria and, on 14 May last, Miss Germany. Invited to Palm Beach, she walked off finally with ... the title of Miss International beauty. Ingrid received a prize of ten thousand dollars ... These ten thousand dollars, they will be the dowry which Miss Beauty offers to the little Ingrid.

Whatever the defects of the literary style, the accompanying photographs show both Ingrid and Roland to be very beautiful young people indeed.[4]

Female Hollywood stars of the fifties were certainly beautiful, but, with the explosive exception of Marilyn Monroe, they tended to conform to a rather limited range of types consonant with all-American ideals of domesticity: big breasts were highly respected, but preferably allied to an air of innocent wholesomeness. The only challenge to Monroe as the great sex goddess came from European stars: first Gina Lollobrigida, then Vadim's 'discovery', Brigitte Bardot. A more interesting case for our present purposes is that of Monica Vitti, star of Antonioni's film of 1959, *L'Avventura*. She had a prominent Roman nose and a lean, intensely sensitive look, and struck audiences at the time as being 'different'; different types of beauty were becoming acceptable as never before. At the same time as Vitti, there appeared a rather special type of mature Italian male beauty, soulful, a tad vulnerable, that of Marcello Mastroianni.

As new types of beauty, both male and female, forced their way onto the screens of some commercial cinemas, Hollywood grasped the virtues of international film making, where the low costs and high talents of European countries could be exploited. Paramount's 1960 film about alleged female collaborators in the Second World War, *Five Branded*

Women, called for five actresses so intrinsically beautiful that they could appear with their hair shorn. *Life* identified it as

> a good example of the new international look in moviemaking. It was pro-
> duced by Italy's Dino DeLaurentiis, directed by America's Marin Pit, and
> photographed in Italy and Austria. Its five shorn actresses were recruited
> from three countries – two each from the US and Italy, one from France.[5]

The same magazine, in January 1966, had a cover story on 'The New Freewheeling Film Beauties of Europe'. In the comments attributed to, or made about, these actresses, uninhibited expression is given to the notion of the autonomous value of beauty; the talent of these strikingly different women, it is made clear, lay fundamentally in their personal appearance. As Catherine Deneuve summed up: 'I owe my start in movies entirely to my face and body'.[6] Each of the British stars who gained international renown also represented very different types of beauty: among women, Julie Christie and Vanessa Redgrave; among men, Peter O'Toole, Terence Stamp, Michael York and, as already mentioned, Sean Connery. If ever there was a time when one particular convention of beauty reigned above all others (and I have suggested that in real life among flesh-and-blood people such conventions matter much less than the theorists of relativism maintain), that time was destroyed in the sixties with films, and television, presenting beauty in its manifold varieties. (I shall come to non-Caucasian types shortly.) Many of the themes informing this chapter run through the English-language film which Antonioni made in 'swinging London' in 1967, *Blow Up.* For the part of photographer, Thomas, Antonioni had wanted Terence Stamp, but settled for the equally beautiful (though sweetly featured rather than toughly macho) David Hemmings. Of these British male figures Antonioni said: 'They are the heroes of the age, they have invented new canons of beauty'.[7] Actually, they had not invented new canons but had revealed what many had always known: that beauty comes in many varieties and is to be found in males as well as females.

Because of rising living standards and better medical care, young people growing up in the later fifties and early sixties were stronger and healthier than ever before. Those born with a good bone structure and balanced features were less likely now to fall victims along the way to some wasting or deforming disease, or even to bad teeth. Thus the proportion of beautiful people in developed societies went up. More important, the proportion of the personable, those whose attractiveness lay in their healthy youthfulness and general vivacity, rather than any rare distinction of beauty, also went up. At the same time the youthful fashions of the day, which older people, if they could, were keen to espouse, exposed natural endowments – male as well as female – and, accordingly, were cruel to natural imperfections. As *New York Times* fashion expert Marilyn Bender summarised in 1967:

> The purpose of fashion used to be dissimulation, the pretence that women were pretty, had perfect bodies, romantic spirits and that they were essentially helpless. Pop fashion, like pop art, lays the subject on the line. Fatty knees, wrinkled elbows, ruthless natures are exposed for all to see.[8]

Pop fashion for men entailed, among other things, tight, unpleated, hip-slung trousers, admirably suited to shapely young men, but doing nothing to conceal scrawny legs or protuberant stomachs. Notably, however, while the general shape of the male leg was now shown off (as it had been prior to the Victorian period), the leg itself remained concealed. There was almost no concealment in the miniskirt, invented for female wear by the British designer Mary Quant in 1965.

This book is deliberately confined to western societies because it is within those societies that the modern evaluation of beauty, now dominant throughout the world, evolved. But what of the minority community within the United States, that of the Afro-Americans, blacks, or, in the language of both white Americans and of themselves at the beginning of the 1960s, 'Negroes'. My main source is the 'Negro' publication, *Ebony*, which by the later fifties had become a lavish monthly colour magazine; owned by a black family and produced by a mixed staff on which blacks were in a majority, it was selling three quarters of a million copies, and probably reaching a total of five million readers. Consistently, there is throughout a very heavy emphasis on questions of personal appearance, discussed at two quite different levels. Most of the items are relatively trivial in nature, mainly aimed at black women exercised by the problem of securing a husband; but some articles firmly tie the question of personal appearance with that of civil rights – as blacks became more assertive and more powerful, they must, the argument was, present an appearance of which all blacks can be proud.

Ebony carried a large number of advertisements featuring black models; it also carried a very large number of advertisements for hair straighteners, skin whiteners, and many other 'beauty aids' designed to help blacks look as much like whites as possible – the accepted ortho-doxy was that black women, if not black men, should always straighten their hair. As well as regular articles on grooming and make-up, and on fashion, there were frequent articles on beauty competitions, on the personal appearance of famous black women, on 'best-dressed Negro women', on such questions as 'what is the best age for beauty?' (treated with a down-to-earth wit, typical of the magazine – 'beauty experts say women, like wines, improve with age', but 'science, skin specialists, even Doctor Kinsey, have not succeeded in dousing the average male's enthu-siasm for a young bustling companion'),[9] and, each June, an article on 'eligible bachelors'. This series did not in any way take the line that men should be assessed on their looks – in fact most of those selected were earnest, bespectacled and distinctly unglamorous, what they stood for being economic success; the main thrust of each article concerned what such men were looking for in a woman. Again we have a touch of the usual down-to-earth wit: 'baseball player Willie McCobey, 24', one of the 1962 eligible bachelors, 'of the San Francisco Giants describes his ideal woman as sports minded, honest and understanding, with charm and beauty. Being a realist he says he'll sacrifice a little beauty if the woman has all the other qualities'. The summing-up for 1964 was: 'As with last year's round-up, the bachelors placed a premium on brains and personality but admitted that beauty still rates a strong considera-tion'. The following year there was the standard endorsement of brains and character, followed in block capitals by: 'NOT ONE OBJECTS TO BEAUTY'.[10] At the core of all this lies the assumption (never in any way stated explicitly) that a black woman will have a struggle to secure even a plain, though economically successful and upwardly mobile black man. Her energy should be directed to making herself look as much like a white woman as possible. It is recognised that a black man may occasionally marry a white woman; this will happen when the black man is economically very successful, so the marriage will actually represent an economic and social advancement for the white woman concerned. In December 1965 there was a sad letter from a black girl ('I'm considered pretty'), lamenting that black men were going after white girls and ignoring black ones, while white men were not going after black girls.[11] When, at the end of the decade, Hollywood did get round to treating this issue in *Guess Who's Coming to Dinner* (an honourable and witty film, though reviewed by one black critic as 'warmed over white shit'), the relationship was black man and white woman, and the man was mature and very distinguished, the woman very young.

The successful black women featured in *Ebony* all had the look of imitation whites; this is particularly evident in the cover and illustrating article of October 1961 on – and the pun may have been intended – 'Ebony Fashion Fair Beauties'. Wherever black girls did well in beauty competitions open to both blacks and whites *Ebony* was there reporting enthusiastically; invariably what the black girls won was never more than a consolation prize; but, then, as seen in *Ebony*'s highly professional photographs, they were never particularly beautiful. The puzzle is explained when it is appreciated that these competitions featured 'talent' – usually singing ability – as well as mere beauty. It seems that black women were not actually expected to look beautiful, though they were expected to be able to sing. Some black women *were* very beautiful, and in the less prejudiced international scene at Cannes black models won titles as International Queen of the Cannes Film Festival in 1959 and again in 1960. When, in February 1966, *Ebony* featured a cover story entitled 'Are Negro Girls Getting Prettier?', the six models on the cover and most of the women whose photographs appeared inside were of the usual type. The basic message was that 'better nutrition' and 'grooming know-how' have 'elevated today's young lady of hue to a place of prominence among the most pulchritudinous'.[12] Three bombs exploding in the letters column of the subsequent issue signalled that the revolution was under way:

> Your February, 1966 issue ... asks the question: 'Are Negro Girls Getting Prettier?' Why don't you put some Negro girls so we can see (instead of the half white)? Are you ashamed of the Negro girl? Or do you go along with the white man's premise that a Negro can only be good-looking when he/she is mixed with the white race?

> The cover of your (Feb) issue delivered today made me (and a lot of other people I'll wager) wince. It should be titled 'Are Negro Girls Getting Whiter?'

Come to my high school and I'll show you some girls to photograph who will illustrate, I believe, that Negro girls have always been pretty.

Yes, Negro girls are getting prettier! But your cover is a refutation of the statement. The majority of us are dark brown with bold features. The girls on your cover do illustrate various types of beauty. You have, however, omitted several other beautiful types which are much more typical of our people.[13]

In June 1966 *Ebony* itself, editorially, made the break. The cover story was: 'The Natural Look: New Mode for Negro Women'. In an earlier discussion of this I then continued:

The cover photograph was of the most beautiful black woman I personally have ever seen, an absolutely beautifully proportioned and intensely appealing face, surmounted by close-cropped fuzzy hair.[14]

Certain feminists, and one pompous, hide-bound historian, unable to envisage personal appearance being treated as a serious subject, mocked this sentence as subjective and unscholarly,[15] ignoring my explanation that I had intended to back this judgement with a copy of the photograph, but that, because of invasion of privacy legislation, had been denied the print I requested. Sometimes one is forced to rely on having gained the trust, or at least the forbearance of one's readers: all I can say is that I have no doubt that the majority of readers, female as well as male, would agree with me if they could see this photograph (which, I may add, is supported by a series of other photos of her inside that June 1966 issue of *Ebony*. For once this was no model or blues singer, but a twenty-year-old Chicago civil rights worker (some of my feminist critics, I fancy, took the view that it was demeaning to comment on the good looks of someone doing such an estimable job). The main article, 'The Natural Look: Many Negro Women Reject White Standards of Beauty', is of seminal significance:

throughout the ages, American women of color have conspired to conceal the fact that their hair is not like any other ... for the girl in the street – the coed, the career woman, the housewife, the matron and even the maid who had been born with 'bad' or kinky hair, the straightening comb and chemical processes seemingly offered the only true paths to social salvation.

Not so today, for an increasing number of Negro women are turning

their backs on traditional concepts of style and beauty by wearing their
hair in its naturally kinky state ...

'We, as black women, must realize that there is beauty in what we are,
without having to make ourselves into something we aren't,' contends
Suzi Hill, 23-year-old staff field worker with the Southern Christian Lead-
ership Conference. 'So many little Negro girls feel frustrated because their
hair won't grow, or because they have what is called "bad hair" ... By the
time they're adults, this feeling has become so much a part of them they're
even afraid to answer the telephone if their hair hasn't been done. Negro
women are still slaves in a way.'

The sentiments are ones I totally agree with, though, obviously, 'beauty'
is being used in the traditional way, embodying moral and 'spiritual'
qualities rather than mere physical ones. So, of course, with the slogan
of the black liberation movement, 'Black is Beautiful'. And, despite age-
old convention, hair is not the single most important element in making
a woman truly beautiful (though it may be the most important – and
highly desirable – element making a woman who is not beautiful more
attractive). As we know today, a beautiful woman can shave her head
and remain beautiful. Some black women were very beautiful and had
no need to imitate white women; many black women, like many white
women, were not beautiful – that's life. The key development of the sixties was that new choices were being opened up, and beauty was being
recognised as a natural physical quality, not something attained by the
slavish imitation of convention.

It was part of the new sensibility, tied also to further advances in the
status and emancipation from tradition of women, that the basic personal appearance of men, apart from their dress and grooming, was
receiving more and more attention. In March 1964 a top male film actor
had this written about him:

While most people who have seen him agree that his boyish face belies his
37 years, they would disagree with his self appraisal of 'averageness'. At six-
foot-two, he is four inches taller than the average American male and there
is nothing average about the feline grace of contained power with which
he moves his lean frame across the stage or screen.

Undoubtedly one of Poitier's biggest assets in today's climate of changing racial values is the dark complexion of his handsome clean-cut face.

Black actor Sidney Poitier had himself modestly said: 'I am blest with a kind of physical averageness that fits Negroes between 18 and 40. I look like what producers are looking for'.[16] The real point was that Poitier's colour was no longer an obstacle to the perception on all sides that he was a very beautiful man. And whatever the confusion still enveloping many black women in America (protests over *Ebony's* support for natural hair were prolonged and furious),[17] one, a model from Detroit, had established herself on the European scene by mid-1966 as one of the most photographed models of the time: Donyale Luna.

This really does drive home the point that the many varieties of beauty were now being recognised. It is simply not a matter of Jean Shrimpton's type of beauty being 'in' one year, and that of Twiggy the next. Such being the way of the fashion industry, and such the way of the mass media, it is true that one type would be very strongly featured at one point in time, and another at another; but for ordinary people with ordinary reactions, both Twiggy and Jean Shrimpton, and many, many others in all sorts of different types, were beautiful *all of the time.* Thanks to the Cultural Revolution of the Long Sixties there was less pressure than ever before to conform to dictates and conventions in this matter.

I concentrate for a moment on Jean Shrimpton ('The Shrimp') and Twiggy (born Lesley Hornby) partly because, in respect of recognition in the annals of history, they will stand with Veronica Franco, Nell Gwyn, Lillie Langtry and Marilyn Monroe (that they, *as models*, should do so, is in itself an historical phenomenon of significance), but also because, though they were exceptionally gifted and exceptionally fortunate, their careers give insights into the way in which opportunities for the beautiful had again broadened and changed. First there is the great, and insufficiently recognised paradox to which I have already alluded several times. In the climate of explicitness,[18] the relationship between beauty and sexuality was more openly paraded than ever before; among the highest compliments was to call someone 'sexy' and sexual attractiveness and sexual success were among the most envied and the most highly prized attributes. Yet whereas the fame and fortune of Veronica Franco, Nell Gwyn, Lillie Langtry and, to some degree at least, Marilyn Monroe, had depended on sexual transactions with men, the sheer economic demand now for beautiful faces meant that women, while openly exposing their sexuality (as, indeed, did men in similar roles), were not required to grant actual sexual favours. This had been a long process: some actresses (Sarah Siddons and Ellen Terry, for instance) had made it on looks and talent alone, as subsequently did many film stars, including, for example, Greta Garbo.

The rise in importance and prestige of the photographic model was intimately connected with the enormous expansion in advertising. Of similar significance in creating job opportunities for the good-looking was the proliferation of television commercials, soap operas and situation comedies, the growth of public relations, the advent of boutiques, bistros and fast-food outlets aimed at the young, and the boom in pop music. The appreciation of the marketability of beauty is revealed in the sudden development in the late fifties of agencies of various sorts, and especially modelling agencies: for example those of Catherine Harlé in Paris and Lucie Clayton in London. The opportunities I am speaking of were opportunities for men as well as women. If a woman is selling herself essentially on her beauty, then, in the last analysis, it is men she will have to please: but, if it is clothes she is modelling, it is women who will be choosing the clothes. Modelling agencies and modelling schools were often run by women. Such is the background to the striking fact that Jean Shrimpton and Twiggy, and also, for that matter, dress designer Mary Quant, owed a great deal to the perceptiveness and support of the particular men with whom they were personally associated.

Jean Shrimpton was born in November 1942, into 'the extended upper class',[19] her father being a businessman and Buckinghamshire farmer; she went to a convent school and was brought up with horses – in David Bailey's words, 'a county chick, all MGs, daddy, and chinless wonders'.[20] A social phenomenon of the post-war world had been the way in which the upper class had moved into the various branches of the media and advertising (as well as more traditional pursuits such as banking, accountancy and the higher levels of the law). The term 'model' was widely used to connote expensive prostitute (in a famous letter to *The Times*, at the height of the Profumo affair, whose central protagonist was the high-class prostitute Christine Keeler, always referred to in the press as a 'model', Lucie Clayton wrote that she presumed it would be only fair if the models in her agency referred to Keeler as 'the well-known journalist'),[21] yet modelling was already recognised as a proper career for a respectable upper-class English girl, and the rewards of photographic modelling were already much higher than those of the traditional (and often aristocratic) mannequin. However, like so many other young women, in 1960, at eighteen, Shrimpton enrolled on a course in shorthand and typing. There are plenty of family snaps of her from a very early age. She was very much in the upper-class English style, long-legged and slim, with a lovely innocently sexy face. She was also well brought up, and shy; belonging to an affluent environment in which most of the girls were personable and well groomed, she was probably not fully aware of her own beauty. Others were. While sitting in the lunchtime sun in Hyde Park, she was spotted and approached by film director Cy Endfield and persuaded to meet his producer; however, the latter turned her down. She was then approached by a photographer: taking the cue, and being both fed up with shorthand and typing, and under no pressing necessity to earn her own living, she enrolled at a modelling school.

It is customary in guides to modelling to say that models do not have to be stunning beauties – indeed Jean Shrimpton says this herself in *The Truth about Modelling*.[22] It is also always pointed out that photographic models have to be on the slim side since it is one of the quirks of the camera that it represents a person as if with an additional fine layer of flesh, making them look heavier than they really are, by as much as ten pounds.[23] Still this scarcely adds up to a case that models are socially constructed, or manufactured by the media, or whatever: they sell on what they look like in their photographs, that is to say, with this 'extra layer of flesh', so it is absurd to argue that a new style of scrawniness is being constructed. Anyway, slimness has always been highly regarded, fatness never praised. The notion that almost anyone, given the right circumstances, can be constructed into a model is best met by Shrimpton's own fairly gentle words: 'A heavy jaw-line, or squashy or bumpy nose is not helpful', and the eyes 'mustn't squint or disappear when you laugh'.[24] Certainly there is a quality of being photogenic which, it seems, some people have and others do not; but, principally, being photogenic means being able to appear natural in front of the camera, not freezing. Shrimpton went to a good modelling school, she signed up with a top agent, Lucie Clayton, she had contacts, she was beautiful, she was photogenic. Without her association with David Bailey, Jean Shrimpton would probably have had at least a moderately successful career as a photographic model. Bailey having risen from the working class to become an elite photographer, they moved in the same circles, without Bailey at first being struck by her potential. But when they did team up, he exerted an enormous influence over her and it seems reasonable to accept her own estimate that he played a crucial part in her rise to a position of being for several years the world's top model.

Lesley Hornby was born in 1949 into an entirely different family background, not working class as was often said, but suburban lower middle class. Her father's job (he was a master craftsman from Bolton) was in essence working class, but his post-war employment at the MGM studios in Boreham Wood gave him rather higher status and income (contrary to Marxist nonsense the middle classes recruit from a wide range of backgrounds, and lower middle class and working class are often close). The family owned their own house in the quintessentially lower middle-class suburb of Neasden, and they had a car. Lesley's mother had come from a poor background and had worked as a shop assistant in Woolworth's; she had been a most attractive woman (she got engaged four times). Not being able to afford make-up, she used to put soot from the fireplace round her eyes, and always pinched her cheeks before entering a room (the way in which beautiful women sometimes had to live through their beautiful daughters – or sons! – is a topic worthy of further study). Twiggy – she was not called this in her childhood although, contrary to what is often said, she acquired this nickname before being launched as a model – was much more integrally involved in the sixties youth revolution than Shrimpton, making her own dresses in order to conform to the style of her peer group. She claims that she 'really hated what I looked like as teenager ... In all these pictures of me at around twelve I am wearing a brassière with Kleenex stuffed in'.[25] Nonetheless, such were her neat figure and sweetly perfect looks that several people thought that she was, or ought to be, a model.

In March 1965, when she was fifteen and a half, and still at school, she met Nigel John Davies, or Justin de Villeneuve, as he was already calling himself. He was twenty-five and came from an incontrovertibly working-class family. Britain remained very much a society divided up by social class, but it was a consequence of the welfare and educational reforms of the 1940s that a kind of classless group was formed of tough, independent-minded, young individuals, taking jobs on the fringes or in the interstices of the class structure – general building and decorating, antique dealing, hairdressing, bouncing at clubs, pop music (inevitably), photography, and often on the edges of the law. Justin de Villeneuve had led a tough, colourful and sometimes semi–villainous life. At the time of his meeting with Twiggy he was working on an antique stall with Graham Morris-Jones, with whom he also had a partnership in interior decoration. Villeneuve's rise obviously owed much to his personality, intelligence and guts; but, arguably, the particular roles he filled were (another case to be noted in passing) dependent on his great natural beauty. Of his partnership with Morris-Jones he says: 'He was an architect, he did the jobs, and I was the front man, I would talk the deal and wear the nice clothes. I always looked smart. First impressions are important'.[26] Twiggy met Justin at the hairdressers where his brother Tony was working. Twiggy's reaction was: 'I thought he was lovely. Everyone liked him – everyone always does.' Justin's reactions: 'There was this lovely little girl, so tiny and so beautiful. She was breathtaking.' These developments show the force of contingency – as well as that of human beauty – in history.

It happened that brother Tony had a friend who dabbled in photography, and Twiggy was taken down to Wimbledon Common to pose for a few shots. Villeneuve claimed (admittedly much later, but there is no reason to doubt the testimony): 'When I saw her being photographed on Wimbledon Common that day, that was the moment I knew I would crack it ... Twiggy just had something about her that was absolutely right'.[27] It will be observed that Villeneuve's reactions were utterly self-centred, entirely oriented towards his own promotion, just like the calculations of the roué Du Barry in eighteenth-century Paris. He was not looking at Twiggy as a sex object for his personal gratification but as someone with a marketable value that could make his own fortune. It was actually quite independently of Villeneuve that, while Twiggy was buying herself an old fur, a photographer – seeing her as she looked before there was ever any question of her being 'constructed' into a public figure – took a picture of her for an article in *London Look* about young girls wearing old clothes. Photographer Michael Molyneux, to whom Twiggy was introduced by Villeneueve, expressed a view shared by most who met her: 'She's got a lovely face, she could have a chance'. However, the wisdom of the day was that a model must be at least five foot seven tall, with not less than a thirty-three-inch hip. On the other hand, the rage of the times was for youth, the trend in fashion towards the sort of clothes which perfectly suited Twiggy, and which, indeed, she herself was adept at making. Maybe an element of artifice and grooming did help resolve the impasse. Twiggy had an eight-hour session at exclusive hairdressers Leonard's, the time being largely taken up with repeated drying out, to see if the very, very short style being designed for her was exactly right. It was, as Villeneuve recorded:

> She really looked extraordinary when she emerged at the end of that day. I had always thought her head was the most wonderful shape, but now her hair was cut so cleverly to show the shape – she was an amazing sight. All the clients at Leonard's just turned and gasped. There was this little cockney girl in a little white gown, with her long neck and her huge, huge eyes – she looked like a fawn. She looked like Bambi: I knew then that she really was going to make it.[28]

She did. The *Daily Express* hailed 'the face of '66 – Twiggy the Cockney kid with the face to launch a thousand shops and she's only sixteen'. A successful visit to Paris, and a stupendous one to the United States followed. The witty and the jealous laid great emphasis on her alleged skinniness and absence of breasts. The American line was: 'From the neck down, forget it'; the funnier, but scarcely more tasteful English one, 'Forget Oxfam. Feed Twiggy'.[29] It has been argued that somehow, by commercial chicanery and deliberate contrivance, men were led to switch from loving big breasts to loving none at all. Actually, Twiggy, with her thirty-one-inch bust, had small, but perfectly proportioned breasts; and, as we have seen, girlish breasts have always been very highly rated.

Without their looks, Shrimpton and Twiggy would have been nowhere; with Twiggy beauty lifted her out of her class into fabulous fame and riches. This process is particularly evident among the most famous male celebrities of the day, including David Bailey, and such actors as Terence Stamp, David Hemmings, Michael Caine and Sean Connery, all from solidly working-class backgrounds. Important ingredients in their successes were talent and the opportunities offered by the current cultural context, but the inescapable conclusion is that personal beauty now operated as a characteristic which could out-trump the old imperatives of class. An even more important conclusion is that, because these highly socially mobile and successful males were in fact personally beautiful, beauty became closely identified with success, as a necessary, or at least likely, component of it.

As with Monroe, Presley and Twiggy, special attention must be given to the pop group the Beatles, three working-class lads, and one lower middle-class one (John Lennon). From the time of their two stunningly successful American tours in 1964, the Beatles were international figures of the first order, soon conquering all of Europe.[30] An American female student who saw them on tour commented: 'It was really fun to watch them. At first I couldn't tell them apart ... They were cute; they were charming; they were clever; they were talented ... They had different characters. Like John, the strong, sort of satirical, and then, of course, Paul, the cutest one'.[31] 'Cute' is another word in the everyday and inevitably flexible vocabulary, which includes 'pretty', 'lovely', 'handsome' and 'good-looking' ; one relies on the context to decide if what is really meant is 'beautiful'. This girl had got it right (photographs of the group, not to mention film, are legion): Paul McCartney was uniquely beautiful; George Harrison was darkly beautiful in a rather conventional way; John Lennon was personable and sensitive looking; Ringo Starr, who had been specially recruited into the original group as a brilliant drummer, was less well favoured. But Ringo sat at the back, and collectively the Beatles presented an appearance of youthful good looks and charm in which the sexuality was not too stridently stressed. The Beatle haircut, not short back and sides, and not long and Italianate, but a clean-looking mop which linked them together in a collective image, was a real innovation. Later in the decade, the Beatles switched to the hippy, long-haired image. The essence here is that a great deal of attention was concentrated on their appearance. A particular 'look' taken after some famous and beautiful female had long been known; but the idea of a male, Beatle look was relatively new. It testifies to the way in which masculine appearance was now becoming almost as relevant a consideration as feminine appearance. Pop groups of all types, travelling around the country and from country to country, often attracting enormous audiences, and also appearing on television, offered standards of male appearance with which the large number of watching females could compare the boys known to them.

It was actually in Portugal that the footballer George Best, born in the slums of Belfast, was christened the 'Footballing Beatle'. But many of the assessments of him in England saw him in exactly that way, as a handsome, sexy mass entertainer, with a particular appeal for youth, and above all female youth. In a reference to Pelé, the incredibly brilliant but far from beautiful Brazilian star who dominated the footballing scene in these years, Best remarked: 'If I'd been born ugly you would never have heard of Pelé. I don't mean that women weakened me or anything like that, I simply mean that without them I might have concentrated more on the game and therefore lasted longer in the game'.[32] Here Best is, as it were, presenting himself as the young Lloyd George of football, so attractive to women as to be running the risk of being distracted from his main task in hand. Shortly he was to become the Duke of Monmouth or Marquis de Cinq-Mars of his profession: his career collapsed into disgrace and ignominy as he succumbed to drink, womanising, and illusions as to his invincibility. However, though he ceased to be a footballer, he remained something of a celebrity. In that he made a substantial, though by twenty-first century standards modest, income from merchandising and commercial endorsements, he was the forerunner of the multi-million pound footballing celebrities of forty years later. The point again is the association between success, or, more accurately in this case, the combination of celebrity and notoriety, and good looks. Best would not have become the only true pop superstar of football in that remote era without 'it', that inextricably bonded package of looks and sexuality.

One other sportsman of the sixties commands attention. The black American Cassius Clay was one of the greatest heavyweight boxers of all time, remarkably lithe and agile. He was also witty and voluble. He became an activist on behalf of the Black Muslim movement, taking the name Muhammad Ali. He said of himself that he was 'the greatest', and proved it over and over again; he also said, and this is the critical issue here, that he was 'the prettiest'.[33] This was also true. Muhammad Ali was yet another example of much publicised male celebrity and male beauty appearing as two sides of the same coin. The consequence was to put a premium on male good looks. Most men did not have the looks of Terence Stamp, David Bailey, George Best or Muhammad Ali, and almost none had their talent; but, as opportunities expanded in all the ramifications of advertising, pop culture and public relations, those who did have the appearance of a Poitier or a Connery, a Presley or a Caine stood in line for at least modest advancement.

The honesty and clarity fostered by the Cultural Revolution, the recognition of the bare realities of beauty, and of the lack of it, were symbolised in the 1972 film *The Way We Were*, which may fruitfully be compared with Marty. Movie star Robert Redford was a top box-office attraction, universally recognised as the epitome of one type of male beauty (there is a cross-reference to him as the ultimate in masculine desirability in another film, *Alice Doesn't Live Here Any More*). Barbra Streisand had a wondrous singing voice but less than harmonious features, including a too-prominent nose. Her first great Broadway success *Funny Girl* (which became an Academy Award-winning film) opened with the chorus singing, 'If a Girl Isn't Pretty'; in one of her song hits she lamented 'Nobody Makes a Pass at Me'. No longer was it an unassailable convention that a successful female star must also be beautiful. In *The Way We Were*, Hubble Gardner (Redford) is a smooth, conservative, all-American college boy; Katie Morasky (Streisand) is at the same college in the 1930s, President of the Young Communist League, a pacifist, and anti-Fascist activist. Hubble is an oarsman and athlete, and always has a gorgeous coed on his arm; Katie persuades a large gathering of students to take the Peace Pledge. She tells him that he is 'decadent and disgusting', yet the film pointedly shows us that she finds it difficult to take her eyes off him. He is the model of the White Anglo-Saxon Protestant, always smiling, to whom everything comes easily (at college he sells a short story, and shortly afterwards a novel; he is invited to Hollywood); she is Jewish, intense and serious, ill at ease in the social world of the conservative rich. Unlike Clara in *Marty*, she is no passive wallflower; and, of course, unlike Betsy Blair, Streisand looks the part.

She gets a job as an assistant radio producer (the opening sequence of the film), goes to a nightclub, and sees him there, now a Second World War sailor, drunkenly asleep. A flashback establishes the background points about their college days; then, in the next sequence, she takes him home and, as the phrase might be, were the sexes reversed, 'takes advantage of him'. An edgy, difficult, though obviously deeply felt relationship begins. On one occasion when they are apart she phones him at night and begs him to come over to her, promising in a characteristic sixties-and-after role reversal, 'not to touch him'. There follows an absolutely central passage of dialogue. 'It's because I'm not attractive enough, isn't it?' He does not reply to this, and after a pause she continues: 'I'm not fishing ... I know I'm attractive ... sort of ...' There's a further pause. 'I'm not attractive ... I'm not attractive in the right way ... am I?' He still makes no response. 'I don't have the right style for you ... do I?' Still no response and she adds: 'You're my friend'. Now he comes in. 'No ... you don't have the right style'. 'I'll change', she responds. Then, moments later: 'Why can't I have you?' He says nothing about looks, but responds: 'Because you push too hard.' He adds, 'You expect too much.' To this she replies, 'But look what I've got', and it is clear that by this she means such a beautiful sex object as him. They marry and live together for a time in the Hollywood of the McCarthy era. They separate and then, in the final sequence of the film, bump into each other again some years later in New York, where she is now a Ban the Bomb activist. He is with a beautiful woman; she is no longer straightening her hair.

Films apart, evidence of the critical change in the way personal appearance was being recorded and evaluated is to be found in three main areas: the empirical studies carried out by university psychology and sociology departments; the guides to grooming which flourished still more than ever before; and the worlds of business and political life. The academic orthodoxy of the 1950s was that embodied in Erving Goffman's 'matching hypothesis', that is that in contemplating marriage a plain person will choose another plain person, a slightly more attractive person a slightly more attractive person, and so on; in other words, that, in marriage choices, levels of attractiveness will exactly match.[34] A massive challenge to this comforting fairy tale was mounted through an experiment whose results were published in 1966 as 'Importance of physical attractiveness in dating behavior'.[35] The experiment sounds fun for those who organised it; it was obviously fun for some of the subjects and presumably quite painful for others. College freshmen (and women) were invited to buy tickets for what was billed as a 'computer dance', that is a dance where they would be paired with an ideal partner selected by computer. In fact the students were secretly rated in advance on personality, intelligence and social skill, and then also, as they purchased their tickets, on physical attractiveness. The students were then paired on a random basis, save that great pains were taken to avoid the solecism of having a short man dancing with a tall woman. Half way through the dance the students filled in questionnaires relating to how much the subject liked his or her partner and whether he or she would like to continue the relationship. Follow-up interviews four to six months later established whether or not the relationships had indeed been continued. The conclusion was clear: the only apparent determinant of how much each student liked his or her partner, how much he or she wanted to see the partner again, and how often they did in fact see each other, was how physically attractive the partner was. The more physically attractive the partner, the more he or she was liked.[36]

Attempts to find additional factors which might possibly predict attraction were not successful; for example, students with exceptional social skills and intelligence levels were not liked any better than those with lower levels. Nevertheless, the correlation between physical attractiveness and liking was not perfect: a perfect correlation would be represented by the figure 1; in fact it came at .78 for men and .69 for women. The most judicious summing-up would be that, in the particular conditions of this experiment, physical attractiveness quite clearly was the key element for both men and women, but in slightly lesser degree (of the order 9 per cent) for women than for men. A critical point about the 'computer dance' experiment was that the subjects were not constrained by the pressures and inhibitions of real life and so could reveal their inmost inclinations. Subsequent researchers stressed that the computer dance situation minimised, or indeed practically obliterated, the risks of rejection – those who by chance secured partners more attractive than themselves were 'assured not only of social contact, but of the fruits of social courtesy norms for the duration of the dance'.[37] In addition, 'those who had achieved their ideal goal of a physically attractive partner may have shown more interest in *retaining* it than they might have shown in trying to *attain* it initially'.[38] Two experiments were conducted to see whether the matching principle might reassert itself if the individual were required actively to *choose* a partner, rather than simply respond to one already laid on, and to discover what the effects would be if the possibility of rejection by a desirable partner were emphasised. The conclusion was still that physically attractive partners were markedly preferred by everyone, women as much as men, but that *within* this general trend it was apparent that men and women of lesser attractiveness did tend to choose less attractive partners than did the highly attractive students.[39] Further experiments confirmed that men generally preferred to date the most physically attractive women, but that this was most pronounced when they were assured of acceptance; subjects who were not thus guaranteed believed that the highly physically attractive women would be significantly less likely to want to date them than would be the moderately attractive or the unattractive women.[40] In the cold, calculating prose of social psychology:

> As in any bargaining situation the participants in the dating game have to learn the range of outcomes available to them. Being turned down or never asked for a date is embarrassing and frustrating, and the less attractive individuals, in order to avoid further frustration, possibly learn to stop trying for the most desirable and unavailable dates.[41]

A third type of experiment examined people who were already committed to genuine real-life relationships, engaged or going steady. Here it was found that people of relatively similar levels of attractiveness did indeed tend to associate with each other, with such other factors as attitude similarity and role compatibility coming fully into play. In the icy jargon:

> The results indicate that physical attractiveness, both as subjectively experienced and objectively measured, operates in accordance with exchange-market rules. Individuals with equal market value for physical attractiveness are more likely to associate in an intimate relationship such as premarital engagement than individuals with disparate values.[42]

It is not unknown for academics to misunderstand or misrepresent their own results. The group who had conducted the original, brilliant computer dance experiment now came up with a claim which had the right touch of politically correct cynicism, 'What is beautiful is good'.[43] Sixty students, thirty males and thirty females, had been asked to predict the personality and life chances of persons represented to them in photographs. The researchers had prepared twelve sets of three pictures, half of women of different levels of physical attractiveness, half of men of different levels of physical attractiveness. Half of the mixed group were given female photographs to respond to, half male photographs; that is to say, some of the subjects were rating people of the opposite sex, some people of their own sex. The subjects were told that the purpose of the study was to compare their ability, as untrained college students, to make accurate predictions, compared with that of trained graduates. The experiment unambiguously showed that both male and female students, regardless of whether they were responding to male or female photographs, assumed that physically attractive persons possessed more socially desirable personalities than unattractive ones, and predicted that their lives would be happier and more successful in both the social and professional sphere. This, of course, was entirely a matter of perceptions; and the students perceived the beautiful to be, not '*good*', but as socially acceptable and likely to be *successful* in all aspects of life. That is the modern view: beauty has market, not moral, value. A person can be very beautiful and very bad; and a person can be very good and very ugly.

Some studies simply concentrated on the long-held suspicion that, in a male-dominated world, beautiful female students were likely to have advantages over less beautiful ones. An investigation of the sixties indicated that even in large classes where it was very difficult for the instructor to know students individually, beautiful girls tended to get the benefit of the doubt in the grading of papers, and suggested that this was because their names and faces stuck in the minds of instructors. In a more systematic experiment, reported in 1974, male college students were given either a notably well written essay or a notably badly written one to evaluate, both supposedly written by female students: one third of the essays of both types had a photo of an attractive girl attached to it, as the alleged author of the essay, one third had no photo, and one third had the photograph of an unattractive girl attached.

> The subjects who read the good essay evaluated the writer and her work more favourably than the subjects who read the poor essay. The subjects also evaluated the writer and her work most favourably when she was attractive, least when she was unattractive and intermediate when her appearance was unknown. The impact of the writer's attractiveness on the evaluation of her and her work was most pronounced when the 'objective' quality of her work was relatively poor.[44]

Real academic quality, irrespective of looks, was recognised; but down at the bottom of the scale, where the essay was in fact rather bad, beautiful girls got compensation, while others did not. In all of these academic exercises two features stood out. First they were based on the premise that everyone involved can make, and will accept, distinctions between the beautiful (the 'very attractive') and the lesser levels of attractiveness (that is, the modern conception of beauty in the eyes of *all* beholders). Secondly, beauty, in a cool and dispassionate way far removed from the heated confusions of traditional discourse, is clearly recognised as a characteristic in itself possessed of high value.

In 'beauty' or, rather, grooming guides, the great change of the sixties is that all traces of agonising and moralising disappeared. Their writers simply plunged straight in, taking it for granted that for a woman (to stick with them for a moment) nothing is more natural and sensible than having a preoccupation with her own personal appearance. Some go as far as to insist – rightly, in the light of the other developments we have been discussing – that a good personal appearance is essential for social and business success; others lay as much emphasis on the notion that making-up or dressing up is fun, the sort of fun every woman will instinctively want to indulge in. Much is made of the relationship between a good appearance and sexiness; sex is in itself a good thing, fun like making-up, and the relationship between sex and personal appearance is openly acknowledged.[45] Great stress is placed on health and fitness, dieting and slimming, not in order to achieve an artificial appearance but in order to give natural qualities the best opportunity of shining through. A greater variety than ever before of cosmetics and other aids to beauty was now available, generally marketed with greater restraint, accuracy and supporting information.[46] There is some recognition of the limits of what can be achieved by artifice, with such qualities as 'poise', 'personality' and 'charm', which can be achieved by skill and effort, recognised as not being quite the same as natural beauty (though, as a generic term in magazines and guides, 'beauty' still signifies self-presentation, grooming, make-up and fashion).[47] Cosmetic surgery is now just beginning to come seriously into the reckoning.[48] Brutal though it is to say it, this involved honest (though not necessarily desirable) acceptance that beauty, far from being a matter of surface tweaking, plucking and painting, is a matter of bone structure and distribution of flesh. Slim legs and neat bottoms have always been thought desirable, but, since for most centuries these were scarcely on view, not a great deal of attention was given to them. Sixties styles did focus attention on beautiful legs and girlish posteriors, and therefore, of course, on their opposites; hence, in particular, treatment for the condition which

French medical cosmeticians defined as 'cellulite', though other medical men denied its existence.[49]

The tonnage of 'beauty' materials aimed at women continued to outweigh by far that aimed at men, yet the cultural revolution did bring significant changes, most obvious in the grooming and fashion articles and guides specifically aimed at men. Two major aspects of a man's life, it is argued, require him to pay great attention to his personal appearance: his sexual, and his business and professional activities.[50] A man's appeal, according to one French manual, no longer depends solely upon his intellectual, financial and social attributes. A man conscious that he has made the most of his appearance, it continues, who is relaxed and lively, in good health and attractive, will easily triumph over one who is tired, fat or has obvious physical flaws;[51] if he is confident in his own appearance he will open many doors and many hearts.[52]

We have noted the occupations where beauty could stand a male in good stead. By the sixties, service itself was no longer a major source of employment (though servants with the right appearance were more highly prized than ever by those who could afford them), but service trades were expanding in all directions. The most obvious new occupation was that of male model – Catherine Harlé's agency in Paris started taking on male models in 1957;[53] more critically, the whole pop, fashion, media, agenting, entrepreneurial, public relations world was pervaded by an atmosphere which put a premium on good appearance. Formerly the Chief of Protocol at the White House had tended to be a venerable type, strong on stuffiness, skilled in diplomacy: the new thirty-six-year-old incumbent of 1965, together with his good-looking wife, formed an attractive team, looking, *Life* reported, 'like the former college prom queen and football captain at a five-year class reunion'.[54] Even in the orthodox business world appearance was counting for more and more, a summary of the situation as it existed at the end of the decade being set out in an elaborate French textbook *Professional Success*, which drew mainly on American experience:

> For very many years, in business, little value was accorded to self-presentation, demeanour and appearance in general. However, modern companies have completely revised their outlook on this point and they attach growing importance to the physical appearance of their executives.[55]

No doubt being personable was more crucial than being truly beautiful; but at the same time special opportunities were opening up for the latter.

Obviously there were very many jobs where other qualities were more vital than good looks, and very many ill-favoured men continued to hold positions of power and responsibility. Job opportunities, many of them not specially dependent on a beautiful appearance, were continuing to expand for women. But it was very clear that, even more exclusively than with men, the service, media and public relations posts demanded beauty: two areas of employment which, as feminist attitudes strengthened through the seventies, drew hostile comment for their evident assumption that only beautiful women need apply were those of television presenters – Barbara Walters, the USA's most famous female presenter had briefly been a model – and 'air hostesses' (as the term was in the sixties). For a woman to achieve a senior position anywhere outside of traditional female professions (such as hospital care), and a position of real power anywhere, was still most unusual. What part looks played in the careers of the few who did single themselves out is a subject awaiting further research. I simply note that the two leading women in the British Labour government of 1964–70, Jennie Lee and Barbara Castle, the Labour member of parliament who became the first female Speaker of the House of Commons (Betty Boothroyd), and the first woman University Dean (at Brest in 1968) in France, and subsequently, in 1976, Minister for Universities, Alice Saunier-Seité, were all reputed considerable beauties in their day. Barbara Castle was distinctly ill at ease in company, a dreadful handicap in a politician, but it seems that it was the confidence her good looks gave her which enabled her to ride this out: 'Her appearance was her carapace, her defence against a world in which she did not feel quite comfortable', in the brilliant perception of her biographer, Anne Perkins. Betty Boothoyd, briefly a show dancer, and pretty rather than beautiful, was affable and full of bounce, but had to suffer repeated election defeats before finally making it to the Commons: I suspect that her tough-skinned perseverance owed much to her confidence in her looks.[56] The general conclusion, backed by the recent research in social psychology, discussed in chapters 1 and 10, is that the trend towards the high rating of beauty in both men and women (a kind of rough equality, at least, between the sexes) was eventually stronger than the original

feminist hostility to women being judged on their looks (harder to
maintain when men also were being judged in this way). Few voices
were raised on behalf of ugly men; there were still plenty of them
around – as is evident as we finally focus again on American presidential politics.

When, in the late summer of 1959, it appeared that John F. Kennedy
might beat Hubert Humphrey for the Democratic presidential nomination, the attention of the media, in the traditional way, was focused
entirely on Kennedy's beautiful wife, Jackie.[57] As it happened, Kennedy's
rival, like many politicians before and since, was no impressive example
of male pulchritude. As historian W. L. O'Neill wrote of Humphrey a
decade later, when the days of discreet silence about the harsh facts of
personal appearance were truly over: 'He was overweight, and with his
big balding dome, square little chin, and rat-trap mouth offered a rather
comic appearance'.[58] Kennedy's youthful good looks were at the time
thought by the professionals to be a disadvantage, signifying nothing
other than inexperience.[59] Only with the first televised encounter
between Kennedy and the Republican presidential candidate, Richard
M. Nixon, did the notion of the special appeal of good looks begin to be
canvassed[60] (Nixon may fairly be described as 'unprepossessing'). Yet,
even at the time of the new President's first visit to Canada most of the
attention remained on the beauty of the presidential consort; however,
a Canadian spectator was reported as saying of Kennedy 'He's just a living doll!'[61] Kennedy's victory, and his frequent, and energetic
appearances thereafter in the public eye helped to ratify the association,
to which the other trends we have noted were favourable, between
beauty and success, and Kennedy himself, more particularly after his
assassination, became a metaphor for that success.

In May 1965 *Life* put on its cover John Lindsay, the Republican
aspirant to the mayorship of New York. The article inside declared:

> With youthful verve and the long-legged grace of a heron, John Vliet Lind-
> say, six foot three inches tall, strode into the race for Mayor of New York
> and Republicans all over the country broke into ear-to-ear smiles ...
> Lindsay is 43 years old and possesses enormous personal charm ...
> Women surround him quickly. Their eyes light up and they try to prolong
> his handshake, a reaction that inevitably reminds many of Jack Kennedy's
> campaign days.[62]

Within less than a year, the spotlight was on a candidate, also Republican, for the governorship of California:

> The speaker stands tall on the rostrum ... Across the twenty feet that separate the dais from the first row of tables he looks almost twenty years younger than the fifty four he is ... His face is tanned, his smile dazzling ... He looks strong and youthful and vigorous. He has that new, clean, young look in American politics – the charisma of a John F. Kennedy, a John Lindsay ...[63]

The candidate was the former actor and television presenter, Ronald Reagan.

Reagan was shortly to win the governorship against the Democratic incumbent Edmund G. Brown, leaving Brown to complain bitterly about 'two-dimensional politics', 'packaged politics' and the evil influences of television: in doing so he pinned down that in his appearance (supported by his voice) Reagan had an asset of great value:

> For two-dimensional politics, Reagan ... is blessed with surface features that are immediately appealing: a resonant voice with a tone of natural sincerity and just the right touch of boyishness, a hairline as unmoving as the Maginot Line, and a ruggedly handsome face that is neither unusual enough to jar the viewer nor so deeply wrinkled that it can't be smoothed out with make-up. He will be sixty – the same age as Humphrey – but most Californians would probably guess, on the basis of *appearance*, that he is ten to fifteen years younger ...[64]

The association of Reagan with Kennedy many seem odd, perhaps even offensive. But Kennedy, here, is simply a metaphor for beauty as an autonomous characteristic which, independent of political philosophies, has political value. It may be undesirable that looks should have this value; or it may in fact be an advantage that looks be honestly scrutinised, as a prelude to separating them out from more worthwhile qualities such as integrity or wisdom. Commercialism, misrepresentation, two-dimensional politics and the meretricious packaging of just about everything were inescapable facets of sixties society. Yet there was an admirable honesty, too, in facing up more squarely than ever before to the facts of natural physical endowment (which, by definition, is *not* packaged). To medieval man deformity or disability was a sign of evil; in more recent centuries they were matters to be politely ignored. It was, in fact, at the very end of the sixties that governments instituted the policies that have resulted in special, and quite explicitly advertised, facilities for the disabled.[65]

10

A Gift from the Genes

Little, shy, ten-year-old Fanny Price comes to stay at luxurious Mansfield Park as a much put-upon poor relation. Years later, while her uncle, Sir Thomas Bertram, is on an extended visit to his plantations in Antigua, she blossoms into a very pretty young woman; on his return Sir Thomas is captivated by Fanny's looks. His son Edmund, with whom she is secretly in love, has always been kind to her, but has never been given to paying her compliments. If she wants these, he tells her, she must go to her uncle, warning her that these will be 'chiefly on your person'; she 'must put up with it, and trust to his seeing as much beauty of mind in time'. Fanny and Edmund are two of Jane Austen's most virtuous characters, and both esteem 'beauty of mind' above 'beauty of person'. The point is that Austen never confuses the two; she was, indeed, alive at all times to the power of personal appearance, as against moral or mental qualities. In the same novel James Rushworth is lured by Maria Bertram's beauty into his disastrous marriage with her; Edmund himself is so besotted with Mary Crawford's beauty that he has been pursuing her instead of recognising the devotedness of Fanny (quietly pretty, perhaps, rather than stunningly beautiful). Viewers of the BBC's famous production of *Pride and Prejudice* may have wondered how on earth the calm and scholarly Mr Bennett came to marry the vulgar and foolish Mrs Bennett; it's simple – she was, Jane Austen tells us in the novel, very beautiful when young. Three of the four Bennett daughters are very attractive; Austen is completely ruthless in making it clear that not only is Mary, the odd one out, plain, she doesn't have any 'beauties of mind' either: she is silly, pedantic and boring, and has an embarrassingly awful singing voice.[1] My concern is not with fictional characters, but with how, in creating them, certain novelists express profound truths about the realities of physical beauty. As is well known,

Martin Chuzzlewit by Charles Dickens is about selfishness and
hypocrisy. It is also, unannounced, a story of how those who are beautiful do well compared with those who are not. The happy couples are
Martin ('a good-looking youth') and Mary, John and Ruth. Angelic, but
funny-looking, Tom Pinch ('one of those strange creatures who never
decline into an ancient appearance but look their oldest when they are
very young') is left on the shelf,[2] as is plain, sour-faced Charity Peck-
sniff, for whom is reserved the special humiliation of being left deserted
at the altar, in favour of her lovely sister, Mercy. We do not hear what
happens to Mercy, but since her power over men is made abundantly
clear, we may suspect that, with her evil husband conveniently dead, she
went on to find a nicer man.

We noted the suggestions of Nancy C. Baker and Wendy Steiner that
beauty should be defined in 'a more human sense', to include concern
for others, intelligence, enthusiasm, humour, self-confidence and being
worthy of love. And indeed there is an everyday tendency to run
together 'beauty of the person' and 'beauty of the mind', so that someone can be described as beautiful without in fact being physically very
attractive. This is a very understandable and, indeed, a very human tendency. But if, as a novelist, you are describing human society as it really
is, or, as a historian, you are trying to pin down the value human beauty
has in different eras, it is a very unhelpful one. If you are to compute
the power or the value of beauty, you have to be absolutely clear what
it is, and what it is not. Beauty, defined rigorously, is what Baker herself, in *The Beauty Trap*, recognises as having an independent existence,
using the words 'gorgeous face and figure'; beauty is not an omnibus
word mopping up everything complimentary we can find to say about
a person; if one wants to call someone intelligent, generous, dynamic,
humorous, one should praise each of these qualities by name, but not
confuse them with 'beauty', used in the vague, blanket way of that much
abused epithet, 'nice'. The problem, of course, is that, such is the desire
of almost everyone to be thought sexually attractive, people prefer to be
described as beautiful – the power and value of beauty is so universally
recognised that we all like to lay claim to a piece of it, despite, with most
of us, there being no validity in the claim.

Anyway, in setting out, as no one else has ever done, to assess the
influence on life chances and life opportunities of personal appearance,

as distinct from high status, great wealth, a good education, the psyche of a Rothschild or a Napoleon, education, or the gift of the gab, I was obliged to be rigorous in my definition of beauty. What I have shown is that beauty has always attracted special attention, and, if carefully managed, can bring fame and fortune. It can also bring tragedy; men, at the highest level, often being less adroit than women in exploiting their looks. The one safe generalisation is that exceptional beauty will always bring exceptional outcomes. However, throughout most of the past the power of beauty was overlayed by that of status and that of wealth, by fear of the lust which accompanied it, and by both the hard realities of, and the romanticised conventions about, the separate roles of men and women. When I embarked on my researches, using letters, diaries and memoirs, moral tracts and guides to fashion and beautification, as well as biographies, I accepted the conventional wisdom that standards of beauty vary from age to age, still paraded today in a galaxy of coffee-table books, in feminist treatises, in *The Oxford Companion to the Body*, and by such politically correct worthies as Professor Richard Evans.[3] It was only after doing the work, analysing the evidence, and sorting out my conclusions on paper, that I came to see that, relative to what does change significantly in human affairs – ideologies and institutions, economic and social organisation, and, say, the respective roles of men and women – beauty hardly changes at all, in the western societies I was studying, at any rate. According to Evans this conclusion is 'in the face of a mass of historical evidence'. That is simply not true – I have searched out the evidence, he has not. The 'evidence' handed down from one conventional work to another and, rather lamentably, appearing in *The Oxford Companion to the Body* is simply the familiar hackneyed old stuff about African tribes admiring fatness, South American ones lip plates, Burmese ones necks stretched and ringed like a snake (actually confusing standards of beauty with symbols of wealth and status), about sixteenth-century beauties having high foreheads (confusing beauty with fashion), and (of course!) about the voluptuous flesh paraded in the paintings of Rubens (in chapter 1 I cast doubt on Rubens as, or even setting out to be, an arbiter of early seventeenth-century taste in women, and, throughout, I have argued that just reading off from paintings and fashion plates, without consulting the full range of written sources, is shoddy scholarship).

My conclusion about beauty being a relative constant and a relative universal (though – this is most important – in many varieties) is supported by the latest social psychology research.[4] I am agnostic over the extreme Darwinian theorising and have reservations about some of the individual experiments in which photographs (of, let it be clear, a mix of Caucasians, Orientals, Africans, etc., etc.) are commented on by students (drawn from a similar ethnic mix). Taken together, however, they do strongly indicate that whatever our ethnic background we share the same preferences in picking out the truly beautiful – who come, to repeat, in many types, many ethnicities.[5] Psychologist Nancy C. Etcoff sums up with true scientific caution: 'the assumption that beauty is an arbitrary cultural convention may simply not be true'.[6] My historical researches (always open, of course, to challenge from further such research) suggest that it is very definitely not true. There is one other consideration: songs, sagas, poems speak to us directly across the centuries of the power and fascination of human beauty. Is it really believable that all that passion, all that joy, all that despair was lavished on what was merely a cultural construct? When it comes to people today sharing, whatever their culture or ethnicity, the same perceptions of beauty, it might be argued that common standards are imposed by ubiquitous western-dominated television. I've already recognised the significance of television, and of film before that, in bringing beautiful faces and bodies within the ken of the masses whose acquaintanceship with beauty had previously been severely circumscribed: the effect, however, was not to impose narrow standards, but to familiarise mass audiences with the plurality of beauty. We now know which faces, among a great range of ethnic types, people, themselves from a range of ethnic types, find beautiful: television, seeking always to appeal to larger and larger audiences, and, alas, to sell often disreputable products, responds by displaying the faces people want to see; it does not impose them.

Fashion, and the way it changes, is a fascinating topic. But changes in fashion, despite the morass of unexamined assumptions to the contrary, are not the same thing as changes in beauty. A beautiful woman or a beautiful man out of fashion will look a little odd, but will still be beautiful, will still arouse sexual interest; an ugly person in the height of fashion will still be ugly, and probably hard put to find a choice sexual partner. Personally I regard both make-up and fashion as perfectly legit-imate facets of human existence, but in this book my interest is confined to what they reveal about attitudes towards (not standards of) beauty, and, in particular, about possible differences between the sexes. Though fully aware of it, I have no interest in the continuing (and now rather dated) postmodernist fashion for study of 'The Body' and the way, allegedly, 'that we perceive our bodies through a culturally constructed body image that shapes what we see and experience'.[7] Recent feminist writing, however, no longer representing make-up and fashion as part of male oppression, is illuminating in explaining how women use them to 'express who they are', and are 'active, creative and skillful, experi-encing pleasure and competence in elaborating the self '.[8] It is a fact of contemporary life, from which deductions may or may not be drawn, that women, in the mass, spend more time on make-up and fashion than men do. Female make-up emphasises the eyes and the lips, both of which in women take up a bigger proportion of the face than they do in men; any trace of facial hair is strictly taboo. Large numbers of men dye their hair and many use creams and lotions to fight off ageing; there is increasing deployment of dry shavers in shaping the beard into orna-mental bits and pieces (very restrained, however, compared with the whiskery opulence of the Victorian era).

Possibly there is support here for the claim that what women perceive as beauty in men coincides with an apparent fitness for carrying out 'male' tasks, while what men perceive as beauty in women coincides with an apparent suitability for fulfilling 'female' roles.[9] But if beauty is unchanging, 'tasks' and 'roles' certainly are not: quite manifestly there are beautiful women athletes, beautiful women soldiers, certainly beau-tiful women company directors and beautiful women footballers, though it can be noted that while male tennis champions are often (not always) beautiful male specimens, female champions are infrequently beautiful women – back in the 1920s, Suzanne Lenglen, being young, female, French, and a slim symbol of the flapper age, was a media sen-sation, but she wasn't in fact specially good-looking.[10] Then there is some evidence that, while men always rate good looks in women as the quality they most desire, women are more flexible, more discriminating in being prepared to give weight to mental and moral qualities.[11] His-torically, as I have stressed throughout the book, women were particularly limited in their choices, and had to find men who would be 'protectors' and principal breadwinners, with only the exceptionally powerful, like Catherine the Great, going for young and beautiful bed-mates. The historical evidence demonstrates that as they have achieved greater economic and social freedom women have tended more and more to judge men as men have always judged women – that is on looks.

Placed on the silver screen, Scarlett O'Hara had to be beautiful and Vivien Leigh, we noted, certainly was that. Yet the opening words of Margaret Mitchell's novel actually were: 'Scarlett O'Hara was not beau-tiful, but men seldom realized it when caught by her charm ...'[12] What a gloriously encouraging start for thousands of readers, aware that they too were not beautiful! It is the age-old reassurance in the power, not just of cosmetics and dress sense, not just of 'beauty of mind', but, above all, of 'charm', of what used to known as 'feminine wiles'. It's all of a piece with the nonsense we have encountered once or twice about famously sexy women being 'not conventionally beautiful', or possessed of 'that indefinable quality sex appeal', about Harriette Wilson not being beautiful but able 'to persuade men that she was'. In most cases the women referred to actually were beautiful – for those able to see beyond the artificial and often snobbish dogma of their day. Men can be lured by qualities other than sheer beauty, and, in desperate straits, by simple availability, but they are not such fools as to see beauty where it does not exist. One can understand women, working so hard on their own appearance and sex appeal, wanting to believe in their appeal and, still more, in their own cunning. Here we have another myth which is fad-ing away under the searching lights of modern society, where women needn't waste their cunning on men, but can direct it to furthering their careers, and where no film or television producer would commission a less than beautiful Scarlett O'Hara, nor trust men (the millions in the audience) confronted with a less than beautiful actress 'not to realise it'.

So we return to the central theme of this book: the way in which, out of the old ambivalences and confusions about beauty, there emerged a modern attitude, a modern evaluation, in which the hallowed myths are ripped away, and in which beauty, in men as well as women, is recog-nised as an independent personal characteristic whose value rivals that conferred, traditionally, by status, or wealth, or, more recently, by education, or by some other marketable talent, in, say, music, or story-telling, or property development, or stock manipulation, or, to come bang up to date, football. Within the bedroom, beauty is the greatest aphrodisiac there is, a fact understood by the masses outside, for whom it is possessed of enormous vicarious sex appeal, which explains why it can command such high prices. Throughout most of history, women could only exploit their beauty through providing powerful men with sexual services; now that there are mass audiences, masses of customers and clients, all paying to enjoy sex appeal at a distance, provision of such services is no longer the essential precondition of success. This is a broad historical truth: in no way am I so silly as to claim that the casting couch, or its equivalent for, say, the young political researcher with major political ambitions, or the young executive with her eye on the boardroom, has totally disappeared. Nor am I going to deny the boom in an ever more imaginative and diversified sex industry, involving, say, female (carefully shaven) lap-dancers, male strippers frantically striving to hold up their erections, male prostitutes on home visits, whose vital statistics can be ascertained in advance, 'cut or uncut'. Of one 1960s sex worker we learn that he had 'the two necessary attributes that led him into male prostitution: good looks and an extraordinary physical endowment'.[13] But, on the whole, as women have rightly claimed the sexual freedoms which men formerly reserved for themselves, sexual activity, even within, as it were, the workplace, has become more of a lifestyle choice rather than a career obligation.

In western societies today the overwhelming majority enjoy moderate prosperity, or at least television sets and sound systems for playing pop music. They provide the basis upon which has grown a structure of sponsorships, icons, celebrities, bestsellerdom, blockbusterdom, high-rating television shows, public relations and spin, multi-ethnic purchasers, international audiences, popularity polls on almost everything, from new talent to old books. Grafted onto, and partially replacing, the old class system, is a new breed of super-rich, mostly drawing their vast incomes from the interconnected entertainment, fashion, communications, sport and service business. The opportunities to seize fame and fortune are considerable; so, commensurately, are the possibilities of failure and disappointment. Much is superficial, on the surface, as in the deference shown in the academic world to the self-promoting French darlings of intellectual fashion and, in the wider world, to the icons of pop and football. Beauty, as I have insisted throughout this book, *is* only skin deep, is only a surface characteristic. Where image is all-important, natural beauty is a specially valuable component – it comes without extra cost, and it is the human quality with the most powerful, the most immediate supercharge, being *the* instant visual aphrodisiac. All the more so where complete sexual freedom is effectively an organic law (within the sanctions imposed by death-dealing sexually transmitted diseases). As extreme feminist theory breaks down where pleasure rather than power is manifestly the male objective, extreme Darwinism breaks down where copulation, not procreation, is clearly the primal urge; and, indeed, where overeating, which *now* – whatever may have been the case with primitive man – has only terrible evolutionary consequences and is a major contemporary problem; and what about smoking, drinking and drug-taking – pleasurable, but surely not demanded by our genes? Let me make myself absolutely clear: beauty is most certainly a matter of basic genetic inheritance – a few have it, most don't. We all (most of us anyway), given a free run, seek out beauty (in others), respond priapically to it – that is certainly a basic instinct, but whether it has evolutionary benefits as distinct from – like drugs – providing short-term gratification, I am less sure (and, so what? – economy of explanation is what all historians, and all scientists, should go for).

The lure of fundamentalist belief systems (which probably *once* did have an evolutionary pay-off in ensuring the solidarity of the group) is still strong among human beings, as in Islam, oriental religions, the more exotic brands of Christianity, Marxism and postmodernism, but a key characteristic of the contemporary world is the dissolution of traditional beliefs, of old conventions and orthodoxies; many of the new faiths, indeed, are characterised by the way, however misguidedly, they challenge traditional thinking – radical feminism and radical postmodernism, for instance. Abroad in the world, very much as a consequence of the Cultural Revolution of the Long Sixties, there is an honesty, a frankness, a willingness to look at things as they are, despite PR, despite spin; there is never a perfect society, and historical trends, both desirable and undesirable, never go entirely in the same direction. All of the trends itemised in this paragraph have combined to confirm the modern evaluation of beauty, of beauty as nothing but itself, a physical, biological quality. 'Know thyself', is an age-old injunction. People today are more likely than ever before to know the truth about themselves, that they are not beautiful (never a completely cheering thought – but not the end of the world), and that the small minority that they clearly can see are beautiful are not specially good, not specially wicked, not specially stupid,[14] just bloody lucky. It is noteworthy that on television chat shows or when expressing themselves through interactive TV, women consistently state that their aspiration is to be 'sexy' (though to be beautiful is inevitably to be sexy, one can be sexy without being beautiful).

That, in a range of ordinary employment, there is, for men as much as women, a financial advantage to being good-looking, and a disadvantage to being plain or ugly, was established by empirical studies carried out in the 1990s, with the way being led by the two American National Bureau of Economic Research Working Papers, 'Beauty and the Labor Market' and 'The Economic Reality of the Beauty Myth' (both 1993), with the authors of the former following up with an article of the same title in the *American Economic Review* (1994). (The 'reality' of the 'Beauty Myth' was that, being realisable in hard cash, it was no myth, and certainly not invented by men, as Naomi Wolf had claimed; not a myth but, no doubt, deeply unfair, as life tends to be.) A decade of further work was summarised in a short article in the *Economist*, 'Pots of Promise', 24 May 2003. Earlier research had suggested that good looks tended to have beneficial results in terms of promotion for military cadets at West Point and that in business management tall males scooped the best salaries.[15]

Veronica Franco, Nell Gwyn, Madame Du Barry, Lady Hamilton – their successes were celebrated within very restricted circles; the *Grandes Horizontales* – they led their lavish lives outside mainstream society; beautiful men did sometimes do well out of their looks, but before Byron no man was openly recognised as owing part of his celebrity to his beauty, and Byron remained a unique figure. Rudolph Valentino and some of the Hollywood stars, male and female, came close to the contemporary position where mass appeal, celebrity and beauty are inextricably intertwined. Movies remained the essential vehicle, until joined by pop music (which, in an unprecedented way, became inescapably woven into contemporary culture, featuring, for example, in the most high-brow TV quizzes as well as the most low-brow), modelling and celebrity soccer. Among the transitional figures are Presley, McCartney, Shrimpton, Twiggy and Best; among their successors are Robbie Williams, Britney Spears, Kylie Minogue, Victoria Beckham (pop singers), Naomi Campbell, Kate Moss, Nick Kamen, Travis Fimmel (models), David Beckham (footballer), with a whole gallery of gorgeous film celebrities, Richard Gere, Brad Pitt, Jude Law, Ewan McGregor, Julia Roberts, Helena Bonham-Carter (the one 'maturely attractive', the other with, in sharp contrast, a 'babyish face'),[16] Catherine Zeta-Jones (old-fashioned seductress). Among the most striking facets of the way these celebrities are presented is the attention paid to their natural endowments, with the males being treated in a manner which had once been reserved for females. Nudity, or semi-nudity, has maximum impact, and maximum commercial value, when displayed in conjunction with a beautiful face. Perfect shape, perfect lovely face, and fundamental physical attributes were vital to actress Liz Hurley posing without visible means of support in her notorious minimalist 'safety-pin dress' styled by celebrity designer Gianni Versace, to Shila Tennant modelling the Chanel micro-bikini, and to 'Wonderbra girls', Eva Hertzigova and her successor Caprice Boulet;[17] David Beckham's transfer to Real Madrid was accompanied by a medical examination which allowed for a public airing of his pectorals (clearly heterosexual, he is also known as a 'gay icon'); gorgeous male supermodel Travis Fimmel filled his Calvin Klein briefs with manifest abundance,[18] while in the film *Boogie Nights* (1997), the actor Marc Wahlberg displayed a truly prodigious penis.

Only slightly less up-front were the polls to establish 'the sexiest man on earth' or 'the men women would most like to marry'; in one of the former run by women's magazine *Cosmopolitan*, Ewan McGregor, who had been seen full-frontally in the film *Trainspotting*, and who was sometimes known, suggestively, as 'Big Mac', came third, behind actors George Clooney and Keanu Reeves; in one of the latter McGregor came first ahead of actor Colin Firth and Clooney.[19] David Beckham was another regular number one in sexiest man polls. I make absolutely no hostile judgements here; indeed I celebrate the new openness and sense of equality of treatment between the sexes; furthermore I enthusiastically recognise the brilliance in their profession of all the actors mentioned here. Equally, the irreducible basis of the fame of David Beckham is the talent he has displayed as a footballer, with Manchester United, with England, with Real Madrid. But then, without the looks he could not have become a fashion icon; and as a fashion icon he changed his hair style and his dress as frequently as any female celebrity had been wont to do (and also – crucial differences will always remain – the arrangement of his facial hair). The male selling sex in the manner traditionally associated with the female was featured in the Richard Gere film *American Gigolo*, and, most obviously, in *Boogie Nights*. In *Bridget Jones's Diary* the two gorgeous characters are the men, played by Colin Firth and Hugh Grant – while Renée Zellweger, as Bridget, had to deliberately put on weight to play the less than beautiful Bridget, for whose delectation the two beauties disport themselves.

I have no wish to exaggerate the importance of beauty – if success only came to the beautiful, the world would quickly grind to a halt, there not being enough beautiful people to do all the things that need to be done. Politics, manifestly – one just has to look around, does not depend on pulchritude; and pop music is so omnipresent, so central to contemporary life, that those with talent, but no great beauty, can be successful. The outstanding example is mega-celebrity Madonna, a large part of whose appeal to girls was her demonstration that a woman could be bold, sexually predatory and immensely successful without being beautiful. In December 2003 the British Pop Idol competition (again conducted by popular poll – the winner being awarded a lucrative recording contract) was won by Michelle McManus; in commenting on her victory Michelle referred to adverse comments which had been made on her 'weight', and expressed the hope that she was opening the way for 'bigger girls' also to be judged entirely on the quality of their voices.[20] If a magnificent voice is what is wanted, then those with magnificent voices should be recognised, whatever their looks – as indeed some always have been even in the contemporary era. ('Whenever I First Saw Your Face', was a ravishing number by Roberta Flack, but whenever one first saw her face it was very far from ravishing.) If beauty is what is wanted (and, in the domain where fashion, looks and celebrity are inextricably intertwined and success depends on mass visual appeal, it *is* what is wanted), then fat is not beautiful, never has been and, I suspect, never will be. Most of us don't have ravishing voices, as most of us

are not (to resort to the two jocular but symbolic examples) rocket scientists or brain surgeons. Those with special gifts are lucky and should
do their best with them; there is no point those of us who are not beautiful complaining that those who are earn rewards that are not open to
us. Attacks on the slender, enticing, human appearance are as common,
and often as banal, as attacks on bottled mineral water. Young girls and
women starving themselves into illness and death is a tragedy and we
should do our best to prevent it – but not by pretending that every
shape and every configuration is beautiful in its own way. Young girls
and women desperately seeking a career in modelling when they simply
don't have the attributes for it is another tragedy, and what is needed is
more honesty and less comforting (for a time) illusion. The growing
emphasis on exercise and on healthy eating is one of the more desirable
customs of today, with 'feeling good' being conjoined to 'looking
good'. Overeating is far more prevalent than anorexia, and nearly as
dangerous. Salivate over the lovelies (male and female) on display all
around; by all means strive to look as *nearly* like them *as possible*, but,
as indeed most people in their moderately sensible and moderately contented way, do, bear the 'nearly' (yet also, 'so far!') and the 'as possible'
firmly in mind. Cosmetic surgery, as everyone knows, is now mega business. It has its uses and its abuses. I confine myself to repeating that its
prevalence confirms the perception that beauty is purely a physical matter, whose absence can only be remedied, if at all, by drastic physical
methods.

It is partly because we retain the power of rational thought that we
are in no danger of kalocracy – political rule by the beautiful. Let us
recall the fundamental facts: politicians do have to submit themselves
for approval to mass electorates; but to get into that position they have
to have been selected and approved by party bosses, bureaucrats, PR
men and spin doctors. Two rather contradictory aspects of the modern
evaluation of beauty then come into play. We know that good looks do
have a definite immediate appeal for the general public,[21] and we do
know that that appeal is more than ever convertible into votes in an age
when television takes the politician into every household; the party
bosses and PR men know this as well (image consultants, of course,
being employed to remedy what nature forgot). At the same time it is
part of the modern evaluation that beauty is not mistaken for what it

is not: intelligence, decency, integrity. Pushed to it we are just about able to recognise that a politician can be dishy *and* deeply deceitful. And ultimately in politics, competence is the quality which counts. The point is that a good appearance (including, in a man, height), short of evidence to the contrary, does initially suggest competence and inspire confidence. Good looks serve to enhance certain perceived personal qualities, ill-looks will often overemphasise perceived weaknesses. However distrusted eventually by large sections of his own electorate, President Bill Clinton in America came over as a friendly, all-smiling, decent, considerate, unpretentious guy, an impression greatly strengthened by his outstanding, all-American, boyish, good looks. Something of the same is true of British Prime Minister Tony Blair, whose looks are sweet rather than saturnine, who seems straightforward and human in television chat shows, and who is genuinely gracious to all, including political opponents.[22]

In projecting oneself as a nice guy, looks are an enormous help. On the other hand the two discarded men of recent British politics, Labour leader Neil Kinnock and Conservative leader William Hague, both had in personal appearance a touch of Hubert Humphrey, which served to compound their political miscalculations and irritating mannerisms.[23] What is different about today is the way in which personal appearance is openly discussed and recognised as a factor which should enter all calculations. One obvious victim of this was former Labour cabinet minister, Robin Cook: his resemblance to a garden gnome being widely commented on and cited as *one* reason for his not being a likely prime ministerial candidate.[24] Is California home of the future or of the fruit-cake? After Ronald Reagan (who, it may be noted, won the California Mr Atlas Body Beautiful competition in 1941), former body-builder, then film star, Arnold Schwarzenegger.[25] The body (and face) beautiful, have always had their fascination: that fascination is more explicit, and less concealed in moralistic mumbo-jumbo than ever before. Ordinary life goes on. What most people, polls indicate, look for in long-term relationships is not beauty but 'kindness'.[26] We are more open and more helpful in our treatment of the disabled than we used to be. But the disadvantaged, as well as the plain and the ugly, do suffer more than they should.[27] Some people speak of 'body fascism' and 'beauty fascism', and perhaps will apply that label to this book. 'Fascism' is a word which is as easy to abuse, as the truth is difficult to face. My faith is in facing up to the truth, as indeed certain novelists and critics continue to try to do, excellent examples being provided by the study, *Plain and Ugly Janes: The Rise of the Ugly Woman in Contemporary American Fiction* (New York, 2000), by Charlotte M. Wright.[28]

Let's face it. Say you're watching a programme like University Challenge – aren't you disappointed if among the drab-looking swots and wrinkled older students there isn't at least one bright (and beautiful) young thing? Say you're watching a television drama and congratulating it for its integrity in presenting leading characters who aren't any better looking than you or I – don't you begin to regret that there isn't just one smasher to lift your spirits and maybe initiate the tiniest fantasy? What a drag these Sunday supplements are – only just redeemed, don't you agree, by page after page of stylish lovelies of both sexes with which to titillate your libido? Whether that is so or not, I hope this book has held your attention, and made you think about your most cherished, most comforting beliefs. For the last time: the beautiful minority have always attracted special attention, though beauty could not compete with status and wealth, and was suspect for engendering lewdness. Today beauty, in men as well as women, has established itself as possessing high independent value. Compared with institutions, ideologies, economic and social systems, which undergo massive changes from age to age and culture to culture, it is relatively constant, relatively universal, but, as we increasingly appreciate as we shed old shibboleths and conventions, it comes in many varieties. It is a gift, like the gifts of musicianship, mathematical skill or kindness, so rare and prized that in ancient Rome (where standards of beauty were similar to our own, as we know from Roman paintings, notably those in the Vatican), the poet Ovid called it 'a gift from the gods'. In our secular, scientific age, we know it to be a gift from the genes.

Notes

Notes to Chapter 1: Fascination

1. Keats to Fanny Brawne, 8 July 1819, *The Letters of John Keats*, ed. Hyder Edward Rollins (Cambridge, Massachusetts, 1958), i, p. 403.
2. See in particular Harold Perkin, *The Rise of Professional Society: England, 1870–1950* (London, 1982).
3. Arthur Marwick, *Beauty in History: Society, Politics and Personal Appearance, c. 1500 to the Present* (London, 1988).
4. J. H. Lupton (ed.), *The Utopia of Sir Thomas More: in Latin from the Edition of March 1818, and in English from the first Edition of Ralph Robynson's Translation in 1551* (Oxford, 1895), ii, pp. 225–27, 232.
5. H. T. Finck, *Romantic Love and Personal Beauty* (New York, 1887), ii, pp. 187, 374–75.
6. Marcel Braunschvig, *La femme et la beauté* (Paris, 1919), p. 135. Much the same view is expressed by Theodore Zeldin, *France, 1848–1945*, ii (Oxford, 1977), p. 44.
7. Simone de Beauvoir, *Le Deuxième Sexe* (Paris, 1947), ii, p. 345.
8. J. O. Thompson (ed.), *Dr Salter of Tolleshunt D'Arcy: Diary and Reminiscences, 1849–1932* (London, 1933), 29 December 1859.
9. Lois W. Banner, *American Beauty* (New York, 1983; Chicago, 1984), p. 269.
10. Joanna Pitman, *On Blondes* (London, 2003).
11. Anton Chekhov, *Uncle Vanya* (1899), Act 3.
12. Sonnet 1: 'From fairest creatures we desire increase, / That thereby Beauty's rose might never die ...'
13. Elaine Scarry, *On Beauty and Being Just* (Princeton, New Jersey, 1999), p. 52.
14. Ibid., p. 4.
15. Stendhal (Henri Beyle), *De l'amour* (Paris, 1822; 1853 edn), pp. 33–34.
16. Voltaire, *Dictionnaire philosophique portatif* (1764), 'Beau, beauté', p. 47.
17. Georges Bataille, *Death and Sexuality: A Study of Eroticism and the Taboo* (New York, 1957), pp. 142–43.

18. Charles Darwin, *The Descent of Man and Selection in Relation to Sex* (London, 1871; revised and augmented edition, New York, 1879), pp. 573–87.

19. Marcel Braunschvig, *La femme et la beauté* (Paris, 1919), p. 221; Emile Bayard, *L'art de reconnaître: la beauté du corps humain* (Paris, 1926), p. 10; Bernard Bosanquet, 'The Aesthetic Theory of Ugliness', *Proceedings of the Aristotelian Society*, 1, no. 3 (1891), p. 36.

20. My arguments are to be found in my *The New Nature of History: Knowledge, Evidence, Language* (Basingstoke, 2001).

21. See Keith Roberts, *Rubens* (London, 1977), p. 3; and Marwick, *Beauty*, pp. 53–58.

22. Peter Paul Rubens, *Théorie de la figure humaine, considerée dans ses principes, soit en repos ou en mouvement, ouvrage traduit du Latin de Pierre-Paul Rubens* (Paris, 1773), pp. 1, 9.

23. Ibid., pp. 14–15.

24. Ibid., pp. 49–50.

25. Rubens to Pierre Dupuy, 15 July 1526, *The Letters of Peter Paul Rubens*, translated and edited by Ruth Saunders Magurn (Cambridge, Massachusetts, 1955), p. 136.

26. See Christopher White, *Rubens and his World* (London, 1962), p. 101.

27. Roberts, *Rubens*, p. 3.

28. Ibid., p. 4

29. *Economist*, 24 May 2003.

30. National Bureau of Economic Research, *Beauty and the Labor Market*, working paper no. 4518 (Cambridge, Massachusetts, 1993), abstract.

31. Naomi Wolf, *The Beauty Myth: How Images of Beauty are Used Against Women* (New York, 1992), pp. 2–4.

32. Ellen Zetzel Lambert, *The Face of Love: Feminism and the Beauty Question* (Boston, 1995), p. xi.

33. Wendy Steiner, *The Problem with Beauty* (London, 2001), p. 217.

34. Nancy C. Baker, *The Beauty Trap: How Every Woman Can Free Herself from It* (New York, 1984), p. 9.

35. Elaine Hatfield and Susan Sprecher, *Mirror, Mirror: The Importance of Looks in Everyday Life* (Albany, New York, 1986), pp. 303–6.

36. Ibid., p. 307.

Notes to Chapter 2: Plato, Augustine and Mrs Astell

1. Charles Perron, *Les Franc-Comtois: leur caractère national, leur moeurs, leur usages* (Besançon, 1892), p. 85.

2. See, generally, Anthony Andrewes, *Greek Society* (London, 1971);

K. J. Dover, *Greek Popular Morality in the Time of Plato and Aristotle* (London, 1974).

3. Plato, *Greater Hippias*, 287e. Throughout I use the accepted method of citation, common to all editions and translations. My English versions (I do not read Greek) are drawn from *The Dialogues of Plato Translated by Benjamin Jowett* (Oxford, 1871; 4th edition, revised, 1964), and J. S. Blackie, *On Beauty: Three Discourses ... with an Exposition of the Doctrine of the Beautiful According to Plato* (Edinburgh, 1858) – more the latter than the former.

4. *Greater Hippias*, 289b, 295c.

5. *Phaedras*, 250de, 251a.

6. K. J. Dover, *Greek Homosexuality* (London, 1978), pp. 12–13, 161 n. 11.

7. Plato, *Symposium*, 210, 211, 212a.

8. Plato, *Charmides*, 154de, 155de.

9. Dover, *Greek Homosexuality*, p. 115.

10. See the exhibits and supporting text in the Roman section of the Museum of London.

11. Saint Augustine, *Confessions*, iii, p. 16. Generally my references are to the *Encyclopaedia Britannica* translation, Saint Augustine, *The Confessions; The City of God; On Christian Doctrine* (Chicago, 1952, 1990), with occasional resort to other translations, e.g., *The City of God Against the Pagans*, edited and translated by R. W. Dyson (Cambridge, 1998); otherwise my references are taken from Carol Harrison, *Beauty and Revelation in the the Thought of Saint Augustine* (Oxford, 1992), and Kim Power, *Veiled Desire: Augustine's Writing on Women* (London, 1995).

12. *Confessions*, v, p. 30.

13. Ibid.

14. Saint Augustine, *De vera religione*, p. 3.

15. Ibid.

16. *The City of God*, xiv, p. 447.

17. Ibid., pp. 447–48.

18. Saint Augustine, *Contra Academicus*, ii, p. 6.

19. *The City of God*, xv, p. 22.

20. Walter C. Curry, *The Middle English Ideal of Personal Beauty* (Baltimore, 1916), p. 3.

21. Ibid., pp. 4–5.

22. Ibid., p. 3.

23. Cited in Georges Duby, *Le chevalier, la femme et le prêtre: le mariage dans la France féodale* (Paris, 1981), p. 18.

24. E. Rodocanachi, *La femme italienne a l'époque de la Renaissance* (Paris, 1907), p. 90.

25. Curry, *Middle English Ideal*, p. 7.

26. Ibid., p. 26.

27. 'Certayne Rewles of Phisnomy', from British Library, MS Sloan 213, fos 118v–121v, reprinted by M. A. Nanzakaoui, *Secretum Secretorum: Nine English Versions*, Early English Text Society (Oxford, 1977), i, pp. 10–17.

28. Curry, *Middle English Ideal*, p. 5.

29. In the Museo Correr, Venice, reproduced in Marwick, *Beauty*, p. 69.

30. Giovanni Marinelli, *Gli ornamenti delle donne: tratti delle scritture d'una reina greca* (Venice, 1562), p. iii.

31. Ibid., p. iii.

32. *Trois livres de l'embellissement et ornament du corps humain pris du latin de M. Iean Liebaut docteur médecin à Paris* (Paris, 1582), pp. 316–18; Marinelli, *Gli ornamenti*, iv, part 2.

33. *Trois Livres*, p. 318.

34. Ibid., p. 357.

35. Ibid., p. 432.

36. Gabriel de Minut, *De la beauté, discours divers ... voulans signifier, que ce qui est naturellement beau, est aussi naturellement bon* (Paris, 1587), pp. 210–12.

37. David de Flurance Rivault, *Art d'embellir* (Paris, 1608), i, fos 2–3.

38. Minut, *De la beauté*, p. 214.

39. Ibid., p. 213.

40. Ibid., pp. 255ff.

41. Ibid., pp. 261–62.

42. Ibid., p. 270.

43. Quoted in Jefferson Butler Fletcher, *The Relations of Beauty in Women and Other Essays on Platonic Love in Poetry and Society* (New York, 1911), p. 3.

44. A. G. Dickens, *The Age of Humanism and Reformation* (Englewood Cliffs, New Jersey, 1972), p. 125.

45. The original edition *Il libro de cortegiano del conte Baldesar Castiglione* (Venice, 1528) has no folio or page numbers, and this is also true of *The Book of the Courtier: From the Italian of Count Baldessare Castiglione Done into English by Sir Thomas Hoby* (London, 1561). My page references therefore are to the 1900 reprinting of the latter. I have some quibbles with George Bull, *The Book of the Courtier: Baldesar Castiglione* (London, 1977).

46. *The Courtier*, pp. 343, 348, 349.

47. Introduction, by Theodore Child, to the abbreviated English translation of Agnolo Firenzuola, *Dialogue on the Beauty of Women* (London, 1892).

48. Niccolò Franco, *Dialogo dove si ragiona delle bellezze* (Venice, 1542); Lodovico Domenichi, *La nobiltà delle donne* (Venice, 1549); Federigo Luigini, *Il libro della bella donna* (Venice, 1554; English translation, 1909); Niccolò Campani, *Bellezze della donna* (Venice, 1566).

49. 'I ritratti di Giovan Giorgio Trissino', in *Tutti le opere di Giovan Giorgio Trissino*, ii (Verona, 1729), pp. 269–77.

50. Agnolo Firenzuola, 'Dialogo delle bellezze delle donne', in *Prose di M. Agnolo Firenzuola Fiorentino* (Florence, 1540), fol. 75.

51. Castiglione, *The Courtier*, p. 216.

52. Firenzuola, *Dialogo*, fos 67–71.

53. Ibid., fol. 74.

54. Niccolò Franco, *Dialogo delle bellezze*, fol. 23.

55. Ibid., fol. 43.

56. Domenichi, *La nobiltà*, fol. 24.

57. Firenzuola, *Dialogo*, fol. 63.

58. Ibid., fol. 62.

59. Jean de La Bruyère, *Les caractères de Thréophaste traduits du grec: avecs les caractères et les moeurs de ce siècle* (Paris, 1688), p. 134.

60. Shakespeare, *As You Like It*, Act I, Scene 3.

61. Discussed further in Chapter 3

62. Rodocanachi, *La femme italienne à l'époque de la Renaissance*, p. 103.

63. Henry Fielding, *History of Tom Jones* (London, 1749), i, chapter 12.

64. Mary Astell, *Some Reflections on Marriage* (London, 1700), pp. 10, 13, 18, 19, 21.

Notes to Chapter 3: Kings and Concubines

1. Georges Montgredien, *Marion de Lorne et ses amours* (Paris, 1940), p. 186; Marie Dormoy, *La Vraie Marion de Lorne* (Paris, 1934), p. 25.

2. Alison Weir, *The Six Wives of Henry VIII* (London, 1991), p. 152.

3. Antonia Fraser, *The Six Wives of Henry VIII* (London, 1992), p. 94.

4. Quoted in Weir, *Six Wives*, p. 497. In general see *The Love Letters of Henry VIII: Edited with an Introduction and Comments by Henry Savage* (London, 1949).

5. See reproductions and comments in David Starkey, *Elizabeth: Apprenticeship* (London, 1992), pp. 31, 35, 67–68.

6. Weir, *Six Wives*, p. 82.

7. David Starkey, *Six Wives: The Queens of Henry VIII* (London, 2003), pp. 263, 564; Weir, *Six Wives*, pp. 151–52; Fraser, *Six Wives*, pp. 150–51.

8. Fraser, *Six Wives*, p. 268; Weir, *Six Wives*, p. 274.

9. Starkey, *Wives*, pp. 618–36.

10. Starkey, *Wives*, pp. 639–44. On Anne's appearance I tend to follow Mary Saaler, *Anne of Cleves: Fourth Wife of Henry VIII* (London, 1995).

11. Reproduced by Starkey, *Six Wives*, between pp. 564 and 565.

12. Starkey, *Six Wives*, pp. 711–59.

13. *Souvenirs et correspondance de Madame de Caylus* (annotated edition, Paris 1881), passim; Henri Carré, *Mademoiselle de la Vallière* (Paris, 1938) and *Madame de Montespan* (Paris, 1939); Pierre Gaxotte, *La France de Louis XIV* (Paris, 1974), chapter 5; Lucy Norton, *The Sun King and his Loves* (London, 1972).

14. All of these paintings are reproduced in Gaxotte, *Louis XIV*.

15. Carré, *Montespan*, pp. 21, 24.

16. Carrée, *La Vallière*, p. 45.

17. *Journal d' Olivier Lefèvre d'Ormesson*, ii, *1661–1672* (Paris, 1861), p. 422, entry for Wednesday 27 January 1666; p. 603, entry for Wednesday 14 December 1670.

18. G. Braux, *Louise de la Vallière de sa Touraine natale au Carmel de Paris* (Chambray-les-Tours, 1981), p. 52.

19. Portraits are reproduced in Gaxotte, *Louis XIV*, and Norton, *Sun King*.

20. *Souvenirs de Madame de Caylus*, p. 27.

21. Reresby and Boyer respectively, quoted in Brian Masters, *The Mistresses of Charles II* (London, 1979), p. 53.

22. *The Diary of Samuel Pepys*, edited by Robert Latham and William Mathews, 11 vols (London, 1970–83), iii, p. 175 (23 August 1662); iv, p. 63 (1 March 1662); vi, p. 191 (16 August 1665); iii, p. 139 (16 July 1662).

23. Masters, *Mistresses*, p. 51.

24. Quoted in Masters, *Mistresses*, p. 10.

25. R. B. Beckett, *Lely* (London, 1951), pp. 14–17, esp pp. 19 and 23.

26. *Memoirs of the Life of Eleanour Gwinn* (London, 1752); *Dictionary of National Biography*, xxiii (1890), pp. 401–3.

27. *DNB* (1890), p. 403.

28. Quoted in J. P. Kenyon, *The Stuarts* (London, 1958; 1966 paperback edn), p. 51. In general see Roger Lockyer, *Buckingham* (London, 1981).

29. Philippe Erlanger, *Le mignon du roi* (Paris, 1967), p. 51. My account is based mainly on this book.

30. Madame D ... [D'Aulnoy], *Mémoires de la cour d'Angleterre* (Paris, 1695), i, pp. 3–6; ii, pp. 225–27.

31. Useful accounts are W. MacDonald Wigfield, *The Monmouth Rebellion* (Bradford-on-Avon, 1980); Robin Clifton, *The Last Popular Rebellion* (London, 1984).

32. Bryan Bevan, *Marlborough the Man* (London, 1975), p. 15.

33. I reproduce a substantial paragraph in *Beauty in History*, p. 116; in general see Duc de Castries, *La Pompadour* (Paris, 1983), Jean Nicolle, *Madame de Pompadour et la société de son temps* (Paris, 1980).

34. Pidonsat de Maurobat, *Anecdotes sur Madame la Comtesse Dubarré* (Amsterdam, 1776), p. 22. In her excellent *Madame du Barry: The Wages of Beauty* (London, 1991), Joan Haslip reproduces, from private collections, four ravishing portraits of Du Barry.

35. Cited by Jacques Levron, *Madame Du Barry: ou la fin d'une courtisane* (Paris, 1961, 1974), p. 31.

36. For example, *The History of the Intrigues and Gallantries of Christina, Queen of Sweden and of her Court, whilst she was at Rome. Faithfully Render'd into English from the French Original* (London, 1697).

37. Clearly demonstrated in the Bernini sculpture in the National Museum, Stockholm.

38. Georgina Masson, *Queen Christina* (London, 1968), p. 321.

39. My account is based on Robert Coughlan, *Elizabeth and Catherine* (London, 1974); Joan Haslip, *Catherine the Great* (London, 1977); *The Memoirs of Catherine the Great* (London, 1955), ed. Dominique Maroger, translated by Moira Budberg, with an introduction by G. P. Gooch.

40. *Memoirs of Catherine the Great*, pp. 60, 70.

41. Ibid., p. 200.

42. Ibid., p. 215.

43. *Mémoires secrets et inédits de Stanislas Auguste, Compte Poniatowski* (Leipzig, 1862), p. 7.

44. Haslip, *Catherine the Great*, p. 273.

Notes to Chapter 4: Something Handsome and Cheap

1. Brian Bevan, *Nell Gwyn* (London, 1969), p. 22.

2. Margaret F. Rosenthal, *The Honest Courtesan: Veronica Franco, Citizen and Writer in Sixteenth-Century Venice* (Chicago, 1992), p. 6. In general see Dacia Mairini, *Veronica Franco: Courtesan and Poet*, translated by J. Douglas Campbell and Leonard G. Sbrocchi (New York, 2001). For an English traveller's first-hand account of Venice at the time, see *Coryat's Crudities. Reprinted from the Edition of 1611* (London, 1776), ii, esp. pp. 38–50.

3. Rosenthal, *The Honest Courtesan*, p. 55. I have used Rosenthal's translation, anglifying her Americanism, 'ass'.

4. Marie Dormoy, *La vraie Marion de Lorne* (Paris, 1934); Georges Montgredien, *Marion de Lorne et ses amours* (Paris, 1940); Emile Magne, *Ninon de*

Lanclos: édition définitive (Paris, 1948); Françoise Hamel, *Notre dame des amours: Ninon de Lenclos* (Paris, 1998).

5. Simone de Beauvoir, *Le Deuxième Sexe* (Paris, 1948), ii, p. 345.

6. Tallement de Reaux, *Historiettes* (1662; published Paris, 1854), ii, p. 34.

7. Janet Aldis, *Madame Geoffrin: Her Salon and her Times, 1750–1777* (1905), esp. pp. 3–17. A portrait by Nattier shows her, at thirty-eight, an agreeable-looking woman. In the famous and powerful Chardin she is a severely plain old lady.

8. *Lettres de Mlle de Lespinasse precédées d'une notice de Sainte-Beuve et suivies des autres écrits de l'auteur et des principaux documents qui le concernent* (Paris 1893), p. 393. In general see Duc de Castries, *Julie de Lespinasse: Le drâme d'un double amour* (Paris, 1985).

9. Camilla Jebb, *A Star of the Salons: Julie de Lespinasse* (London, 1908), p. 212.

10. *Lettres de Mlle de Lespinasse*, p. 405.

11. John Christopher Herold, *Mistress to an Age: A Life of Madame de Staël* (New York, 1958); Ghislain de Diesback, *Madame de Staël* (Paris, 1983).

12. Herold, *Mistress to an Age*, p. 51.

13. Comtesse Jean de Plauge, *Monsieur de Staël* (Paris, 1932), pp. 40, 41.

14. Irving Wallace, *The Nymphs and Other Maniacs* (New York, 1971), p. 67.

15. My account is based on those of Duc de Castries, *Madame Récamier* (Paris, 1985), and Françoise Wagener, *Madame Récamier, 1777–1849* (Paris, 1986).

16. Castries, *Madame Récamier*, p. 331.

17. J. Steven Watson, *The Reign of George III, 1760–1815* (Oxford, 1960), p. 271 n. 1.

18. Amanda Foreman, *Georgiana: Duchess of Devonshire* (London, 1998), esp. pp. 3, 80–81; Brian Masters, *Georgiana, Duchess of Devonshire* (London, 1981), p. 34; *DNB*, ix (1887), p. 348; Hugh Stokes, *The Devonshire Home Circle* (London, 1917), pp. 73–76.

19. *Diary and Letters of Madame D'Arblay* (Fanny Burney) (London, 1891), iii, p. 369 (20 August 1791); *Letters of David Garrick*, ed. D. M. Little and G. M. Kahrl (London, 1963), p. 1035. For a survey of great and (sometimes) lovely ladies in eighteenth-century Britain see Rosemary Baird, *Mistress of the House: Great Ladies and Grand Houses, 1670–1830* (London, 2003).

20. Katie Hickman, *Courtesans* (London, 2003), p. 151, an excellent book, particularly relevant to my chapter 6; Frances Wilson, *The Courtesan's Revenge: Harriette Wilson, the Woman who Blackmailed the King* (London, 2003); Valerie Grosvenor Myer, *Harriette Wilson: Lady of Pleasure* (Haddenham, Cambridgeshire, 2003).

21. Jean-Pierre Gutton, *Domestiques et serviteurs dans la France de l'ancien régime* (Paris, 1981), pp. 73, 164.

22. Merlin Waterson, *The Servants Hall: A Domestic History of Erddig* (London, 1980), p. 170.

23. Cissie Fairchilds, *Domestic Enemies: Servants and their Masters in Old Régime France* (Baltimore 1984), pp. 91–92.

24. Fairchilds, *Domestic Enemies*, p. 91

25. Sarah C. Maza, *Servants and Masters in Eighteenth-Century France* (Princeton, 1983), pp. 35–36.

26. Henry Fielding, 'A Journey from this World to the Next', *Miscellanies*, ii (1743), p. 48.

27. Quoted by Flora Fraser, *Beloved Emma: The Life of Emma, Lady Hamilton* (London, 1986), p. 57.

28. Waterson, *The Servants' Hall*, p. 170.

29. Pamela Horn, *The Rise and Fall of the Victorian Servant* (Dublin, 1975), p. 84.

30. Donald E. Sutherland, *Americans and their Servants: Domestic Service in the United States from 1800 to 1920* (Baton Rouge, Louisiana, 1981), p. 42.

31. See Gordon Grimmet in Rosina Harrison (ed.), *Gentlemen's Gentlemen* (London, 1976), p. 33.

32. George Washington, in Harrison, *Gentlemen's Gentlemen*, p. 176. See Anne Martin-Fugier, *La place des bonnes: la domesticité feminine à Paris en 1900* (Paris, 1979).

33. Edward Ward, *The London Spy: The Vanities and Vices of the Town Exposed to View* (London, 1703), cited by Alison Adburgham, *Shoppping in Style* (London, 1979), pp. 14–21.

34. Pepys, *Diary*, v, p. 264 (6 September 1664).

35. James Peller Malcolm, *Anecdotes of the Manners and Customs of London during the Eighteenth Century* (London, 1808), p. 133.

36. Lois W. Banner, *American Beauty* (Chicago, 1984), pp. 32–33.

37. Louis Fissner Journals, 14 April 1854, Stanford University Libraries Special Collections, M89.

38. Henry Mayhew, *The Shops and Companies of London* (London, 1865), p. 86.

39. Reproduced in Marwick *Beauty*, p. 246.

40. John Bird Thomas, *Shop Boy: An Autobiography* (London, 1920), p. 163.

41. *Pick-me-up*, 1 December 1888, reproduced in Adburgham, *Shopping*, p. 169.

42. Bevan, *Nell Gwyn*, p. 22.

43. Pepys, *Diary*, vi, p. 73 (3 April 1665); viii, p. 193 (1 May 1667), p. 463 (5 October 1667), p. 91 (2 March 1667).

44. Henriot, *Portraits*, pp. 63ff.

45. Quoted by Henriot, *Portraits*, p. 65.

46. Macklin and Richard Cumberland respectively, quoted in Carola Oman, *David Garrick* (London, 1958), pp. 25, 93.

47. Oman, *David Garrick*, p. 330.

48. *The Life of Mrs Abington (formerly Miss Barton) Celebrated Comic Actress ... by the Editor of the 'Life of Quin'* (London, 1888), p. 6.

49. 'A modern writer', quoted in *Life of Mrs Abington*.

50. *Life of Mrs Abington*, p. 32.

51. Ibid., p. 37.

52. Thomas Davies, *Memoirs of the Life of David Garrick* (London, 1780), i, p. 188; ii, pp. 169, 171.

53. Quoted in *The Testimony of Truth to Exalted Memory: or A Biographical Sketch of the Right Honourable the Countess of Derby in Refutation of a False and Scandalous Libel* (London, 1797), p. 23; see also Suzanne Bloxham, *Walpole's Queen of Comedy: Elizabeth Farren, Countess of Derby* (London, 1988).

54. Quoted by Roger Manvell, *Sarah Siddons: Portrait of an Actress* (London, 1970), p. 23. In general see Robyn Asleson (ed.), *A Passion for Performance: Sarah Siddons and her Portraitists* (Los Angeles, 1999).

55. Sebastien Mercier, *Tableau de Paris* (Paris, 1781), ii, pp. 7, 11.

56. Antonia Fraser, *The Weaker Vessel: Women's Lot in Seventeenth-Century England* (London, 1984), p. 410.

57. *Harris's List of Covent Garden Ladies* (London, 1793), p. 24.

58. *Covent Garden Ladies*, p. 35.

59. Ibid., p. 25.

60. *Ranger's Impartial List of the Ladies of Pleasure in Edinburgh* (Edinburgh, 1775) (Miss Fraser, Miss Cobb).

61. *Covent Garden Ladies*, pp. 93.

62. *Covent Garden Ladies*, pp. 31, 40; *Ranger's Impartial List* (Miss Nairn, Mrs Dingwall, Miss Smith).

63. Fraser, *Weaker Vessel*. p. 413.

64. *Covent Garden Ladies*, p. 25.

65. Roy Porter *English Society in the Eighteenth Century* (London, 1982), p. 282.

66. Quoted Porter, *English Society in the Eighteenth Century*, p. 280.

67. Quoted Derek Parker, *Casanova* (Stroud, 2002), p. 240; see also, J. Rives Childs, *Casanova: A New Perspective* (London, 1989); Giacomo Casanova, *History of My Life*, translated W. R. Trask, 6 vols (London, 1967–72).

68. Pat Rogers, *An Introduction to Pope* (London, 1975), p. 2.

69. Ralph M. Wardle, *Oliver Goldsmith* (Lawrence, Kansas, 1957), pp. 12–13, 20–21, 70–71, 90–91, 184–85, 292–93.

70. Lisa Jardine, *The Curious Life of Robert Hook* (London, 2003).

Notes to Chapter 5: Getting Married

1. Quoted in R. B. Outhwaite (ed.), *Marriage and Society: Studies in the Social History of Marriage* (London, 1981), p. 10. A collection of seventeenth-century letters in which attitudes to marriage and wealth, status and beauty emerge most distinctly is *Barrington Family Letters, 1628–1632*, edited for the Royal Historical Society by Arthur Searle, Camden Fourth Series, 28 (London, 1983).

2. Quoted in Outhwaite, *Marriage and Society*, p. 10.

3. Roger Thompson, *Women in Stuart England and America* (London, 1974), p. 117.

4. Kathleen M. Davies, 'Continuity and Change in Literary Advice on Marriage', in Outhwaite, *Marriage and Society*, pp. 55–80; Lawrence Stone, *The Family, Sex and Marriage in England, 1500–1800* (London, 1977), p. 188.

5. Mary Astell, *Some Reflections on Marriage* (London, 1700), pp. 10, 13, 18, 21.

6. Peter Borsay, 'The English Urban Renaissance: The Development of Provincial Urban Culture, *c.* 1680–1760', *Social History* (May 1977), p. 595.

7. Henry Fielding, *History of Tom Jones* (London, 1749), book 1, chapter 12.

8. Henry Fielding, 'To a Friend on Choosing a Wife', in *Miscellanies*, i (London, 1743), pp. 27ff.

9. Edward Shorter, *The Making of the Modern Family* (New York, 1976), p. 144.

10. Charles Perron, *Les Franc-Comtois: leur caractère national, leur meours, leurs usages* (Besançon, 1892), p. 85.

11. Olwen Hufton, 'Women, Work and Marriage in Eighteenth-Century France', in Outhwaite, *Marriage and Society*, pp. 198–99.

12. Mary Hallock to Helena de Kay, undated (1869), Mary Hallock Foote Papers, Stanford University Libraries Special Collections and University Archives, M115, box 1, letter 7.

13. Mary Hallock to Helena de Kay Gilder, undated (1870?), Mary Hallock Foote Papers, box 1, letter 14.

14. Mary Hallock to Helena de Kay Gilder, 7 December 1876, box 8, letter 130.

15. *The Journal of Katherine Mansfield*, ed. J. Middleton Murry (London, 1954), p. 5.

16. *The Diary of Thomas Turner, 1754–1765*, ed. David Vaizey (Oxford, 1984), 30 August 1755 (p. 13); 1 January 1756 (p. 21).

17. Ibid., 10 February, 15 October, 1756 (pp. 17–18, 66).

18. Ibid., 17 January 1762 (p. 243).

19. Ibid., 23 June 1763 (p. 274).

20. Ibid., 13 August 1764 (p. 300).

21. Ibid., 10 November 1763, 17 January 1762 (pp. 281, 243).

22. Ibid., 19 March 1764 (p. 288); 24 March 1765 (p. 317).

23. Ibid., 5, 6 April 1765 (p. 318).

24. Ibid., 14 April 1765 (p. 318).

25. Ibid., 14 April 1765 (pp. 318–19).

26. Ibid., 24 April 1765 (p. 320).

27. Ibid., 11 May 1765 (p. 321).

28. Ibid., 31 July 1765 (p. 323).

29. Nicolas-Edmé Rétif de la Bretonne, *La vie de mon père* (Paris, 1779, ed. Gilbert Rouger, Paris, 1970), pp. 19, 33–48.

30. *Daily Advertiser*, 1750, quoted in Derek Jarett, *England in the Age of Hogarth* (London, 1976), p. 103.

31. Mercier, *Tableau*, ii, p. 164.

32. *The Diary of Dudley Ryder, 1715–1716*, ed. William Mathews (London, 1959), 4 and 11 April 1716 (pp. 213–14).

33. Ibid., 22 May 1716 (p. 240); 3 April 1716 (p. 211).

34. Ibid., 23 May 1716 (p. 241).

35. 'Memorial of James Howard of Manchester (1738 to 1822)', typescript in the possession of Mrs J. E. Nurse, Tunbridge Wells.

36. James Gall, 'Journal, 1809–1813', January 1809, National Library of Scotland, Acc. 8874. H. T. Finck, *Romantic Love and Personal Beauty* (New York, 1887).

37. Diary of E. E. Graham, 1872–1932, 12 March 1875, Robert Graham Diaries, National Library of Scotalnd, Acc. 9077.

38. Graham Diary. entries for 7, 11, 12, 13, 16 April, 5 August 1875.

39. Anderson Papers, boxes 1, 2, 6, 7, 60, Stanford University Libraries, Special Collections and University Archives, M51.

40. Louis de Sainte-Ange, *Le secrèt de triompher les femmes et de les fixer* (Paris, 1825), p. 2.

41. Ibid., pp. 10–17.

42. Ibid., pp. 135–44.

43. *Dictionary of American Biography*, vi (New York, 1931), pp. 383ff; Henry Theophilus Finck, *My Adventures in the Golden Age of Music* (New York, 1926), pp. 270–72.

44. Finck, *My Adventures*, p. 270.

45. Ibid., pp. 271–72.

46. Horace Bleackley, *The Beautiful Duchess: Being an Account of the Life and Times of Elizabeth Gunning, Duchess of Hamilton and Argyle* (London, 1927), pp. 6–7.

47. *Life and Character of the Late Illustrious Duchess of Kingston … Collected from Authentic Sources* (London, 1788), p. 15.

48. Anon. [K. Hamilton, 6th Duke of Hamilton], *The Charms of Beauty of The Grand Contest between the Fair Hibernians, and the English Toasts: A Poem Occasioned by the Marriage of his Grace the Duke of Hamilton with Miss Elizabeth Gunning; and the Expected Marriage of her Elder Sister with a Certain Noble Earl* (London, 1752).

49. *DNB*, xliv (1895), p. 419.

50. Ibid., p. 418.

51. Cited by Ernest John Knapton, *Empress Josephine* (Cambridge, Mass. 1963), p. 18. In general see Andrea Stuart's brilliant *The Rose of Martininque: A Life of Napoleon's Josephine* (London, 2003).

52. Knapton, *Empress Josephine*, p. 19.

53. Ibid., p. 25.

54. Ibid., pp. 127–28.

55. Ibid., p. 113.

56. Nina Epton, *Josephine: The Empress and her Children* (London, 1975), p. 1.

Notes to Chapter 6: *Grandes Horizontales*

1. See Claude Dufrêsne, *La divine scandaleuse: Hortense Schneider* (Paris, 1993); Jean-Paul Bonami, *La Diva d'Offenbach: Hortense Schneider, 1833–1920* (Paris, 2002).

2. Both quotations are in Bernard Grebanier, *The Uninhibited Byron* (London, 1970), p. 199; see also Leslie A. Marchand, *Byron: A Biography* (London, 1957), i, p. 370, and, generally, the magnificent biographies Benita Eisler, *Byron: Child of Passion, Fool of Fame* (London, 1999), and Fiona MacCarthy, *Byron: Life and Legend* (London, 1997).

3. Biographical information from Cornelia Otis Skinner, *Elegant Wits and Grand Horizontals* (London, 1963); Joanna Richardson, *The Courtesans: The Demi-Monde in Nineteenth Century France* (London, 1967); Virginia Rounding, *Grandes Horizontales: The Lives and Legends of Four Nineteenth-Century Courtesans* (London, 2003); Charles Castle, *La Belle Otéro: The Last Great Courtesan* (London, 1981); Michael Harrison, *Fanfare of Strumpets* (London, 1971); Auriant, *Les lionnes du second empire* (Paris, 1935).

4. Edgar Holt, *Plon-Plon: The Life of Prince Napoleon* (London, 1973), p. 121.

5. Marie Colombier, *Mémoires: fin d'empire* (Paris, 1898), chapter 2 for her obscure origins.

6. Yolaine de la Bigne, *Valtesse de la Bigne: ou le pouvoir de la volupté* (Paris, 1999), pp. 218–19, 236.

7. Richardson, *The Courtesans*, p. 64; Rounding, *Grandes Horizontales*, chapters 4 and 9; Janine Alexandre-Debray, *La Paiva: Ses amants, ses maris* (Paris, 1986), esp. pp. 61ff.

8. Rounding, *Grandes Horizontales*, p. 82.

9. Richardson, *The Courtesans*, p. 52.

10. 'Zed', *Le Demi-Monde sous le second empire: souvenirs d'un sybarite* (Paris, 1892), p. 53.

11. Hickman, *The Courtesans*, pp. 5–6.

12. 'Zed', *Le Demi-Monde*, p. 14.

13. Paul Gsell, *Mémoires de Mme Judith de la Comédie Francaise* (Paris, 1911), p. 221.

14. This account is based on Poiret-Dalpach, *Marie Duplessis: 'La dame aux camélias'* (Paris 1981); Rounding, *Grandes Horizontales*, chapters 2 and 3.

15. Romain Vienne, *La vérité sur la dame aux camélias* (Paris, 1888), pp. 105–6.

16. Céleste Mogador, *Mémoires* (Paris, 1858–59), i, pp. 240–41.

17. Ibid., i, p. 173

18. Ibid., ii, p. 38.

19. Richardson, *The Courtesans*, chapter 1.

20. Henry Blyth, *Skittles, the Last Victorian Courtesan: The Life and Times of Catherine Walters* (London, 1977), pp. 21–22.

21. See Ishbell Ross, *The Uncrowned Queen: The Life of Lola Montez* (New York, 1972).

22. R. P. Pzewaski, preface to Liane de Pougy, *My Blue Notebooks* (London, 1979), p. 14.

23. See Jean-Louis Vaudoyer, *Alice Ozy: ou l'Aspasie moderne* (Paris, 1930), pp. 77ff.

24. Ross, *The Uncrowned Queen*, pp. 273ff; Lola Montez, *Memoirs* (New York, 1860), and Lola Montez, *The Arts and Secrets of Beauty* (New York, 1853); James F. Varley, *Lola Montez, the Californian Adventures of Europe's Notorious Courtesan* (Spokane, Washington, 1996).

25. Rebecca West, *1900* (London, 1982), p. 154.

26. Pzewaski, preface to de Pougy, *Blue Notebooks*, p. 14.

27. Skinner, *Elegant Wits and Grand Horizontals*, pp. 188ff.

28. Ibid., p. 188.

29. Sam Waagenaar, *The Murder of Mata Hari* (London, 1964), p. 172. Other

supporters of Mata Hari's innocence are Russell Howe, *Mata Hari: The True Story* (New York, 1986), Julie Wheelwright, *The Fatal Lover: Mata Hari and the Myth of Women in Espionage* (London, 1992, and Lionel Dumarcet, *L'affaire Mata Hari* (Paris, 1999). For reasoned indications of some guilt see Ronald Miller, *Mata Hari* (Geneva, 1970), Fred Kupferman, *Mata Hari: songes et mensonges* (Brussels, 1982), and Philippe Collas, *Mata Hari: Sa véritable histoire* (Paris, 2003).

30. For Castiglione see Claude Dufrêsne, *La Comtesse de Castiglione* (Paris, 2002); for de Mérode and Sabatier see respectively Cléo de Mérode, *Le ballet de ma vie* (Paris, 1955) and Rounding, *Grandes Horizontales*, chapters 5 and 6.

31. Lois W. Banner, *American Beauty* (New York 1983, Chicago 1984), chapters 6–8.

32. Ibid., p. 128.

33. Ibid., p. 135

34. Ibid., p. 135.

35. Ibid., p. 136.

36. Clarence Day, quoted in Banner, *American Beauty*, p. 136.

37. Banner, *American Beauty*, plate 19 and caption.

38. Ibid., p. 136.

39. Ibid., p. 257.

40. Ibid., p. 258.

41. Ibid., p. 138.

42. Ibid., p. 138.

43. *Spirit of the Times*, 15 November 1882, quoted in Banner, *American Beauty*, p. 138.

44. James Brough, *The Prince and the Lily* (New York, 1975), pp. 141–42.

45. See Tom Prideaux, *Love or Nothing: The Life and Times of Ellen Terry* (New York, 1975), and Ellen Terry, *My Life* (London, 1910).

46. Prideaux, *Ellen Terry*, p. 113.

47. Philippe Julianne, *Sarah Bernardt* (Paris, 1977), p. 34. My account is based on this excellent biography, amplified by André Castelot, *Ensourcelante Sarah Bernhardt* (Paris, 1973), *Ma double vie: mémoires de Sarah Bernhardt* (Paris, 1907), and Pierre Spirakoff, *Sarah Bernhardt vue par les Nadar* (Paris, 1982).

48. Mérode, *Ballet*, pp. 88–89.

49. Jan Marsh, *Pre-Raphaelite Sisterhood* (London, 1985), pp. 15–32, 117–20, 244–48.

50. The visual sources cited are reproduced in Marwick, *Beauty*, pp. 254–59, where my arguments are developed more fully. On the undoubted good

looks of Lizzie Siddall see also Gay Daly, *The Pre-Raphaelites in Love* (London, 1989), p. 34.

51. Derek Hudson, *Munby, Man of Two Worlds: The Life and Diaries of Arthur J. Munby, 1828–1910* (London, 1972), pp. 40–41.

52. Quoted in Hilary Evans, *The Oldest Profession: An Illustrated History of Prostitution* (Newton Abbot, 1979), p. 121.

53. Ibid., p. 121.

54. B. Pierce Egan, *Life in London* (London, 1869), pp. 88–90.

55. Renée Jeanne, Charles Ford, *Histoire du Cinéma* (Paris, 1947–55), i, pp. 208, 486; ii, pp. 29–30; iii, pp. 107, 405.

Notes to Chapter 7: The Tallest Wins

1. *DNB*, xlv (1896), pp. 258–59, 365.

2. Quoted by Louis Kronenberger, *The Extraordinary Mr Wilkes* (New York, 1974), p. 4.

3. Quoted by Audrey Williamson, *Wilkes: 'A Friend to Liberty'* (London, 1974), p. 72.

4. Williamson, *Wilkes*, p. 18

5. Donald Nicholas, *The Portraits of Bonnie Prince Charlie* (London, 1973), p. 1.

6. Herbert Agar, *The American Presidents from Washington to Harding* (London, 1933), p. 3.

7. Robert Darnton, *George Washington's False Teeth* (New York, 2003).

8. David K. Bruce, *Sixteen American Presidents* (London, 1962), p. 39.

9. Agar, *The American Presidents*, p. 3.

10. Ibid., pp. 61–62.

11. *Dictionary of American Biography (DAB)*, x (New York, 1933), pp. 17–18.

12. Agar, *American Presidents*, p. 87.

13. Quoted in Bruce, *Sixteen American Presidents*, p. 178.

14. Agar, *The American Presidents*, p. 113.

15. John and Alice Durant, *Pictorial History of American Presidents* (New York, 1958), p. 75.

16. Durant, *Pictorial History of American Presidents*, p. 82.

17. Ibid., p. 94

18. Agar, *The American Presidents*, p. 157.

19. Bruce, *Sixteen Presidents*, p. 290.

20. Agar, The *American Presidents*, p. 243; Durant, *Pictorial History of American Presidents*, p. 177.

21. Durant, *Pictorial History of the American Presidents*, p. 193.

22. Quoted by, among many others, Agar, *The American Presidents*, p. 74.

23. Agar, *The American Presidents*, p. 94.

24. *Cyclopaedia*, v, p. 283; Agar, *The American Presidents*, p. 130.

25. Bruce, *Sixteen Presidents*, p. 240.

26. Bruce, *Sixteen Presidents*, p. 260.

27. Durant, *Pictorial History of American Presidents*, p. 137.

28. Durant, *Pictorial History of American Presidents*, p. 145; Agar, *The American Presidents*, p. 223.

29. Durant, *Pictorial History of the American Presidents*, p. 183; Agar, *The American Presidents*, p. 247.

30. Agar, *The American Presidents*, p. 260; Durant, *Pictorial History of the American Presidents*, p. 188.

31. Agar, *The American Presidents*, p. 174.

32. Ibid., p. 180.

33. Reproduced in Marwick, *Beauty*, p. 237.

34. *Cyclopaedia*, iii p. 726; *DAB*, xi (1933), pp. 246–47.

35. Quoted by Stephen B. Oates, *Abraham Lincoln: The Man Behind the Myths* (New York, 1984), pp. 50–51.

36. Dwight C. Anderson, *Abraham Lincoln* (New York, 1982); Cullom David (ed.), *The Public and Private Lincoln* (London, 1979): Oates, *Abraham Lincoln*.

37. Cited by Oates, *Abraham Lincoln*, p. 35.

38. Richard N. Current, *The Lincoln Nobody Knows* (New York, 1958), pp. 2, 4–5.

39. The election is summarised in Arthur Schlesinger jr (ed.), *The Coming to Power: Critical Presidential Elections in American History* (New York, 1981).

40. Robert W. Johannsen, *Stephen A. Douglas* (New York, 1973), p. 4.

41. Schlesinger, *The Coming to Power*.

42. Johanssen, *Stephen A. Douglas*, p. 781.

43. James M. McPherson (ed.), '*To the Best of My Ability': The American Presidents* (New York, 2000), p. 104.

44. Larry Gara, *The Presidency of Franklin Pierce* (Lawrence, Kansas, 1991), p. 29.

45. *DAB*, xiv, p. 577; *Cyclopaedia*, v, p. 9.

46. *DNB*, lvi (1898), p. 17.

47. 'Memoirs from Lord Shaftesbury', in The Hon. Evelyn Ashley, *The Life of Henry John Temple, Viscount Palmerston, 1846–1865* (London, 1876), ii, p. 316.

48. Kenneth Bourne, *Palmerston: The Early Years* (London, 1982), pp. 185, 434. Hot off the press is James Chambers, *Palmerston* (London, 2004).

49. Ashley, *Palmerston*, ii, p. 288.

50. *DNB*, xv (1988), p. 10.

51. Robert Blake, *Disraeli* (London, 1966), p. 473.

52. *DNB, 1941–1950* (1959), p. 528.

53. W. P. R. George, *My Brother and I* (London, 1976), pp. 94–95. In general see John Grigg, *The Young Lloyd George* (London, 1973) pp. 58–59, and *Lloyd George: The People's Champion, 1902–1911* (London, 1978), esp. p. 189.

54. Grigg, *The Young Lloyd George*, p. 59.

55. David Duff, *Eugénie and Napoleon* (London, 1978), p. 98.

56. Duff, *Eugénie and Napoleon*, p. 72; Jasper Ridley, *Napoleon III and Eugénie* (London, 1979), p. 157.

Notes to Chapter 8: Movies

1. Arthur Marwick, *The Sixties: Cultural Revolution in Britain, France, Italy and the United States, c. 1958 to c. 1974* (Oxford, 1998).

2. René Jeanne, *Les Grandes Vedettes du cinéma: beauté masculine* (Paris, 1929), p. 3.

3. E. Charles-Roux, *Chanel* (Paris, 1976), pp. 151–53.

4. Robert Roberts, *The Classic Slum* (London, 1971), p. 181.

5. Ella Adelin Fletcher, *The Woman Beautiful* (New York, 1899), p. 1.

6. Harriet Hubbard Ayer, *Harriet Hubbard Ayer's Book: A Complete and Authentic Treatise on the Laws of Health and Beauty* (Springfield, Massachusetts, 1899 and 1902), p. 57.

7. Mrs C. E. Humphry, *How to be Pretty though Plain* (London, 1899), p. 12.

8. C. Sherman Big, *Face and Figure* (London, 1879), p. 21.

9. *Harriet Hubbard Ayer's Book*, pp. 50ff.

10. Femina-Bibliothèque (preface by Henri Duvernois), *Pour être belle* (Paris, 1913), pp. i–ix; Arthur Lefèbvre, *L'art d'être belle* (Paris, 1901), p. 7; Humphry, *How to be Pretty*, p. 14 ('work well done has made many a plain face beautiful'; Comtesse de Traver, *Que veut la femme; être jolie, être aimée, et dominer* (Paris, 1911), p. 9; Alice M. Long, *My Lady Beautiful* (Chicago, 1906), passim. The advice offered to Italian women did not greatly change over one hundred and fifty years: see, for example, *La bellezza e di mezzi di conservarla ossia la toalette delle signore* (Milan, 1827), and Prof. George Banhoff, *L'eterno feminino: una guida alla bellezza* (Rome, 1958).

11. Madame Athena, *Pour se faire aimer* (Paris, n. d., c. 1920), p. 11.

12. Hortense Odlum, *A Woman's Place* (New York, 1939), pp. 218–20.

13. US War Department *Education Manual, EM982: Establishing and Operating a Beauty Shop* (Madison, Wisconsin, n. d., c. 1944), p. 2.

14. Ibid., pp. 2–3

15. Louis Léon-Martin, *L'Industrie de la beauté* (Paris, 1930), p. 230.

16. See in particular the four boxes of advertisements, leaflets, handbills, etc., entitled 'Beauty Parlour', in the John Johnson Collection, Bodleian Library, Oxford.

17. Nose machine, and supporting advertisements, etc, in Museum of London.

18. Madame Vriac-Lecôt, *Pour être belle à tout âge* (Paris, 1929), p. 7; Allied Newspapers, *Beauty for Every Woman* (Manchester, 1929), p. 7.

19. Vriac-Lecôt, *Pour être belle*, pp. 24–25.

20. Paula S. Fass, *The Damned and the Beautiful: American Youth in the 1920s* (New York, 1977), p. 281.

21. Letter to *Le Petit Parisien* quoted by Léon-Martin, *Industrie*, pp. 236–68.

22. Herbert Andrews, General Manager Screen Advertising Inc., to Hon. Ernest Lundeen, 23 January 1918, Ernest Lundeen Papers, box 91, Hoover Institution Archives.

23. *New York Tribune*, 7 December 1923, clipping in Mark Sullivan Papers, box 1, Hoover Institution Archives.

24. Edward Pessen, *The Log Cabin Myth: The Social Background of the Presidents* (New Haven, Connecticut, 1984), p. 156.

25. W. E. Leuchtenberg, *The Perils of Prosperity, 1914–1932* (Chicago 1958), p. 89.

26. Mark Sullivan Diary, 12 September 1923, Mark Sullivan Papers, box 1, Hoover Institution Archives.

27. *New York Tribune*, 7 December 1923, Mark Sullivan Papers, box 1, Hoover Institution Archives.

28. *Kansas City Journal*, 14 September 1932, Mark Sullivan Papers, box 233; *New York Times*, 6 November 1932, and other clipppings in Raymond Moley Papers, boxes, 5, 11, Hoover Institution Archives.

29. *New York Times Magazine*, 6 November 1932.

30. *Seattle Star*, 26 September 1932; *Chicago Sunday Tribune*, 21 August 1932; *Cleveland Plain Dealer*, 21 August 1932; *Cleveland Sunday News*, 21 August 1932; clippings in Moley Papers, boxes 5, 4, 11.

31. Friends of Franklin Roosevelt, *Franklin D. Roosevelt: Who He Is and What He Has Done* (New York, 1932), Moley Papers, box 11.

32. *World Telegram*, 23 August 1932, Moley Papers, box 4.

33. *Chicago Sunday Tribune*, 21 August 1932, Moley Papers, box 4.

34. See *DNB, 1931–1940* (Oxford, 1949), p. 569.

35. See David Marquand, *Ramsay MacDonald* (London, 1977), pp. 285–87.

36. Ibid., pp. 69, 6.

37. David Carlton *Anthony Eden: A Biography* (London, 1981; paperback 1986)), p. 111; David Dutton, *Anthony Eden: A Life and Reputation* (London, 1988), p. 461; D. R. Thorpe, *Eden: The Life and Times of Anthony Eden, First Earl of Avon, 1897–1977* (London, 2003), who attributes Eden's 'handsome being' to his mother's having been a 'society beauty', p. 19.

38. *DNB.*

39. Carlton, *Anthony Eden*, p. 111; Dutton, *Anthony Eden*, p. 461. For Eden on TV see Michael Cockerell, *Live from Number 10: The Inside Story of Prime Ministers on Television* (London, 1988), p. 31.

40. There is an excellent, up-to-date discussion of the Suez episode in Thorpe, *Eden*, chapters, 17, 18, 19.

41. Arthur Marwick, *Class in the Twentieth Century* (Brighton, 1986), p. 23.

42. Cited in Robert Hessler, *Yesterday's Rulers: The Making of the British Colonial Service* (Syracuse, New York, 1963), pp. 74–75.

43. *Report of the Royal Commission on the Civil Service* (1931), paras 250–56.

44. Marwick, *Class in the Twentieth Century*, chapter 1.

45. H. W. Nevinson, *Running Accompaniments* (London, 1936), p. 124.

46. Ben Pimlott, *Hugh Dalton* (London, 1985), p. 37.

47. Ibid., p. 115.

48. Ibid., p. 31.

49. See John Colville, *The Fringes of Power: Downing Street Diaries, 1939–1955* (London, 1985).

50. Yale University, *The Class of 1913* (New Haven, Connecticut, 1914), p. 17.

51. Fass, *Damned and Beautiful*, pp. 155, 157, 201, 230, 240–41.

52. Gordon Grimmet, 'The Lamp Boy's Story', in Rosina Harrison (ed.), *Gentleman's Gentleman* (London, 1976), p. 16.

53. Ibid., p. 31.

54. Ibid., p. 37.

55. Ibid., pp. 79–80.

56. Edwin Lee, 'The Page Boy's Story' in Harrison (ed.), *Gentleman's Gentleman*, p. 110.

57. Grimmet, 'The Lamp Boy's Story', p. 33.

58. Reproduced in Marwick, *Beauty*, p. 314.

59. Quoted in Frederick Sands and Sven Bromen, *The Divine Garbo* (London, 1979), p. 30.

60. Boston Herndon, *Mary Pickford and Douglas Fairbanks* (London, 1977), p. 68.

61. Ibid., p. 1.

62. Noel Botham and Peter Donnelly, *Valentino: The Love God* (London, 1976), pp. 30–83.

63. Charles Higham, *Bette: The Life of Bette Davis* (New York, 1981), p. 31.
64. Ibid.
65. Laurence Olivier, *Confessions of an Actor* (London, 1982), pp. 32, 96.
66. Ibid., p. 108.
67. *Marty* (United Artists/Hecht-Hill-Lancaster, 1955).
68. See still in Marwick, *Beauty*, p. 336.
69. Clifford Bax, *The Beauty of Women* (London, 1946), p. 95.
70. Barbara Leaming, *Marilyn Monroe* (London, 1998; paperback, 2002), pp. 11ff.
71. Quoted in Anthony Summers, *Goddess: The Secret Lives of Marilyn Monroe* (London, 1985), pp. 35–61.
72. Ibid., pp. 301–68; Leaming, *Marilyn Monroe*, pt 3.
73. Peter Guralnick, *The Last Train to Memphis: The Rise of Elvis Presley* (Boston, 1994), pp. 81, 140.

Notes to Chapter 9: The Swinging Sixties

1. Arthur Marwick, *The Sixties: Cultural Revolution in Britain, France, Italy and the United States, c. 1958–c. 1974* (Oxford, 1998).
2. *Paris Match*, 27 April 1963.
3. Elizabeth Kendall, *Good Looks, Good Grooming* (New York, 1963), p. 25.
4. *Paris Match*, 4 September 1965.
5. *Life*, 11 April 1965.
6. Ibid., 28 January 1966.
7. *Paris Match*, 27 May 1967.
8. Marilyn Bender, *The Beautiful People* (New York, 1967), p. 23. See generally David Bailey, *David Bailey's Box of Pin-Ups* (London, 1965) – most of them are male – and Michael Gross, *Model: The Ugly Business of Beautiful Women* (London, 1996).
9. *Ebony*, November 1958.
10. Ibid., June 1964, June 1965.
11. Ibid., December 1965.
12. Ibid., February 1966.
13. Ibid., April 1966.
14. Marwick, *Beauty*, p. 365.
15. Richard Evans, *In Defence of History* (Cambridge, 1997), p. 72.
16. *Ebony*, March 1964.
17. See Marwick, *Beauty*, p. 367; for portrait photograph of Sidney Poitier see p. 368.
18. 'Explicitness' as well as 'permissiveness' is a characteristic of the 'Cultural Revolution'. See Marwick, *The Sixties*, pp. 381–403.

19. Arthur Marwick, 'The Upper Class in Britain, France, and the USA since World War I', in Arthur Marwick (ed.), *Class in the Twentieth Century* (Brighton 1986), pp. 17–61.

20. Jean Shrimpton, *The Truth about Modelling* (London, 1964), p. 12.

21. Ibid., p. 153.

22. Ibid., pp. 16ff.

23. Ibid., p. 17.

24. Ibid., p. 20.

25. Twiggy, *An Autobiography* (London, 1975), p. 8.

26. Ibid., p. 24.

27. Ibid., p. 25.

28. Ibid., p. 36.

29. For Twiggy, see Marwick, *The Sixties*, pp. 419–21, 465; Twiggy Lawson, *In Black and White* (London, 1997).

30. For the Beatles in America and, in particular, France and Italy, see Marwick, *The Sixties*, pp. 456–71.

31. Peter Joseph, *Good Times: An Oral History of America in the Nineteen Sixties* (New York, 1973), p. 185.

32. Quoted in Michael Parkinson, *George Best: An Intimate Biography* (London, 1975), p. 69.

33. Susan Cleeve, *Growing Up in the Swinging Sixties* (London, 1980), p. 69. In general, see Jack Olsen, *Cassius Clay: A Biography* (London, 1967).

34. Erving Goffman, 'On Calling the mark out: some aspects of adaptation to failure', *Psychiatry*, 15 (1952), p. 456.

35. E. Walster, V. Aronson, D. Abrahams and L. Rottman, 'Importance of Physical Attractiveness in Dating Behavior', *Journal of Personality and Social Psychology*, 15 (1966), pp. 508–16.

36. Ibid., pp. 513–14.

37. E. Berscheid, K. K. Dion, E. Walster and G. W. Walster, 'Physical Attractiveness and Dating Choice', *Journal of Experimental Social Psychology*, 7 (1971), pp. 173–89; W. Stroebe, C. A. Insko, V. D. Thompson and B. D. Laydon, 'Effects of Physical Attractiveness, Attitude Similarity, and Sex on Various Aspects of Interpersonal Attraction', *Journal of Personality and Social Psychology*, 18 (1971), p. 89.

38. Berscheid et al., 'Physical Attractiveness and Dating Choice', pp. 180–81.

39. Ibid., p. 183.

40. J. L. Huston, 'Ambiguity of Acceptance, Social Desirability, and Dating Choice', *Journal of Experimental Social Psychology*, 9 (1973), pp. 32–42.

41. Stroebe et al., 'Effects of Physical Attractiveness', p. 89.

42. Bernard J. Murstein, 'Physical Attractiveness and Marital Choice', *Journal of Personality and Social Psychology*, 22 (1972), p. 11.

43. *Journal of Personality and Social Psychology*, 24 (1974), pp. 205–90.

44. J. E. Singer, 'The Use of Manipulative Strategies: Machiavellianism and Attractiveness', *Sociometry*, 27 (1974), pp. 128–50.

45. Josette Lyon, *La femme et la beauté* (Paris 1965), pp. 9, 12; Helen Whitcombe and Rosalind Lancy, *Charm: The Career Girl's Guide to Business and Personal Success* (New York, 1964); Brigitte Baer, *Grande forme: être bien dans sa peau* (Paris 1970), p. 16.

46. Gilda Lund, *Beauty* (London, 1963), p. 7.

47. E.g. Helen M. McLachlan, *Poise, Personality and Charm* (New York, 1965); Lizabeth Kendall, *Good Looks, Good Grooming* (New York, 1963).

48. Dr Robert Schwartz, *Médecine et beauté* (Paris, 1969); Pierre Desjardin, *Le guide de la santé et de la beauté* (Paris, 1971).

49. Schwartz, *Médicine et beauté*, pp. 157ff.

50. See e.g. Franka Guez, *Masculin quotidien: guide pratique à l'usage des hommes* (Paris, 1969), pp. 7–8; 'Marabout Flash', *Le Guide Flash de l'homme* (Verviers, Belgium, 1970), pp. 8–9.

51. Guez, *Masculin quotidien*, p. 8.

52. *Guide Flash*, p. 11.

53. Catherine Harlé, *Comment devenir modèle* (Paris, 1970), p. 24.

54. *Life*, 12 March 1965.

55. Pierette Sartin, *La Réussite professionnelle* (Paris, 1971), pp. 37–38.

56. Jennie Lee, *This Great Journey: A Volume of Autobiography* (London, 1963), with one portrait; *My Life with Nye* (London, 1980) with several portraits; Wilfred De'ath, *Barbara Castle: A Portrait from Life* (London, 1970); Jean Choffel, *Seille une Femme … Alice Saunier-Seité* (Paris, 1979), p. 96; Alice Saunier-Seité, *En première ligne: de la communale aux universités* (Paris, 1982) – the portrait on the cover shows her as very beautiful; Anne Perkins, *Red Queen: The Authorized Biography of Barbara Castle* (London, 2003), esp. pp. 72–73; Paul Routledge, *Madame Speaker: The Life of Betty Boothroyd* (London, 1995).

57. See e.g. *Life*, 24 August 1959, cover story : 'Jackie Kennedy: A Front Runner's Appealing Wife'.

58. W. L. O'Neill, *Coming Apart: An Informal History of America in the 1960s* (Chicago, 1971), p. 387n.

59. Kathleen Hall Jamieson, *Packaging the President* (New York, 1984), pp. 139–41.

60. Ibid., pp. 153 ff.

61. *Life*, 26 May 1961.

62. Ibid., 28 May 1965.
63. Ibid., 21 January 1966.
64. Edmund G. Brown, *Reagan and Reality: The Two Californias* (New York, 1970), pp. 40–41.
65. Marwick, *The Sixties*, p. 790.

Notes to Chapter 10: A Gift from the Genes

1. Jane Austen, *Mansfield Park* (1814), Oxford World's Classics edition (2003), p. 154; *Pride and Prejudice* (1813), Penguin Classics edition (1996), pp. 9, 21, 98.
2. Both quotations are on p. 16 of the Oxford University Press edition (1984) of Charles Dickens, *Martin Chuzzlewit* (1844). For an approach to beauty in literature very different from mine see Lennard J. Davis, *Resisting Novels: Ideology and Fiction* (New York, 1987), pp. 122ff.
3. Examples are Arline and John Liggett, *The Tyranny of Beauty* (London, 1989); Julian Robinson, *The Quest for Human Beauty: An Illustrated History* (New York, 1998); Kate Mulvey and Melissa Richards, *Decades of Beauty: The Changing Image of Women* (London, 1998); Robin Tolmach Lakoff and Raquel L. Scherr, *Face Value: The Politics of Beauty* (Boston, 1984); Colin Blakemore and Sheila Jennett (ed.), *Oxford Companion to the Body* (Oxford, 2003); Richard Evans, *In Defence of History* (Cambridge, 1997), p. 72
4. *Nature*, 368, pp. 186–87 and 240–41; see references in note 5, and also Elaine Hatfield and Susan Sprecher, *Mirror, Mirror: The Importance of Looks in Everyday Life* (Albany, New York, 1986).
5. Among the most important research reports are J. F. Cross and J. Cross, 'Age, Sex, and Race, and the Perception of Physical Attractiveness', *Developmental Psychology*, 5 (1971), pp. 433–39; J. M. Thatcherer and S. Iwawaki, 'Cross-Cultural Comparisons in Interpersonal Attraction of Females towards Males', *Journal of Social Psychology*, 108 (1979), pp. 121–22; Michael K. Cunningham, 'Measuring the Physical in Physical Attractiveness: Quasi-Experiments in the Sociobiology of Female Facial Beauty', *Journal of Personality and Social Psychology*, 50 (1986), pp. 925–41; D. M. Jones and K. Hill, 'Criteria of Facial Attractiveness in Five Populations', *Human Nature*, 4 (1993), pp. 271–96; V. S. Johnston and M. Franklin, 'Is Beauty in the Eye of the Beholder?', *Ethnology and Sociobiology*, 14 (1993), pp. 183–99; D. E. Perrett, K. A. May, S. Yosgikava, 'Facial Shape and Judgements of Female Attractiveness', *Nature*, 368 (1994), pp. 239–42. There is a brilliant general study by

Nancy C. Etcoff, *Survival of the Prettiest: The Science of Beauty* (Boston, 1999).

6. *Nature*, 368, p. 186.

7. Nicola Sault, 'Introduction' to Nicola Sault (ed.), *Many Mirrors: Body Image and Social Relations* (New Brunswick, New Jersey, 1944), p. 1.

8. Natalie Beausoleil, 'Makeup in Everyday Life: An Inquiry into the Practices of Urban American Women of Diverse Backgrounds' in, Sault (ed.), *Body Image*, p. 55; Ellen Zetzel Lambert. *The Face of Love: Feminism and the Beauty Question* (Boston, 1995), p. xii.

9. Lee Sigelman, Carol K. Sigelman and Christopher Fowler, 'A Bird of a Different Feather? An Experimental Investigation of Physical Attractiveness and the Eligibility of Female Candidates', *Social Psychology Quarterly*, 50 (1987), pp. 32–43.

10. Claude Annet, *Suzanne Lenglen* (Paris, 1927).

11. Daniel McNeill, *The Face* (1998), p. 340, summarising the recent social psychology research.

12. Margaret Mitchell, *Gone With the Wind* (London, 1936), p. 1.

13. *Confessions of a Kept Man as told to John O'Day, with Psychological Evaluations by Dr Leonard A Lowag, PhD, LPD* (Los Angeles, 1964).

14. See correspondance in *Independent*, 3, 4 April 2003.

15. National Bureau of Economic Research, *Beauty and the Labor Market* and *The Economic Reality of the Beauty Myth*, Working Papers 4518 and 4523 (Cambridge, Massachusetts, 1993); Daniel S. Hammesh and Jeff E. Biddle, 'Beauty and the Labor Market', *American Economic Review*, 84 (1994), pp. 1174–94; *Economist*, 24 May 2003; A. Mazur, J. Mazur and C. Keating, 'Military Rank Attainment of a West Point Class: Effects of Cadets' Physical Features', *American Journal of Sociology*, 90 (1984), pp. 125–50; I. H. Frieze, J. E. Olsen, and D. C. Good, 'Perceived and Actual Discrimination in the Salaries of Male and Female Managers', *Journal of Applied Social Psychology*, 20 (1990), pp. 46–47.

16. Daniel McNeill, *The Face*, p. 281.

17. Kate Mulvey and Melassa Richards, *Decades of Beauty: The Changing Image of Women* (London, 1998), pp. 191, 202–3.

18. *Independent*, 18 March 2002.

19. Laura Jackson, *Ewan McGregor: A Force to be Reckoned With* (London, 1999), p. 113; see also Andy Dougan, *The Biography of George Clooney* (Basingstoke, 1997); and, for the Beckhams, Andrew Morton, *Posh and Becks* (London, 2003).

20. *Independent*, 23 December 2003.

21. Sigelman and Sigelman, 'Bird of a Different Feather'.

22. Nigel Hamilton, *Bill Clinton: An American Journey* (2003); John Rentoul, *Tony Blair, Prime Minister* (2001). For interesting comparisons see the *jeu d'esprit* by Grail Marcus, *Double Trouble: Bill Clinton and Elvis Presley in a Land of No Alternatives* (London, 2000).

23. Eileen Jones, *Neil Kinnock* (London, 1994); Jo-Anne Nadler, *William Hague in his Own Right* (London, 2001).

24. John Kampfner, *Robin Cook* (London, 1999).

25. Nigel Andrews, *True Myths: the Life and Times of Arnold Schwarzenegger* (London, 1995).

26. McNeill, *The Face*, p. 344, summarising the empirical evidence.

27. Ill-fated sixties pop star Janis Joplin 'was very uncomfortable about what she felt was her physical unattractiveness, her marred, pitted skin and her bulky body. Her concern was obsessive that men wouldn't find her appealing'. Myra Friedman, *Buried Alive: The Biography of Janis Joplin* (London, 1974), p. 52.

28. Charlotte M. Wright, *Plain and Ugly Janes: The Rise of the Ugly Heroine in American Fiction* (New York, 2000).

Note on Sources

I don't like the antique word 'Bibliography' – an original work of history is based on archives, artefacts, visual sources, etc. and not just other people's books. The Sources listed at the end of my *Beauty in History: Society, Politics and Personal Appearance, c. 1500 to the Present* take up twenty double-column pages, and serious scholars are referred to this. Here I simply summarise the kinds of evidence my work is based on, also noting some recent books relevant to the more controversial issues. When place of publication is not given, it is London.

PRIMARY SOURCES

These fall into four broad categories:

1. Portraits

(Wherever possible I have sought to study originals; photographs and etchings, of course, naturally occur as reproductions in books, newspapers, etc.). Principal Galleries visited:

City Art Gallery, Birmingham
City Art Gallery, Manchester
Dulwich Art Gallery, London
Frick Collection, New York
Galleria Nazionale, Rome
Kenwood House, London
Musée Carnavalet, Paris
Musée Cognac-Jay Paris
Musée des Beaux Arts, Orléans
Musée des Beaux Arts, Nancy
Musée de Saint-Omer

Musée d'Orsay, Paris
Museo Archeologico, Naples
Museo Correr, Venice
Museum of Brussels
National Gallery of Art, Washington
National Gallery of Scotland, Edinburgh
National Museum, Stockholm
National Portrait Gallery, London
Palazzo Bianco, Genoa
Scottish National Portrait Gallery
Uffizi Gallery, Florence
Vatican Museum, Rome
Wallace Collection, London

2. Letters, Diaries, Memoirs and Contemporary Artefacts

(a) Archives and Museums:

Archivio Diaristico, Pieve Santo Stefano, AR, Tuscany
Anna Avallone, 'Il mio sessantotto: ricordi di un "madre" e "insegnante"'
Ivana Cavaletti, 'Diario di una teenager, 1958–1960'
Silvana Sabatini, 'Pagini e giorni: diario di una donna borghese'

Bancroft Library, University of California at Berkeley
Henry Nash Smith Papers, 87/136C
Social Protest Collection, 68/157C

Bodleian Library, Oxford
John Johnson Collection: 'Beauty Parlour' (4 boxes)

British Library, London
Department of Prints and Drawings
Political and Personal Satires 5373–6720

Hoover Institution Archives, Stanford University, California
George Barr Baker Collection
Mrs Edsall P. Ford, Diary
Ernest Lundeen Papers
Raymond Moley Papers

Ronald Reagan Papers (most of this collection was closed, but press releases, clippings, etc., proved very useful)

Mark Sullivan Papers

Karl H. von Wiegand Papers

Imperial War Museum, London
War Diary of Ann Meader, 1940–41

Istituto Ferruccio Pari, Bologna
Video materials relating to 'the economic miracle' and the 1960s

Maison de la Villette, Paris
Various *témoignage*s (oral histories and interviews)

Musée Nationale des Arts et Traditions Populaires, Paris
Various documents on popular culture

Museum of London
Various artefacts, leaflets, etc.

Lincoln County Record Office
Monson Papers

National Gallery of Scotland
Diary of E. C. Batten, 1837 (Acc. 8129)
Diary of E. E. Graham, 1872–1932, Robert Graham Diaries (Acc. 9077)
James Gall, 'Journal 1809–1813' (Acc. 8874)
Traverse Theatre Archive (Acc. 4850 and 10365)

Schlesinger Library, Radcliffe College, Cambridge, Massachusetts
Barbara Seaman Papers

Betty Friedan Papers

Susan Bolotin Papers

MS Magazine Letters

Stanford University Libraries, Special Collections and University Archives
Anderson Papers (M51)
Bound Manuscripts: Two Commonplace Books, 1779–82 (box 4, item 6) and 1837 (box 2, item 10 (M290))
James E. Bouldu Diary (M84)
Joseph Henry Steel Papers (M167)

'Journal of a Tour in France, Switzerland, Italy and a Part of Germany in the
    Year 1824' – anonymous holograph (M290, box 6, item 31)

Louis Fissner Journals (M289)

Mary Hallock Foote Papers (M115)

Robert Stephen Harlin Diaries (M86)

Private Collection

'Memorial of James Howard of Manchester (1738 to 1872)', written between 1853
    and 1862 by his daughter Rachel Barrow (1789–1870), in the possession of Mrs
    J. E. Nurse, Tunbridge Wells

(b) There are many published collections of letters, diaries, memoirs (or auto-
biographies). Here is an extremely brief sample (the list in *Beauty in History*
runs to three double-column pages):

Jane Austen, *Austen Papers*, ed. R. A. Austen-Leigh (1942); *Barrington Family
Letters, 1628–1632*, edited for the Royal Historical Society by Arthur Searle,
Camden Fourth Series (1932); Sarah Bernhardt, *Ma double vie: mémoires de
Sarah Bernhardt* (Paris, 1907); Comte de J. N. Dufort Cheverny, *Mémoires sur
les règnes de Louis XV et Louis XVI*, ed. R. de Crevecoeur (Paris, 1886); William
Cole, *The Bletcheley Diary of the Reverend William Cole 1756–67*, ed. F. C. Stokes
(1931); Madame D'Aulnoy, *Mémoires de la cour d'Angleterre*, 2 vols. (Paris,
1695); Marquise du Deffand, *Correspondance complète de la Marquise du
Deffand* (Paris, 1865); Dreux de Radier, *Recréations historiques* (Paris, 1767);
Helen Forrester, *Twopence to Cross the Mersey* (1974); David Garrick, *Letters of
David Garrick*, ed. D. M. Little and G. M. Kahol (1963); Rosina Harrison (ed.),
Gentlemen's Gentlemen (1976); Madame de Hausset, *Mémoires de Madame de
Hausset: femme de chambre de Madame de Pompadour* (Paris, 1824); Mme
Judith, *Mémoires de Mme Judith de la Comédie Française*, ed. Paul Gsell (Paris,
1911); John Keats, *Letters of John Keats*, ed. Hyder Edward Rollins (Cambridge,
Massachusetts, 1958); Olivier Lefèvre d'Ormesson, *Journal d'Olivier Lefèvre
d'Ormesson* (Paris, 1861); Celeste Mogador, *Mémoires* (Paris, 1858–59); Lady
Monkswell, *A Victorian Diarist: Extracts from the Journals of Mary, Lady
Monkswell, 1873–1895*, ed. Hon. E. C. F. Collier (1944); *The Paston Letters*, ed.
John Warrington, 2 vols (1924); *The Diary of Samuel Pepys*, ed. Robert Latham
and William Mathews, 11 vols (1970–83); *Correspondance de Mme de Sévigné*, 12
vols. (Paris, 1972–78); Tallement de Réaux, *Historiettes* (Paris, 1662; 1854);
Horace Walpole, *The Letters of Horace Walpole*, 9 vols (1857–59).

3. Guides, Treatises, Surveys and other Contemporary Published Materials

These take up over six double-column pages in *Beauty in History*. Some of the most important can be found in my chapter notes; here I give a brief sample:

Giovanni Marinelli, *Gli Ornamenti delle donne. Tratti delle Scritture d'una Reina Greca* (Venice, 1562); Mrs Susan D. Power, *The Ugly Girl Papers: or Hints for the Toilet* (New York, 1874); Plato, *The Dialogues of Plato, translated by Benjamin Jowett* (Oxford; 1874, 4th edition revised, 1964); Saint Augustine, *The Confessions; The City of God; On Christian Doctrine* (Encyclopaedia Britannica, Chicago, 1952; 1990); Mary Astell, *Some Reflections on Marriage* (1700); Germaine Greer, *The Female Eunuch* (1970); Naomi Wolf, *The Beauty Myth: How Images of Beauty are Used Against Women* (New York, 1992); Agnolo Firenzuola, *Prose di M. Agnolo Firenzuola Fiorentino* (Florence, 1540); Marilyn Bender, *The Beautiful People* (New York, 1967); Charles Perron, *Les Franc-Comtois: leur caractère national, leur moeurs, leurs usages* (Besançon, 1892); William Acton, *Prostitution Considered in its Moral, Social and Sanitary Aspects* (1857, 1870). Garland have published an invaluable facsimile series in 44 volumes, *Marriage, Sex and the Family in England, 1660–1800* (New York, 1984–86).

4. Research Reports (mainly in social psychology): The main ones I have used can be found in the notes for chapters 9 and 10.

5. Newspapers and Periodicals: Some sense of the range used can be gathered from my chapter notes.

6. Novels, Plays, Poems, Stories, Operas and Films.

There is scarcely a creative work which does not, even if only negatively, comment on beauty. For direct references, see my chapter notes.

SECONDARY SOURCES

These fill over six double-column pages in *Beauty in History*. My work depends heavily on biographical dictionaries and biographies: the most directly relevant of these will be found in the chapter notes. Here I confine myself to offering two brief lists of recent books:

A Books which are opposed to the views I put forward of human beauty as an independent biological attribute, a relative constant and relative universal, though in many varieties, and which instead espouse the conventional philosophical or cultural construction of beauty positions.

B Books which tend to support my views (there aren't many of them).

The **A** list can be divided into Works of Philosophy and Aesthetics, Postmodernist and Feminist Works (concentrating, for example, on 'The Body'), Histories of Fashion, Grooming and Cosmetology. Books purporting to be on sexuality are astonishingly silent on physical attractiveness: e.g. Jeffrey Weeks, Janet Holland, and Mathew Waites, *Sexualities and Society: A Reader* (Cambridge, 2003), Jeffrey Weeks, *Making Sexual History* (Cambridge, 2000), Tim Hitchcock, *English Sexualities, 1700–1800* (1997).

A

Philosophy and Aesthetics

Bill Beckley with David Shapiro, *Uncontrollable Beauty: Towards a New Aesthetics* (New York, 1998); Umberto Eco, *Art and Beauty in the Middle Ages* (New Haven, Connecticut, 1986) – actually written in the 1950s, reeks of academic aesthetics; Ellen Scarry, *On Beauty and Being Just* (Princeton, NJ., 1999) – runs together all possible meanings of beauty; John Armstrong, *The Secret Power of Beauty* (2004) – a brilliant book which yet fails to see that human beauty just is different from all other kinds of beauty.

Postmodernism and Feminism

Colin Blakemore and Sheila Jennett (eds.), *The Oxford Companion to the Body* (Oxford, 2001); Carol Harrison, *Beauty and Revelation in the Thought of Saint Augustine* (Oxford, 1992). This, and Kim Power, *Veiled Desire: Augustine's Writ-*

ing on Women (1995), are very helpful; Harold Koda, *Extreme Beauty: The Body Transformed* (New York, 2001); Ellen Zetzel Lambert, *The Face of Love: Feminism and the Beauty Question* (Boston, 1995); Thomas Laqueur, *Making Sex: Body and Gender from the Greeks to Freud* (Cambridge, Massachusets, 1990); Jan Marsh, *Pre-Raphaelite Sisterhood* (1985), superb scholarship; Nicole Sault (ed.), *Many Mirrors: Body Image and Social Relations* (New Brunswick, New Jersey, 1994); Peter N. Stearns, *Fat History: Bodies and Beauty in the Modern West* (New York, 2002); Wendy Steiner, *The Problem with Beauty* (2001).

Fashion, Grooming and Cosmetology

Elizabeth Haiken, *Venus Envy: A History of Cosmetic Surgery* (Baltimore, 1997); Kate Mulvey and Melassa Richards, *Decades of Beauty: The Changing Image of Women* (1998); Julian Robinson, *The Quest for Human Beauty: An Illustrated History* (New York, 1998); Philip Scranton (ed.), *Beauty and Business: Commerce, Gender and Culture in Modern America* (New York, 2001); Valerie Steele, *Fetish, Fashion, Sex and Power* (New York, 1996).

B

Nancy Etcoff, *Survival of the Prettiest: The Science of Beauty* (Boston, 1999). This magnificent book by a psychologist supports everything I myself have been saying about beauty. Elaine Hatfield and Susan Sprecher, *Mirror, Mirror: The Importance of Looks in Everyday Life* (New York, 1986) is similarly supportive, even if it is slightly too Darwinian. Daniel McNeill, *The Face* (Boston, 1998) is an impressive compendium of the latest research, lacking however in precise references, and finally copping out with the old jazz: 'People are beautiful because of their character, their insight, their ability to delight, their capacity for affection'.

Finally, SPECIALIST WORKS OF ART HISTORY, PARTICULARLY THOSE ANALYSING PORTRAITURE are invaluable. At the top of the tree three books by Roy Strong: *Gloriana: The Portraits of Queen Elizabeth I* (1987); *Artists of the Tudor Court: The Portrait Miniature Rediscovered* (1988); and *The Tudor and Stuart Monarchy: Pageantry, Painting and Iconography*, 3 vols (1995, 1998).

Index